ARBITRATION IN PRACTICE

ARBITRATION IN PRACTICE

R.S. POONIA

REGAL

REGAL PUBLICATIONS
New Delhi

ARBITRATION IN PRACTICE

ISBN 978-81-8484-326-2

Typeset by
RAHUL COMPOSERS
New Highway Apartments, Lakshmi Niwas
760, Pocket-D, Lok Nayak Puram, New Delhi - 110 041

Printed in India at
MAYUR ENTERPRISES
WZ Plot No. 3, Gujjar Market, Tihar Village, New Delhi - 110 018

Published by
REGAL PUBLICATIONS
F-159, Rajouri Garden, New Delhi - 110 027
Phone : 45546396, 25435369
E-mail : regalbookspub@yahoo.com, regaldeepbooks@yahoo.com

Contents

Preface

Long back the great social thinker Rousseau wrote in "The Social Contract" "man is born free, but and he is everywhere in chains". Looking back upon the society, we may muse how human beings can remain free yet live together where no one person has right to dictate other persons. Members of society acquire certain rights in return for giving up certain freedom. The contractual system too is very similar to social contracting where there is play of rights and obligations.

Contract law is one of the most essential and integral component of our life. It is the bedrock of modern economies and basis of our day-to-day interactions. In fact, one cannot think of a comfortable life in the absence of contract system. However, we must be sure of our rights under contract law because we do not know when the bargain will be breached and what can we do about it. Breach or non-fulfilment of the promise is the most discomforting part of contract law.

During the course of performance of contract, situations do arise which lead to differences between parties. The reason for disputes could be several. Primarily it is the misunderstanding of facts or law, misrepresentation, mistakes or deliberate mischief known as fraud. For maintaining peace in society and faith in the contractual system, resolution of disputes in amicable manner is essential. To this end the mechanism of arbitration has been devised. In order to successfully contest one's case in the arbitration, its nuances should be clearly understood. Since disputes arise out of contract, the solution also lies mostly in the contract law or contract Act. The key to a successful arbitration so far as parties to contract are concerned is to prove that **"breach of contract occurred on account of other party".**

This book is not the outcome of any research work nor does it contain contributions by legal luminaries. It is in fact, the result of collection of resource material through internet, leafing through books of eminent writers on the subject, study of court cases and of course my personal experience gathered while dealing with contractual and arbitration matters. During the course of proceedings, as arbitrator, it has been realised that the parties to the arbitration are severely handicapped in contesting their cases before arbitrator. There are occasions when a party looks up blankly for support from arbitrator as if arbitrator should supply him the necessary arguments. Parties are found wanting and ill-equipped with rules or doctrines with which they could contest the case effectively. Many are not aware as to what do they have to substantiate. The lack of confidence in arbitrators in disposal of arbitration cases shows up in the form of inordinate delays in bringing them to finality. It is this concern which has impelled me to take up this limited exercise to strengthen the knowledge of people who are engaged in arbitration directly or indirectly, by putting things lucidly. Generally any written material on law will have legal jargons, page length sentences which are unreadable for common man. This book evades all this and makes the matter readable for a lay man. It is intended to empower those executives, in a limited manner, and contractor who never had any exposure to legal matters concerning contracts and are forced by circumstances to arbitration. The book also demonstrates that when law is nothing but common sense then why have we poured into it so much of Greek and Latin and that it can be expressed in simpler manner.

The observations made by the Hon'ble apex court in deciding one case are reproduced which convey as to how judiciary feels helpless about our stale justice dispensing system, the arbitration being part of it.

"The law exists to serve the needs of the society which is governed by it. If the law is to play its allotted role of serving the needs of the society, it must reflect the ideas and ideologies of that society. It must keep time with the heartbeats of the society and with the needs and aspirations of the people. As the society changes, the law cannot remain immutable. The early nineteenth century essayist and wit, Sydney Smith, said, "When I hear any man talk of an unalterable law, I am convinced that he is an unalterable fool." The law must, therefore, in a changing society march in tune with the changed ideas and ideologies. Legislatures are, however, not best fitted for the role of adapting the law to the necessities of the time, for the legislative process is too slow and the legislatures often divided by politics, slowed down by periodic elections and overburdened with myriad other legislative activities. A constitutional document is even less suited to this task, for the philosophy and the ideologies underlying it must of necessity be expressed in broad and general terms and the process of amending a Constitution is too cumbersome and time-consuming to meet the immediate needs. This task must, therefore, of necessity fall upon the courts because the courts can by the process of judicial interpretation adapt the law to suit the needs of the society."

A time tested law is available on contracts and arbitration since British time. Its objective is to protect the rights of the natives and provide remedies wherever rights are infringed. However, law by itself cannot do anything. People have to understand it and use it gainfully. The law does require changes in it to suit to the needs of changing time.

Well, no one is infallible including judiciary since it is also populated by human being. The role of legislature is to enact laws which cannot be taken over by judiciary and the role of judiciary is to interpret it and apply it. But many a time we come across divergent interpretations on same issue of importance. We also happen to see the analysis of legal issues by judiciary in one way, but the application is otherwise. A clear manifestation of difference between thought and action is at display, at times. It is our wishful thinking that institutions will change according to the need of time and society. But for the present we find only fossils all around us.

After enacting law some agency should make rules and procedure for uniform implementation of the abstract law. This happens seldom. For instance, the arbitration act is one but its proceedings are conducted in thousand different ways. Higher judiciary sets precedents and makes rules but arbitrators are not from legal field and are unaware of existence of such dynamic rules. Court rulings are gist of the ideology and reflect the response of society to the law. Surprisingly, and circumstantially party to arbitration are away from this field. When such is the situation, only an easy to read and comprehensive book will enlighten readers and repose confidence in them which is lacking now. In no way it is my intention to impart legal knowledge to the readers but make them learn basics necessities of arbitration so that they do not deliver injustice, suffer injustice.

The book contains rules/doctrines such as errors in making reference to arbitrator, relief in case of waiver of breach, unconscionable terms in contract, application of *res judicata* to awards; relief due to mistake in contracts; adverse inference in case of spoliation of evidence, damages when breach is on employers' account, right of claims due to differing site conditions, etc.

The Act, 96 is a procedural act. It lays out norms for appointment of arbitrator, conducting proceedings, making award etc. It does not equip the warring parties with necessary armaments with which to fight the battle. This is precisely what this book is meant for. I hope, contractors, executives in construction industry and law students would find it very useful.

I am grateful to Dr. Ramesh Rao for contributing 'The law of equity' and Shri Shukla who went through the manuscript several times over and made valuable suggestions. I am indebted to my family members and friends who encouraged me to pen the book. And not the least, I thank profusely my publisher Regal Publications, New Delhi who willingly agreed to publish this book.

The views contained in this book are not of my employer. The views on contract and arbitration have evolved over centuries, by social thinkers and subsequent generations have made it richer.

At the end I dedicate this book to Santosh, my wife; Dr. Meghna and Muddit, daughter and son; and Vimala and Raghu, my aunt and uncle for their everlasting bond of love with me.

R.S. POONIA

1 Commencement of Arbitration

INTRODUCTION

Disputes in contractual matters are inevitable. The root causes for differences to arise are unequal bargaining power, imbalance in contract conditions, lack of transparency and an element of misrepresentation embedded in the fine print of contract which is not informed to the other party. In very few cases parties are able to come together and resolve their differences. In majority of cases, they are unable to hammer out a solution own their own. Their stance gets hardened as they feel that the one party has wronged the other. The necessity for mediation by third party is therefore unavoidable.

For affording speedier and cost effective solution to litigants, a system of arbitration, has been evolved which is popularly known as alternative dispute resolution mechanism. This mechanism has several advantages over normal judicial process. In this mechanism one can fight his case himself without the aid of attorney; much of legal knowledge is not necessary and by presenting facts of the case cogently one can successfully contest the dispute. Legal procedures are not followed rigidly in it.

However, the age old adage that "a job well begun is half done" should not be forgotten. In the entire process of arbitral adjudication the first few steps are most significant. The arbitration should be commenced well.

The arbitration process allows the parties to select an individual or individuals with expertise in the subject matter of the dispute, to listen to the evidence and render a binding decision. In smaller dispute arbitration, there is usually one arbitrator. In complex cases, the parties may request more than one arbitrator, and a panel of arbitrators is appointed. Usually, an arbitration panel consists of three members, one of which is designated as the Presiding arbitrator.

Arbitration proceedings generally begin with a preliminary conference with the arbitrator which is attended by both parties to frame rules and procedures that will be followed during the arbitration process. After the conference, all communication with the arbitrator must be made jointly by both parties and private conversations between the parties and the arbitrator are generally not allowed. "*Ex parte*" conversations may be a cause of action to vacate the arbitration award. Such conduct borders on misconduct of arbitrator.

METHODS OF COMMENCEMENT

Where there is an agreed procedure either in the arbitration agreement or contractual clause, it must be followed for the arbitration to commence. Some rules require parties to commence arbitration by filing notice with the relevant arbitration institutions whereas in other cases notice is required to be filed with the head of organization. The date when the request is received by the institution or head of organization is deemed to be the date of the commencement of the arbitral proceedings. All these rules require a notice of arbitration to be served on the other party.

In the absence of any definition of commencement date, the arbitration is deemed to have commenced when a notice in writing is served by one party on the other, requiring the other party, either:

(1) To appoint an arbitrator; or
(2) To submit the dispute to any person named or designated in the agreement.

This notice read in conjunction with the arbitration agreement, determines the scope of the dispute referred to arbitration and hence the jurisdiction of the arbitrator. Besides, it should be seen that a dispute exists between parties. Where one party raises a dispute and other denies it, it is held that this be treated as dispute. For a dispute to exist, there should be a claim by one party and denial by another party on whatever ground.

Form of Notice

The notice need not be in any particular form. Most often it should be a simple letter containing background of the dispute in brief, the claims and their respective amount. It should identify the arbitration agreement, by clause number or other appropriate reference. It should also identify by reference to other documents and the nature of the dispute to be submitted to arbitration. This need not be in great detail but the recipient of notice should be in a position to understand what is alleged in it.

Claims

Certain arbitration agreements provide for referring all disputes between the parties to arbitration without exception or subject to exceptions. In such cases the arbitrator will have jurisdiction to entertain any claim/counter-claim, even though it is not raised while giving notice. Since agreement provides that no new claims would be entertained, therefore, all claims filed before arbitrator at the commencement of hearing will only be entertained.

Other arbitration agreements require specific disputes to be referred to arbitration and provides that the arbitrator will have the jurisdiction to decide only the disputes so referred. The arbitrator's jurisdiction is therefore controlled by the specific reference and he cannot travel beyond the reference, nor entertain any additional claims or counter-claims which are not part of the disputes specifically referred to arbitration.

The appointing Authority's role is only to appoint the arbitrator. Though the arbitration clause requires the party invoking the arbitration to specify the dispute/s to be referred to arbitration, it does not require the appointing authority to specify the disputes or refer any specific disputes to arbitration.

The act legislates that "Unless otherwise agreed by the parties, either party may amend or supplement his claim or defence during the course of the proceedings. Thus, new claims are barred. In order to have successful arbitration, the parties must chronicle their disputes/differences as the project advances because there are chances of not recalling to memory all claims while filing them. In case there is a doubt about some claims, it is better to include them in the reference and withdraw or modify the same during proceedings, since new claims would not be allowed during proceedings.

It has been held that in case additional claims/counter-claims are required to be added during proceedings, the parties could secure fresh reference regarding dispute which are the subject matter of claims/ counter-claims and that both the original reference and second reference could be consolidated and decided together. It may be noted that arbitrator own his own cannot enlarge the scope of arbitration. Further, *res judicata* operates in arbitration in respect of decided claims.

APPOINTMENT OF ARBITRATOR

When a dispute arises between parties to a contract, the party feeling wronged would like to seek the dispute resolved through third party. The provision for dispute resolution is invariably provided in the contract agreement either as a clause or in the form of a separate arbitration agreement. The essential requirements of arbitral agreement are cover by sec. 7 of Act, 1996. The arbitration clause in the main contract stipulates certain provisions about making application for appointment of arbitrator, what disputes shall not be referred for arbitration even though claimant has sought for resolution of such disputes through arbitration, etc. Since Act, 96 is procedure-oriented, the process should be followed without even slightest departure, else the exercise may get vitiated.

If the parties to an arbitration agreement agree to a method for appointing an arbitrator, that method must be followed unless the method fails. If the parties have not agreed on a method or the agreed method fails or an arbitrator appointed fails or is unable to act and a successor has not been appointed, the court, on motion of a party to the arbitration proceeding, shall appoint the arbitrator. An arbitrator so appointed has all the powers of an arbitrator designated in the agreement to arbitrate or appointed pursuant to the agreed method. An individual who has a known, direct and a material interest in the outcome of the arbitration proceeding or a known, existing and substantial relationship with a party may not serve as an arbitrator since his neutrality is doubtful. If there is doubt about the neutrality of the arbitrator, the objection in this regard should be raised at the first available opportunity before the arbitrator who will take final decision in the matter.

The first step is serving notice by one party to the other intimating that he proposes to invoke arbitration agreement and urges the other party to take steps setting the process in motion. The notice should be addressed to the proper authority and sent to official address. It should be highlighted that all procedures prescribed in the arbitration agreement have been followed. Append a list of disputes that require adjudication together with amount of each claim. It should be made known that in the event of failure to appoint an arbitrator, appropriate remedy would be sought.

If the appointing authority fails or refuses to appoint, then on an application by the one party to the agreement, the CJI or his nominee shall have jurisdiction to appoint arbitrator. The procedure for CJI or his nominee is laid down in sec. 11 of Act, 1996. The court will examine if the applicant has approached proper court; whether there is an arbitration agreement; and party making an application is a party to the agreement.

OBJECTION REGARDING APPOINTMENT OF ARBITRATOR

The objection to the appointment of an arbitrator who is not duly qualified as per arbitration agreement should be raised at the earliest opportunity.

Disclosure by Arbitrator

Before accepting appointment, an individual who has been nominated to serve as an arbitrator, after making a reasonable inquiry, shall disclose to all parties any known facts that a reasonable person would consider likely to affect the impartiality of the arbitrator in the arbitration proceeding, including: a financial or personal interest in the outcome of the arbitration proceeding; an existing or past relationship with any of the parties to the agreement or their counsel or representatives. An arbitrator has a continuing obligation to disclose in writing the circumstances likely to give rise to justifiable doubt as to his independence and impartiality. In case justifiable doubt persists, the arbitrator can be challenged as to his independence and impartiality. In this matter a notice is required to be given within 15 days after becoming aware of the appointment of arbitrator.

Arbitration Limitations

The moment dispute arise and need for appointment of arbitrator is realised the contract agreement must be consulted immediately. There the Arbitration agreement and other contract clauses may contain provisions which require certain acts or a procedure to be completed within a specified period. These provisions would contain limitations and procedure for commencement of arbitral proceedings.

Firstly, the limitations apply to arbitrations in the same way as it applies to other civil actions. These limitations are given in the arbitration agreement and "arbitration and conciliation act" 1996 referred to as Act 1996. For example, a typical arbitration agreement may contain following stipulations:

(i) In the event of any dispute or difference between the parties about the construction or operation of this contract, or any matter in question, dispute or difference on any account or if the respondent fails to make a decision within 120 days, then and in any such case, but except "excepted matters" referred to in conditions, the contractor, after 120 days but within 180 days of his presenting his final claim on disputed matters shall demand in writing that the dispute or difference be referred to arbitration.

(ii) The demand for arbitration shall specify the matters which are in question, or subject of the dispute or difference as also the amount of claim item-wise. Only such dispute or difference, in respect of which the demand has been made, together with counter-claims or set-off, given by the claimant and respondent, shall be referred to arbitration and other matters shall not be included in the reference.

   (a) The claimant shall submit his claim stating the facts supporting the claims along with all the relevant documents and the remedy sought against each claim within a period of 30 days from the date of appointment of the Arbitral Tribunal.

   (b) The respondent shall submit his defence statement and counter-claim(s), if any, within a period of 60 days of receipt of copy of claims from claimant thereafter, unless otherwise extension has been granted by Tribunal and so on.

These limitations are very important for claimant. If these are not adhered to one may extinguish his rights. However for certain acts arbitrator may consider extension of time falling within his jurisdiction. Otherwise courts have the discretion to extend the period under section 43(3) of Act, 1996.

Waiver of Right

According to section 4 of the Act, 1996, if a party, who knows that any requirement under the act has not been complied with and yet proceeds with arbitration without stating his objections to such non-compliance shall be deemed to have waived his right to object. Therefore any objection or submission of reply should be made timely.

Statement of Claims/Counter-claims

This is the second stage of arbitration which is equally important. In the statement of claims the party should indicate brief history of the case, issues in question and item-wise claims. Each claim should be justified by presenting facts. The arguments should be cogent and logical. At end the submission should be summarized by giving claims and their amount and any document required from the respondent. In the similar fashion counter statement should be prepared justifying how claims filed are not justified. At the same time if there are any counter-claims, these should be incorporated in the statement together with their justification. Provisions from contract conditions, arbitration act and case laws should be liberally quoted, if possible, in support of claims/counter claims.

A reasonable amount as cost of litigation may be claimed. Arbitration is considered to be domestic court and is expected to cost least. Tribunals are generally of the opinion that cost should be borne by the parties themselves to the litigation. However, raising such claim is neither barred nor against any principle of law.

Interest for delay in making payment may also be claimed which has always been contentious issue because of restrictive contractual provisions. Law does permit claim of pre-reference, pendente-lite and future interest. Interest should also be claimed as compensation for breach of payment terms. Every breach gives rise to damages and therefore the interest should be part of damages and explained so in the statement of facts.

Similarly, it may be noticed that the disputes which are not covered by arbitration agreement (Excepted matters) should not be referred to and if already referred to then objection should be taken. Issue of jurisdiction should also be raised from time to time as the need arises. And not the least is that parties should come fully prepared for proceedings with relevant references, application, case laws etc.

Effect of not Submitting Claims in Time

Act, 1996 provides that unless otherwise agreed by the parties, where, without showing sufficient cause,—(a) the claimant fails to communicate his statement of claim in accordance with sub-section (1) of section 23, the arbitral tribunal shall terminate the proceedings; (b) the respondent fails to communicate his statement of defence in accordance with sub-section (1) of section 23, the arbitral tribunal shall continue the proceedings without treating that failure in itself as an admission of the allegations by the claimant, (c) a party fails to appear at an oral hearing or to produce documentary evidence, the arbitral tribunal may continue the proceedings and make the arbitral award on the evidence before it.

ARBITRATION PROCESS

An arbitrator may conduct arbitration in such a manner as the arbitrator considers appropriate for a fair and expeditious conclusion of the proceedings. An arbitrator may decide a request for summary disposition of a claim or particular issue if all interested parties agree. While fixing date for hearing, the arbitrator shall set a time and place with the consent of parties and give notice of said hearing not less than five days before the hearing begins. Upon request of a party to the arbitration proceeding and for good cause shown, or upon the arbitrator's own initiative, the arbitrator may adjourn the hearing from time to time as necessary, but may not postpone the hearing to a time later than that fixed by the agreement to arbitrate for making the award unless the parties to the arbitration proceeding consent to a later date. The arbitrator may hear and decide the controversy upon the evidence produced although a party who was duly notified of the arbitration proceeding did not appear.

In certain government departments contract provides that 'excepted' matters and certain other issues should not be referred to arbitration. Therefore, the appointing authority does not refer all the disputes for adjudication. He makes selective reference to arbitration. He has been chosen by the parties simply for the purpose of appointing arbitrator. He is not authorized to filter/scan through the claims of either party. Such a course would amount to passing nil award without the claim being adjudicated. It is only the arbitrator who can decide the admissibility of claims.

In Earnest builders *vs.* UOI & Ors. (2002) the claimant had raised 9 claims. Only 7 claims were referred for arbitration, two claims being excepted matters. The claimant thereofore approached CJI.

Section 11 lays down the procedure for appointment of arbitrators by the parties. Sub-section (6) thereof, *inter alia*, provides that in case of failure of a party to act as required under the appointment procedure agreed upon by the parties, a party may request the Chief Justice or any person designated by him to take the necessary measures for securing the appointment of arbitrator. The scope and ambit of Section 11 of the Act has been Succinctly explained by the Apex Court in the case of Konkan Railway Corporation Limited case, as follows:

> "..... When the matter is placed before the Chief Justice or his nominee under Section 11 of the Act it is imperative for the said Chief Justice or his nominee to bear in mind the legislative intent that the arbitral process should be set in motion without any delay whatsoever and all contentious issues are left to be raised before the Arbitral Tribunal itself. At that stage it would not be appropriate for the Chief Justice or his nominee to entertain any contentious issue between the parties and decide the same. A bare reading of Sections 13 and 16 of the Act makes it crystal clear that question with regard to the qualifications, independence and impartiality of the arbitrator, and in respect of the jurisdiction of the arbitrator could be raised before the arbitrator who would decide the same."
>
> It was further observed:
>
> "Section 16 empowers the Arbitral Tribunal to rule on its own as well as on objections with respect to the existence or validity of the arbitration agreement. Conferment of such power on the arbitrator under the 1996 Act indicated the intention of the legislature and its anxiety to see that the arbitral process is set in motion. This being the legislative intent, it would be proper for the Chief Justice or his nominee just to appoint an arbitrator without wasting any time or without entertaining any contentious issues at that state, by a party objecting to the appointment of an arbitrator....."
>
> "Therefore, in the light of the afore noted decisions, it is clear that under Section 11 of the Act the Chief Justice or his designate, while exercising his power under the said provisions, cannot entertain or decide the issues like existence of arbitration agreement, its validity or scope or the jurisdiction of the arbitrator to decide the disputes that are sought to be referred to his arbitration. All that the Chief Justice or his designate is required to do is to nominate an arbitrator or arbitrators, as the

case my be, if a party to an arbitration agreement has failed to do so, within the specified time after a request to do so had been made and in so doing, regard must be had to the qualifications that are required of an arbitrator by the agreement of the parties. All other issues are to be left to the decision of the arbitrator/ arbitrators. This is so because of the jurisdiction of the Arbitral Tribunal under Section 16 of the Act is very wide. It is not confined to the width of it jurisdiction at all to deal with the matter before it."

"However, in the present case, the appointing authority having nominated the arbitrator, paradoxically enough, himself proceeded to act as an arbitrator to decide that some claims fell within the excepted category and were not arbitrable. In My opinion, the said exercise undertaken by the appointing authority was not illegal if that is the requirement of arbitration agreement. Further, under the scheme of the Act, it is for the arbitrator to decide whether he could adjudicate upon a particular claim in the light of the contract between the parties or not. Similarly, while exercising power under Section 11 of the Act, it is equally not permissible for this Court to go into the afore noted objections raised by the respondents."

In the *State of Goa* v. *M/s. Praveen Enterprises* the Supreme court has held that:

(a) Section 11 of the Act requires the Chief Justice or his designate to either appoint the arbitrator/s or take necessary measures in accordance with the appointment procedure contained in the arbitration agreement. The Chief Justice or the designate is not required to draw up the list of disputes and refer them to arbitration. The appointment of Arbitral Tribunal is an implied reference in terms of the arbitration agreement.

(b) Where the arbitration agreement provides for referring all disputes between the parties (whether without any exceptions or subject to exceptions), the arbitrator will have jurisdiction to entertain any counter claim, even though it was not raised at a stage earlier to the stage of pleadings before the Arbitrator.

(c) Where however the arbitration agreement requires specific disputes to be referred to arbitration and provides that the arbitrator will have the jurisdiction to decide only the disputes so referred, the arbitrator's jurisdiction is controlled by the specific reference and he cannot travel.

As arbitrator is the creature of arbitration agreement, the appointing authority too have to follow the procedure for referring disputes in line with the provisions of arbitration agreement.

Since appointing authority has already appointed the sole arbitrator, he is competent to decide as to which of the disputes are not arbitrable in terms of the agreement between the parties. Withholding of any claim by the appointing authority from the domain of the nominated arbitrator, is in excess of his authority. The applicant would be at liberty to raise the afore noted claims before the nominated arbitrator. Thus, the restrictive clauses incorporated in contracts prohibiting reference of excepted matters, etc. to arbitrator would only negate the legislative intent. The parties should therefore ensure that all of their claims are referred to arbitrator.

SUMMARY

Summing up following important points should be paid adequate attention and contested wherever required:

(i) Application for reference to arbitrator should be proper indicating the claims clearly and distinctly;

(ii) Statement of claims/defence should be comprehensive and claims should match with claims given in notice. In case of specific reference no deviation is permissible;

(iii) Objections, if any, about the independence and impartiality or qualification should be raised immediately;

(iv) Limitation of every kind should be kept in view;

(v) Rules of arbitration should be framed elaborately; and

(vi) Deviations in claims or non conformity should be contested.

2 Duties and Powers of Arbitrator

The arbitration, a faster and cheaper mode of dispute resolution serves social cause. To serve it in an efficient and satisfactory manner, the arbitrators have onerous task before them. While on one hand they are expected to be thorough in their field and possess reasonably good legal knowledge, on the other hand they are not empowered to reprimand a litigant who does not cooperate during proceedings. He should be fair in his approach to the dispute, give equal opportunities to the rival parties, conduct proceedings expeditiously and pass a reasoned award within the framework of rules. He is not entirely like a judicial judge, yet he is held in awe. He does not enjoy as much immunity as a judge do yet he enjoys some support being quasi-judicial in nature. Multifarious duties are cast upon him which he should not violet, at the same time powers are bestowed upon him to enable him to discharge his functions efficiently.

Apart from arbitrator, there is a team of claimant, respondent and their attorneys. Their conduct should also be conducive to business which will be transacted. They should maintain amicable, harmonious and friendly ambiance so that proceedings are held properly and every one gets adequate time to present his point across. In paragraphs that follow, the duties of these personnel have been discussed.

DUTIES OF ARBITRATORS

(i) To act with honesty, integrity, diligence and dignity. The arbitrator shall recognise:

(a) Responsibility to the public, parties and others who are participating in the proceedings;
(b) Do not solicit appointment if he believes that he is adequately competent and qualified to conduct proceedings;
(c) Refrain from entering into any kind of relationship with parties or counsel;
(d) Do not accept any gift or substantial hospitality directly, or indirectly from any party to the arbitration;
(e) Disclose any direct or indirect financial or personal interest in the outcome of the arbitration; and
(f) Disclose any existing relationship.

Other Duties of Arbitrator are :

1. Duty to Follow Rules of Natural Justice

An arbitrator must observe the rules of natural justice. He must act in a judicial manner. His enquiry should not be slip-shod but full and complete. He must give due notices and maintain proper record of the proceedings. He ought not hear one side in the absence of the other side. Any departure from the rules of natural justice is sure to vitiate the award.

2. Duty to Act Fairly to both Parties

The arbitrator must act fairly to both parties. He must not favour parties, or do anything for one party which he does not do for another.

3. Duty not to Delegate

An arbitrator must not delegate his duties to a third person, or to a co-arbitrator. Since one who has an authority to do an act for another, must do it himself and should not delegate to another. This rule is, however, subject to the exception that an arbitrator may delegate to another the performance of an act of ministerial character only.

4. Duty to Decide According to Law

It is the duty of an arbitrator, in the absence of a provision to the contrary, to decide the questions according to legal rights of the parties and not according to what he may consider to be fair and reasonable under the circumstances. If an arbitrator decides honestly, though wrongly, he is not guilty of misconduct. But deliberate disregard of law in matters of arbitration is misconduct.

5. Duty not to Exceed his Authority

An arbitrator should not travel beyond the scope of his authority. He derives his authority from the arbitration agreement and reference. He cannot take upon himself an authority which is not conferred by the submission. If the arbitrators go beyond the scope of reference and decide a dispute not referred to them, the award is bad in law and liable to be set aside.

6. Duty to Decide all Matters Referred

It is the duty of the arbitrator to decide all the matters referred to him. Where he omits to decide some of the important questions referred the award is bad. A partial award is invalid and should be remitted for reconsideration. All referred matters should be decided. Section 28(3) of the Act, 1996 provides that arbitral tribunal should decide all the matters before it in accordance with terms of contract. An arbitrator can not do what he thinks just and right. An arbitrator cannot act arbitrarily, irrationally, capriciously or independent of the contract. His sole function is to arbitrate in terms of the contract. Accordingly award should also conform to terms and conditions of contract. Where all disputes are not decided, the award may be invalid.

7. Duty to Act Together

When there are several arbitrators, all must act together. The presence of all the arbitrators at all the meetings is essential to the validity of the award. If there had been absence of some of the arbitrators to the meeting, an award given by majority is not valid. However, if a party does not raise any objection to the absence of the arbitrator at some of the meeting, it is not open to such a party to contend subsequently that such absence rendered the award ineffective. If some arbitrator is absent due to unavoidable reasons, the presiding arbitrator should obtain the consent of parties to conduct proceedings by rest of the arbitrators and this fact should be recorded in minutes.

8. Duty not to Accept Hospitality

An arbitrator should not accept hospitality from the parties, if the invitation is given with the intention of inducing him to act unfairly. But merely dining or lunching with one of the parties and his witness in the absence of other will not invalidate an award.

9. Where arbitral proceedings come to an end, the tribunal should record in the minutes that both the parties have completed their arguments and that they have nothing more to state. Besides, *"the proceedings are closed and kept reserved for making and publishing award"* should also be recorded.

10. Some arbitrators, after the conclusion of oral arguments, do not call upon the parties to submit written arguments. It is rather in the interest of parties to state their case in writing and request the tribunal to allow them reasonable time within which it is proposed to submit written arguments.

11. Framing of Issues

As per section 19(1) of the Act, 1996 an arbitral tribunal is not bound by the Code of Civil Procedure and therefore it is not necessary for arbitrator to frame issues. It is not expected of arbitral tribunal which is not well versed in law to frame issues. For tribunal, the claims itself are treated as issues and the same are determined.

12. One Party Absent from Meetings

Where a party deliberately abstain from appearing before an arbitral tribunal, it is not expected that the tribunal should wait indefinitely before proceeding with case. On the very first failure of a party to appear on the date and time fixed for hearing, the tribunal could give the defaulting party an opportunity of being present. While granting the opportunity the tribunal should make clear its intentions to proceed with the case on the next date of hearing even in the absence of the said party.

DUTIES OF PRESIDING ARBITRATOR

There can be no doubt that the role of the Chair is pivotal in ensuring a smooth-running and fair arbitration. The Chair of an arbitration is, in a sense, the glue that holds the whole process together. He must oversee all administrative matters as well as all procedural and substantive matters; be the key liaison among the parties and the other arbitrators, between the tribunal and any administering institution, if any, and sometimes must even mediate between the other arbitrators where not everyone sees eye to eye. One might like to consider the Chair as the conductor of the arbitral orchestra.

The role of the Chair can conveniently be considered at the following stages of an arbitration:

— Getting the arbitration on track
— Sorting out administrative and financial details
— Fashioning the first Procedural Order or Terms of Reference
— Supervising submissions
— Planning the hearings
— Conducting the hearings
— Planning the stages subsequent to the hearings
— Drafting the award
— Completing the mandate

It is one of the duties of the presiding arbitrator to do administrative job on behalf of the tribunal and with the full knowledge of all the Arbitrators.

Conduct of Parties

- Should maintain dignity of proceedings and act with honesty and diligence
- Should expedite conduct of proceedings
- Should follow the rulings given by arbitrator during proceedings
- Parties should avoid any dilatory tactics

Code of Ethics for Lawyers

- Should have due regard for the fair conduct of proceedings;
- Should maintain due respect and courtesy towards tribunal and defend the interests of the client honorably;
- Should never give false or misleading information to the tribunal;
- Should fully co-operate with the parties and the Arbitrators; and
- Should be bound by the code of conduct prescribed by BCI.

Conduct of Proceedings

- Adhere to the concept of fairness, patience, courteousness and equality;
- Devise method of record of proceedings;
- Afford full opportunity to other arbitrators;
- Act within the scope of Arbitration Agreement;
- Follow the procedure set out in the Agreement;

- Do not discuss the case with any party in the absence of other party; and
- *Equal treatment of parties*—The parties shall be treated with equality and each party shall be given a full opportunity to present his case.

Powers of Arbitrator

(1) To appoint one or more experts to report to it on specific issues to be determined by the arbitral tribunal;
(2) To terminate proceedings when its continuation becomes impossible;
(3) To take court assistance in taking evidence;
(4) To make interim award;
(5) To pass rulings on the issues brought before it;
(6) To rule on its own jurisdiction;
(7) To rule on objections raised during proceedings; and
(8) To grant interim relief.

In addition to the statutory powers given above, there are some implied and incidental powers, such as:

(a) To obtain legal assistance
(b) To delegate authority limited to the performance of acts of ministerial character
(c) To award interest
(d) To award costs
(e) To allow amendment of the claims
(f) To direct parties to produce relevant documents/evidence sought by other party
(g) To fix place and time of meeting in case of disagreement between parties

The Arbitrators have no Power

(1) To allow withdrawal of the reference
(2) To receive or realize monies
(3) To alter the terms of arbitration agreement
(4) To award damages otherwise than in accordance with law.

Request for Documents

The arbitrator shall direct the party who has the possession of the documents required by other party. For its decision the arbitrator shall be guided by Rules of Evidence. On this basis, the Tribunal considers that the following standards should guide its reasoning:

(i) The request for production must identify each document or specific category of documents sought with precision.

(ii) The request must establish the relevance of each document or of each specific category of documents sought in such a way that the other party and the Arbitral Tribunal are able to refer to factual allegations in the submissions filed by the parties to date. In other words, the requesting party must make it clear with reasonable facts/allegations which the intended document would establish.

(iii) The Arbitral Tribunal will only order the production of documents or category of documents if they exist and are within the possession, power, custody or control of the other party. If this is contested, the requesting party will have to satisfy the Arbitral Tribunal that the document is indeed within the possession, power, custody or control of the other party.

ARBITRATOR'S POWER TO SANCTION UNETHICAL CONDUCT OF PARTIES

The ideal arbitration is efficient, cost-effective and imbued with fairness. To achieve these goals, the arbitrator should be provided with certain powers to control the proceedings. The intention to have power is not for wielding or disciplining but to exercise them in rare cases. Arbitrators generally are not limited to awarding relief allowed by law; they may base their decision upon broad principles of justice and equity. Since arbitrators manage the process, it falls upon them to see that the arbitration process is fair and completed efficiently. It follows from this essential fact that arbitrators should have the authority to address abuses and disruption of the arbitration process. The great discretion arbitrators have over the proceedings is the ability to halt proceedings. If things come to such a pass that making any headway is impossible, the arbitrator might terminate the proceedings under section 32(c) of the Act 1996 or adjourn for some days or draw adverse inference.

When party does not appear before the arbitrator for hearings, the tribunal should not proceed *ex parte* in haste. This may prove fatal to the award as courts start doubting the purpose of tearing haste. The recourse to *ex parte* proceedings should be taken in extreme cases.

ARBITRATOR'S POWER TO SANCTION MISCONDUCT OF ATTORNEY

Arbitrator is not a legal luminary. He may not possess even basic knowledge of law. Whereas the attorney would produce plethora of cited case filled with legal jargons. He is always on the lookout for opportunities so that breaks can be applied to proceedings. His behaviour is irritating and repulsive and makes other feel helpless. At such moments arbitrators think of censuring him. The position however is different. He cannot be debarred or expelled. The position is somewhat like this:

> In any arbitral proceedings, the main figure is attorney who would not allow the proceedings to remain on track especially when he is going to be looser. Being from legal background, they dislike the manner in which proceedings are conducted by arbitral tribunal. They want arbitrator to behave as a judicial judge. Evidence should be taken the way it is taken in court of law.

Attorney's participation in arbitration on behalf of parties who are within the jurisdiction of the arbitral tribunal constitutes consent of attorney. Courts have held that an arbitrator could impose sanctions on a party, but not on a party's attorney. The arbitrator's ability to impose sanctions on attorney may depend on the terms of the arbitration agreement. Fortunately, there are other ways arbitrators can deter unethical conduct by attorney. For example, in lieu of sanctions at the end of the process, arbitrators could bring up the issue of attorney ethics at an early preliminary conference and then ask counsel whether they will agree to be subject to sanctions if they behave unethically during the arbitration. Alternatively, arbitrators could announce, at the preliminary conference, or later in the event of misconduct by attorney, that they will hold the parties responsible for the misconduct of their attorney. Arbitrators also could make clear that unethical behaviour will be viewed with scepticism. Thus, direct sanctions cannot be imposed upon attorney for misconduct.

TERMINATION OF PROCEEDINGS

(1) The arbitral proceedings shall be terminated by the final arbitral award or by an order of the arbitral tribunal under sub-section (2) of Section 32.

(2) The arbitral tribunal shall issue an order for the termination of the arbitral proceedings where:

(a) the claimant withdraws his claim, unless the respondent objects to the order and the arbitral tribunal recognizes a legitimate interest on his part in, obtaining a final settlement of the dispute,

(b) the parties agree on the termination of the proceedings, or

(c) the arbitral tribunal finds that the continuation of the proceedings has for any other reason become unnecessary or impossible.

Subject to section 33 and sub-section (4) of section 34, the mandate of the arbitral tribunal shall terminate with the termination of the arbitral proceedings."

The aforesaid provision specifies the circumstances under which arbitral proceedings shall be terminated. It provides that arbitral proceedings shall stand terminated on Arbitral Tribunal making an award. Besides that, arbitral proceedings can also be terminated in case (a) claimant withdraws his claim, (b) parties agree on the termination of the proceedings. For example, if parties arrive at a settlement and agree for termination of proceedings, in such an eventuality also, arbitral proceedings shall stand terminated, and (c) if Arbitral Tribunal finds that continuation of the proceedings have become unnecessary or impossible for any other reason. In other words, if the arbitral tribunal finds, for any reason which includes non-cooperation of the parties, making the continuation of the proceedings impossible, then it can make an order for termination of the arbitral proceedings. In case of termination of the proceedings, the mandate of Arbitral Tribunal shall also stand terminated as envisaged under Sub-Section 3 of Section 32 of the Act except in cases where Section 33 and Section 34(4) of the Act are attracted.

Arbitral Tribunal has power to terminate the arbitral proceedings under Section 25(a) upon default of the claimant to communicate his statement of claim; under Section 30(2) upon settlement of dispute by the parties and under Section 38(2) upon failure of the parties to pay the amount of deposit fixed by the Arbitral Tribunal. The termination of arbitral proceedings is different from termination of the mandate of arbitrator. The mandate of arbitrator, depending upon the facts and circumstances of a case, may come to an end but not the arbitral proceedings. For example, if the parties to the arbitration agreement had fixed a period of six months for completion of arbitral proceedings and making of an award by the Arbitral Tribunal and the Arbitral Tribunal fails to do so on or before expiry of six months, the mandate of Arbitral Tribunal shall come to an end but not the arbitration proceedings and in such an eventuality, if a substitute arbitrator is appointed than he shall have to continue with the arbitration proceedings from the stage the same had been left by the earlier arbitrator. However, in case arbitration proceedings are terminated within the meaning of Section 32 of the Act resulting in termination of mandate of arbitrator, the same cannot continue merely by appointing another arbitrator. *In such a scenario, first of all, the arbitration proceedings have to be revived after setting aside the order of Arbitral Tribunal terminating the arbitral proceedings.*

Thus substantial powers have been conferred upon arbitral tribunal so that it is capable to run and manage its day to day affairs on its own. Autonomy of the tribunal has been given consideration to improve its efficiency and repose faith in public about this institution.

3 Arbitral Proceedings, Award and Setting Aside of Award

PROCEEDINGS

As soon as an arbitrator is appointed, he should write to both the parties inviting them for preliminary meeting. In this meeting the arbitrator would issue disclosure (S. 12) about his impartiality and independence and also frame rules with the association of parties for conducting proceeding. During this meeting dates for submissions are also decided. Arbitrator's fee, place of holding meetings shall also be decided (S. 20).

Once the submissions are received from both the parties, regular proceedings are held wherein equal and adequate opportunity is given to parties to present their case. Evidences are led coupled with arguments by both sides. The parties may exhibit their proofs. All the arbitrators must meet together, and hear the evidence of parties, but the award of a majority is valid.

If a party to arbitral proceedings refuses to participate (S. 25), or fails to comply with any orders of the tribunal, the tribunal may continue with the proceedings and issue an award without that party's participation. There is a reasonable approach when a party to arbitration fails to turn up to participate in the proceedings. In such cases the arbitrator should not jump to *ex parte* proceedings against him at that sitting. The arbitrator should fix another date of hearing and await the response of the party. If it is suspected that the party is avoiding appearance to frustrate the proceedings, the arbitrator should issue a notice that he intends holding hearing on a particular date at such venue. If the party concerned does not turn up then hold the proceedings in his absence. It remains open to the defaulting party to challenge the award subsequently on the usual grounds. In certain circumstances, the other party to the arbitration may also seek court support, with the permission of the tribunal, to use court powers in aid of arbitration.

The arbitral tribunal may refuse to accept evidence that relates to a fact that is irrelevant or that has already been established. The tribunal shall determine the admissibility, relevance, materiality and weight of the evidence offered. (S.19(4))

Minutes of every meeting are recorded and copy supplied to claimant and respondent. A day comes when nothing more is left for discussion/argument, that day proceedings are closed.

During meetings contentious issues would also be raised by parties. For instance, the issue of non production of documents in the possession of one party which could be used as evidence, admissibility of new claims, charge of misconduct against arbitrator etc. would be raised. These will have to be considered carefully and appropriate rulings given.

While conducting meetings and outside the meetings the arbitrator has to observe certain conduct which has been discussed elsewhere. Having gathered so much of stuff it is now time for the arbitrator to sit down and write the reasoned award. In fact, during the course of hearings, the mist starts clearing up as the evidence builds up and the arbitrator gets firm grip over the whole dispute. Only he has to reduce it in presentable form. In brief the following should be remembered while conducting meetings:

The minutes of the session shall include:

- (i) Any decision of the Arbitral Tribunal and the grounds thereof shall be written down in the minute:
  - (a) a brief description of the proceedings;
  - (b) requests and pleas made by the parties;
  - (c) the reasons underlying the decided measures;
  - (d) the order of the Tribunal; and
  - (e) the signatures of the arbitrators and the Co-arbitrators.
- (ii) The parties are entitled to take knowledge of the content of the minutes and of the documents in the file.
- (iii) Upon the parties' request, the Arbitral Tribunal may amend or complement the minutes of the session by other minutes.

(iv) A copy of the minute of the session shall be delivered to the parties upon their request.

Arbitrators must Act Together

Witnesses and parties must be examined in the presence of all the arbitrators. If there had been absence of some of the arbitrators from the meetings, an award given by the majority is not valid. However, if a party does not raise any objection to the absence of one of the arbitrator at some of the meetings, it is not open to such a party to contend subsequently that such absence rendered the award ineffective *(Gangaram Rathore* v. *Ramji Bondarji*, AIR 1966 MP 177).

Framing Issues

As per S. 19(1) of the act, an arbitral tribunal is not bound by the Code of Civil Procedure and therefore not necessary for it to frame issues. It is not expected of arbitrator which is not well versed in law to frame issues. For arbitral tribunal the claims are the issues to be determined.

Written Arguments

Some arbitrators after the conclusion of oral argument do not call upon the parties to submit written argument. It is rather in the interest of the parties to state their case in writing and request the tribunal to allow them a reasonable time within which it is proposed to submit written arguments.

When the arbitral tribunal proceedings come to an end the tribunal should record in the minutes that both the parties have completed their argument and they have nothing more to add. Besides, *"the proceedings are closed and kept reserved for making and publishing award"* should be recorded.

Writing Award

Making award is the climax of the arbitrator's task. Until the point of decision, the arbitrator has been under a moral and legal duty to keep an open mind. He might have begun to form a view, but that view remains subject to re-examination until the arbitrator has taken the logical steps, required for a sound decision. Award is not one of those areas where the form is more important than the substance. In many ways the whole purpose of arbitration is that decisions are made entirely on substance and not on form. Nevertheless presentation is important, as a courtesy to the arbitrator's employer, the parties who have honoured the arbitrator by inviting him to decide the issues they have been unable to resolve between them.

Courtesy requires a presentable award. It means a presentable document, well finished in appearance. What is more important, however, is that it should be a presentable document in respect of its content. The reasoning should be clear and the discussion polite. There should not be direct attack on any party or individuals. It should be remembered that the arbitrator is there to judge the issues and not the people.

The discussion should begin with a brief description of the background. Strictly, it need contain no more background than is necessary to support the findings of the Award, but it may be appropriate to extend it sufficiently to make sense of the story. Then the arbitrator may set out those facts that are uncontested, but it is important that they are uncontested. If there is any doubt, it is better to make a finding. Following on, from the background and the uncontested facts, the common ground, we turn to the discussion, reasoning and findings.

While writing it, the arbitrator should think about where to begin with. First we should put the loser. He needs to be satisfied that his case was heard and considered and, so far as possible to be satisfied that the arbitrator has been fair and that the Award is right. At the end of a hearing, they will be in a position to give a decision and the reasons for that decision. They should do so at the earliest possible moment. No particular form of Award is required. All that is necessary is that the arbitrators should set out what on their view of the evidence, did or did not happen, and should explain why in the light of what happened, they have reached their decision and what that decision is. This is all that is meant by a 'reasoned award'. It will be quite sufficient that they should explain how they reached their conclusion.... The point is that a reasoned award is completely different from an award in the form of a special case. Secondly, the award is intended for any Court which may have to enforce it or to hear any appeal under Arbitration Act, 1996. That requires the Award to be clear in its legal reasoning, and it requires it to be set out clearly so that the Court can see precisely what is intended. There is a schools of thought which encourages arbitrators to say as little as possible, to avoid giving grounds for appeal. That is not in the spirit of the legislation and is to be deprecated. The arbitrator's job is to be confident and not to try to hush up the reasoning in the hope of getting past a Judge. An arbitral award is a documentary instrument that has legal effect. The requirements an award should satisfy are that it should be cogent, complete, certain and final. In addition, it must be substantively compliant and procedurally compliant. Briefly, these requirements may be summarised thus:

Cogent: The award must be convincing in its reasoning.

Complete: The award must deal with all issues referred to the arbitrator.

Certain: The award must state what has been decided, if it is a declaratory award, and direct what is to be done and by whom, if it is dispositive. There must be no scope for doubt.

Final: The Award must deal finally with all the issues in the reference; nothing should be left to the decision of another.

Substantively Compliant: Broadly speaking, the decisions in the award should be in consonance with the laws or rules of law that the parties have selected. Otherwise, the Court may not enforce them. The other issue is that of Public Policy, which is one of the grounds that may persuade a Court not to enforce an award.

Procedurally Compliant: It is widely accepted that arbitration must be fair. Failure to comply with the agreed process, failure to give each party sufficient opportunity to present his case, all these are reasons for refusing enforcement. Additionally, there are formal requirements, such as that the award shall be signed, on non-judicial stamp paper of requisite amount and the seat of the arbitration recorded on the award (S. 31(4)).

The facts are those that the parties have presented, some of which may have been in the form of evidence by witnesses, some may have been common ground, and some may have been within the arbitrator's own knowledge and experience. When the arbitrator sits down, to commence writing the award, the first task is to marshal the evidence and the arguments.

The other important aspect is the arbitrator's own knowledge and experience. The principles of natural justice require that each party have a sufficient opportunity to present his case and to deal with any matter that may be against them. So, if an arbitrator is aware of something, or becomes aware of something it must be put to the parties if it is to be taken into account.

"The people who go to arbitration desire to have arbitrators who will not decide on evidence alone, but will bring to the consideration of the case a great deal of special knowledge."

The Arbitrator applies his skill and knowledge, but not his special knowledge of particular matters, at least not without some precautions. *"He should not act on his private opinion without disclosing it. It is undoubtedly true that an expert arbitrator can use his own expert knowledge. But a distinction is made in the cases between general expert knowledge and knowledge of special facts relevant in the particular case."*

> *"If the expert arbitrator, as he may be entitled to do, forms a view of the facts different from that given in the evidence which might produce a contrary result to that which emerges from the evidence, then he should bring that view to the attention of the parties".*

At an early stage, the arbitrator will have to consider how he wishes to construct the Award. Broadly speaking there are two choices. One is to set out the reasoning of the award as a flowing narrative, dealing with the evidence as it arises naturally in the sequence of things.

The findings are found throughout the narrative text and may or may not be summarised at the end.

There is an alternative to the narrative form. Where there are many issues, perhaps many disparate issues, the arbitrator may choose to write his reasoning on an issue-by-issue basis, dealing with the evidence and argument applicable to each and, perhaps, even making an award in respect of each one, with a sum of money attached to it. Whether the discussion has been on a narrative basis or on an issue-by-issue basis, it is as well to create a separate section of the Award, a dispositive section, in which to crystallise the decisions made into clear directions, setting out either precisely what has been found, if the Award is declaratory, or precisely who is to pay, how much, and when, if the award is a money Award. How the separation is made is a matter of personal style.

Summarizing, the arbitral award shall be drawn up in writing and shall include:

(a) the names of the members of the Arbitral Tribunal and of the co-arbitrator, the place and date of the rendering of the award; (S. 31)
(b) the full personal or corporate names of the parties and their addresses—residence or head office—as well as the full names of the parties' representatives and of the other persons having attended the hearings of the dispute;
(c) mention of the arbitral agreement underlying the arbitral proceedings;

(d) the object of the dispute and a summary of the parties' respective claims;
(e) the order with reasons (S. 31(3)); and
(f) the affixed signatures of all arbitrators and the signature of the co-arbitrator.

MINORITY DISSENTING VIEW OF ARBITRATOR

Under sec. 31(2) of the 1996 Act, it is stated that the signatures of the majority of the members shall be sufficient "so long as the reason for any omitted signature is stated." Sec. 29(1) states that, unless otherwise agreed, any decision of the arbitral tribunal with more than one member, shall be made by a majority of all its members.

This raises the question whether an arbitrator who is in a minority could avoid signing the award. It appears appropriate that section 31(2) may be amended providing that the dissenting member shall be entitled to submit his dissenting opinion and the same shall be treated as an annexure to the award. If the dissenting opinion is annexed to the award, the court before whom it may be questioned, will have the benefit of the dissenting opinion as well. It appears to be settled law, at any rate in international arbitration, that a dissenting opinion is not part of the award and, if given, it remains on record only as a part of information, unless the arbitration rules provide otherwise.

Award is Final and Binding

An arbitral award is final and binding upon the parties and persons claiming under them respectively(S. 35 of act). When award becomes final, it puts an end to all controversies between the parties and the issues have been arbitrated cannot be re-agitated. The award is final adjudication of a court chosen by parties and until impeached upon with sufficient grounds, in appropriate forum, is conclusive on the merits of the dispute submitted. A valid award operates to extinguish all claims which were subject matter of the reference to arbitration and the award alone furnishes the basis by which the rights of the parties can be determined. The finality and binding of award is subject to any right of appeal and wherever appeal is preferred, it is the appellant's award which becomes final award.

An award if valid, is final adjudication by a competent forum chosen by the parties themselves. It will therefore operate as *res judicata* in subsequent proceedings between the parties either in court or before arbitrator. Thus, if a cause has been decided by the award, a party will be prevented from raising it again in the same forum. Supreme Court of India in *Satish Kumar & Ors.* v. *Surinder Kumar & Ors.* have observed that "all claims which are the subject matter of a reference to arbitration merge in the award which is pronounced in the proceedings before the arbitrator and after an award has been pronounced, the rights and liabilities of the parties in respect of the said claims can be determined only on the basis of the said award. After an award is pronounced no action can be taken on the original claim which had been subject matter of the reference".

In *Seth Kerori mall* v. *Union of India*, the contractor claimant filed his claims before arbitrator. The respondent disputed every claim but had no claim of his own. During proceedings, the respondent wanted to add one claim which was denied by arbitrator on the ground that the claim was not referred to arbitration. As a result he had no jurisdiction to adjudicate the same. Respondent requested for appointment of another arbitrator for which the same arbitrator was appointed.

In the counter statement the opposite party contended inter alia that the claim is barred under the principle of *res judicata* as it was rejected in earlier proceedings. The court held that if the arbitrator, in determining his own jurisdiction considered a particular dispute sought to be raised by one party to be not within the reference, then it cannot be said that the arbitrator has adjudicated that particular dispute. If there has been no such adjudication of the dispute, it cannot be held that the subsequent reference of the dispute is barred by the principle of *res judicata*. It was further held that the same dispute once referred and embodied in an award cannot be the subject matter of a fresh reference and to that extent the rule of *res judicata* applies to proceedings. Further it is not the law that all dispute in relation to one contract must be disposed of in one reference. Failure to raise any such dispute in one reference, does not debar a party from raising other disputes to be adjusted in a subsequent reference.

It follows from the above that the same dispute once referred and embodied in an award cannot be the subject matter of a fresh reference and to that extent the rule of *res judicata* applies to arbitration proceeding. There is no authority for the proposition that disputes which could have been raised but were not raised previously, could not be raised on the principle of constructive *res judicata*. It is not necessary to consider to what extent the rule of constructive *res judicata* is applicable to arbitration proceeding because I hold on fact that the instant dispute was expressly left out of consideration in the previous arbitration proceeding on the ground that the arbitrator lacked jurisdiction to entertain the dispute.

To bar a subsequent reference, it must be shown that the disputes sought to be referred were actually referred and decided in the previous proceeding. If not actually referred, there would be no bar to a subsequent reference.

In the case of *Balmukund Rina* v. *Gopiram Bhotica* (AIR 1920 Cal 808) it was held: "there may be as many awards as there are disputes arising out of the same contract. The sub-mission is not exhausted by reason of the more fact that one award final and complete in itself has issued from it."

In the case of *Pushraj Puranmal* v. *Clive Mills Co. Ltd.*, following observations were made: "One arbitration agreement therefore can produce one or more awards and the law of arbitration, as I understood it, does not nurse any dogma to say that it can never do so under any circumstances because of some fancied universal doctrine of legal merger of the arbitration agreement in the award.

Setting Aside Award

Section 34 of the Act, 1996 deals with the setting aside of an arbitral award on the grounds mentioned there in. The section reads as under:

S. 34 Application for Setting Aside Arbitral Award

(1) Recourse to a Court against an arbitral award may be made only by an application for setting aside such award in accordance with sub-section (2) and sub-section (3).

(2) An arbitral award may be set aside by the Court only if—

(a) the party making the application furnishes proof that—

(i) a party was under some incapacity, or

(ii) the arbitration agreement is not valid under the law to which the parties have subjected it or, failing any indication thereon, under the law for the time being in force; or

(iii) the party making the application was not given proper notice of the appointment of an arbitrator or of the arbitral proceedings or was otherwise unable to present his case; or

(iv) the arbitral award deals with a dispute not

contemplated by or not falling within the terms of the submission to arbitration, or it contains decisions on matter beyond the scope of the submission to arbitration:

Provided that, if the decisions on matters submitted to arbitration can be separated from those not so submitted, only that part of the arbitral award which contains decisions on matters not submitted to arbitration may be set aside; or

(v) the composition of the arbitral tribunal or the arbitral procedure was not in accordance with the agreement of the parties, unless such agreement was in conflict with a provision of this Part from which the parties cannot derogate, or, failing such agreement, was not in accordance with this Past; or

(b) the Court finds that—

(i) the subject-matter of the dispute is not capable of settlement by arbitration under the law for the time being in force, or

(ii) the arbitral award is in conflict with the public policy of India.

Explanation.—Without prejudice to the generality of sub-clause (ii), it is hereby declared, for the avoidance of any doubt, that an award is in conflict with the public policy of India if the making of the award was induced of affected by fraud or corruption or was in violation of section 75 or section 81.

(3) An application for setting aside may not be made after three months have elapsed from the date on which the party making that application had received the arbitral award, or, if a request had been made under section 33, from the date on which that request had been disposed of by the arbitral tribunal:

Provided that if the Court is satisfied that the applicant was prevented by sufficient cause from making the application within the said period of three months it may entertain the application within a further period of thirty days, but not thereafter.

(4) On receipt of an application under sub-section (1), the Court may, where it is appropriate and it is so requested by a party, adjourn the proceedings for a period of time determined by it in order to give the arbitral tribunal an opportunity to resume the arbitral proceedings or to take such other action as in the opinion of arbitral tribunal will eliminate the grounds for setting aside the arbitral award.

When the award has been made, the party or parties after participating in proceedings as per Act, 1996, who feel aggrieved by the award will have an opportunity for re-agitating the issues in respect of which the claims has been unsuccessful before the arbitral tribunal. An award if challenged in appellate court can be set aside on the following grounds as mentioned in S. 34.

(i) Incapacity of party;
(ii) Invalid arbitration agreement;
(iii) Composition of tribunal not in accordance with the agreement;
(iv) Party unable to present its case
(v) Failure to consider vital document;
(vi) Award based on no evidence;
(vii) Arbitrator acting beyond submissions;
(viii) Award made in ignorance of terms of contracts;
(ix) Award contrary to law or substance of dispute;
(x) Inconsistent findings in award;
(xi) Failure to adjudicate;
(xii) Award by illegally constituted tribunal;
(xiii) Matter non-capable of settlement;
(xiv) Award contrary to public policy of India;
(xv) Findings of facts cannot be set aside; and
(xvi) Court cannot look into the merit of award.

If the party making the application furnishes the proof of incapacity, the award may be set aside. If arbitration agreement is not valid ie consideration for entering into an agreement to refer is illegal, the whole agreement and reference is void. In case a party is able to furnish proof that it was not given proper notice of appointment of arbitrator, the award will not be valid and liable to set aside. Appointment of arbitrator made contrary to terms of the agreement would vitiate the proceedings. An award passed without following natural law of justice and without affording full opportunity to either party may be set aside. Award based upon guess work and assumptions and not on evidence will be bad in law. It is also obligatory and mandatory for the arbitrator to stick to the term of the contract and the reference. An arbitrator cannot travel beyond the terms of the contract on the reference and enlarge the scope of his jurisdiction. An arbitrator cannot decide dispute not submitted to it.

An arbitrator must arrive at his findings on the basis of the whole record placed before him by the parties. Arbitrator has no authority to ignore any document or evidence which throws light on the dispute. Whether a particular document is material or not and whether it should be produced before the arbitrator is essentially a matter for the arbitrator to decide. Even if a party does not produce, it is incumbent upon arbitrator to get hold of the said document.

An award could also be set aside if it is so unfair and unreasonable that it shakes the conscience of the court. Where the arbitrator does not decide an important and essential matter but leaves it to the decision of another authority, the award will suffer from serious infirmity making it invalid.

However, the appellate court too has limitations to deal the challenges which are as under:

(i) That court cannot substitute its own decision in case of dispute as to the contract because what is the interpretation of that contract is a matter for the arbitrator. A court cannot take upon itself the burden of saying that the findings of arbitrator are contrary to the contract.

(ii) That only in case of speaking award, court can look into the reasoning of the award but cannot probe mental process of arbitrator where no reasons are given by the arbitrator.

(iii) That in case of challenge to award, there are two distinct and different grounds i.e. (a) an error apparent on the face of the record, and (b) the arbitrator has exceeded his authority.

(iv) That reasonableness of reasons assigned in the award cannot be reviewed by court by sitting as court of appeal.

(v) That where the liability is not denied and the dispute relates only to the amount awarded then certainly there is no error apparent on the face of it.

(vi) Court will not set aside the award because the award amount is high except where the award is perverse or when the awarded amount exceeded the claimed amount.

(vii) It is not open to court to set aside a finding of fact by arbitrator unless these are supported by evidence. The award is not pen to challenge on the ground that arbitrator has reason writing conclusion and failed to appreciate facts.

(viii) A court cannot interfere with the award if its opinion is different from that of the arbitrator.

(ix) The court cannot examine why the arbitrator has claimed certain claims.

(x) The court should not re-appreciate the evidence.

(xi) A court cannot review the award of arbitrator and correct any mistake in his adjudication unless objection to legality or error of law is apparent on the fall of the award itself.

4 Public Policy and Misconduct by Arbitrator

In the earlier Arbitration Act, 1940, the misconduct by arbitrator was a powerful tool to monitor the quality of proceedings and conduct of arbitrator. In new act, this has been taken off. At few places we come across the phrase 'Public Policy'. It is the public policy which plays significant role in guiding the proceedings of tribunal and making of an award. Therefore, it is important to dwell for sometime on it.

The Act, 1996 or the Contract Act, 1872 do not define the expression "Public Policy" or "opposed to public policy." "Public Policy" is not the policy of a particular government. It connotes something which concerns the public good or the public interest.

The concept of the 'Public Policy' denotes that what is good for the public or in public Interest or what would be injurious or harmful from time to time. It implies good and moral conduct conforming to norms than following slipshod approach in arbitration. The concept of 'Public Policy' has very wide and general implications. Anything that hurts collective conscience is against the 'Public Policy'. Hence, the *Acts in violation of law* shall be considered against the 'Public Policy'. 'Public Policy' is equivalent to the "Policy of Law." Therefore any act that have a mischievous tendency so as to be injurious to the interest of the state or the public is stated to be against "Public Policy". Whatever leads to obstruction of justice or violation of a statute or is against the good morals when made the object of contract would be against 'Public Policy of India' and being void, would not be susceptible to enforcement.

Misconduct of "Arbitrator or of the "proceedings before an arbitral tribunal" and "error of law on the face of an arbitral tribunal award" by themselves are not made as grounds for recourse against an arbitral award under section 34 of the 1996 Act. Interpreting the "Public Policy of India" in its broader view, courts of law may intervene permitting recourse against an arbitral award based on irregularity of a kind which the court considers has caused or will cause substantial injustice to the applicant. Extreme cases where arbitral tribunal has gone so wrong in its conduct of arbitration that justice calls out for it to be corrected may justifiably fall within the ambit of the 'Public Policy of India' to enable courts of law to intervene under section 34 of the 1996 Act permitting recourse against arbitral award.

Awards made, signed and Pronounced by the learned sole Arbitrator/Arbitral Tribunal after entering into the reference and conduct of the arbitration Proceedings are challenged considering the awards being against the "Public Policy of India" which has a wider meaning. There is no definition of the term "Public Policy of India" in the Arbitration and Conciliation Act, 1996, except the reference under section 34(2) (b) (ii); 48(2) (b), and section 57(I) (e) stating that the awards made should be not against the Public Policy of India. Similarly, section 75 on confidentiality and section 81 on admissibility of evidence in other proceedings also restrain the sole Arbitrator/Arbitral Tribunal to make award which is against the "Public Policy of India". Therefore, it is desirable that the sole Arbitrator/Arbitral Tribunal should be conversant with the terms "Public Policy of India" and the prevailing law on this, so that the sole Arbitrator/Arbitral Tribunal take care of the same, while making award.

AWARD IN CONFLICT WITH "PUBLIC POLICY OF INDIA"

The legislature has clarified by insertion of explanation to sub-section (2) of section 48 of the Act 1996 that "an award is in conflict with Public Policy of India " if the making of it was induced or affected by fraud or corruption. "Induced by fraud" will mean the arbitral tribunal was led to give the award by the influence of deception practised to secure the award to the detriment of the other party. The expression "Induced by corruption" will mean securing of an award by corrupting arbitral tribunal. The court is empowered to set aside such an award which is induced or affected by fraud or corruption treating these acts as opposed to the public policy of India.

The Act, 1996 restrains an Arbitral Tribunal to make any award which is against the Public Policy of India. Various provisions laid down under Act, 96 are briefly discussed here:

Section 34(2)(b) (ii) of the said Act, 1996 lays down that "*an Arbitral Award may be set aside if the court finds that the arbitral award is in conflict with the Public Policy of India.*"

Explanation to section 34 of the 1996 Act, without prejudice to the generality of sub-clause (ii), it is here by declared, for the avoidance of any doubt, that an award is in conflict with the Public Policy of India if the making of the award was induced or affected by fraud or corruption or was violation of Section 75 or Section 81 of 1996 Act.

In *Oil and Natural Gas Corporation Ltd.* v. *Saw Pipes Ltd.* the Supreme Court has examined this issue critically and exhaustively and have filled many gaps. *Court has observed* : "The clause (ii) of sub-section 2(b) of Section 34 which *inter alia* provides that the Court may set aside arbitral award if it is in conflict with the 'Public Policy of India'. The phrase 'Public Policy of India' is not defined under the Act. Hence, the said term is required to be given meaning in context and also considering the purpose of the section and scheme of the Act. The expression '*public policy*' does not admit precise definition and may vary from generation to generation and from time to time. Hence, the concept 'public policy' is considered to be vague, susceptible to narrow or wider meaning depending upon the context in which it is used.

SCI again observes : "While dealing with the concept of 'public policy', it is noted that Indian Contract Act does not define the expression "public policy" or "opposed to public policy". From the very nature of things, the expressions "public policy", "opposed to public policy", or "contrary to public policy" are incapable of precise definition. Public policy, however, is not the policy of a particular government. It connotes some matter which concerns the public good and the public interest. The concept of what is for the public good or in the public interest or what would be injurious or harmful to the public good or the public interest has varied from time to time. As new concepts take the place of old, transactions which were once considered against public policy are now being upheld by the courts and similarly where there has been a well recognized head of public policy, the courts have not shirked from extending it to the new transactions and changed circumstances."

SCI further observes: "the principles governing public policy must be and are capable, on proper occasion, of expansion or modification. Practices which were considered perfectly normal at one time have today become obnoxious and oppressive to public conscience. If there is no head of public policy which covers a case, then the court must in consonance with public conscience and in keeping with public good and public interest declare such practice to be opposed to public policy. Above all, in deciding any case which may not be covered by authority our courts have before them the beacon light of the Preamble to the Constitution. Lacking precedent, the court can always be guided by that light and the principles underlying the Fundamental Rights and the Directive Principles enshrined in our Constitution."

"The normal rule of Common Law has been that a party who seeks to enforce an agreement which is opposed to public policy will be non-suited. Where a contract is vitiated as being contrary to public policy, the party adversely affected by it can sue to have it declared void. The case may be different where the purpose of the contract is illegal or immoral."

While dealing with the concept of 'public policy' SCI continues to observe: "Public policy does not remain static in any given community. It may vary from generation to generation and even in the same generation. Public policy would be almost useless if it were to remain in fixed moulds for all time." The court adds: "In a case where the validity of award is challenged there is no necessity of giving a narrower meaning to the term 'public policy of India'. On the contrary, wider meaning is required to be given so that the 'patently illegal award' passed by the arbitral tribunal could be set aside. If narrow meaning is given some of the provisions of the Arbitration Act would become nugatory. Take for illustration a case wherein there is a specific provision in the contract that for delayed payment of the amount due and payable, no interest would be payable, still however, if the Arbitrator has passed an award granting interest, it would be against the terms of the contract and thereby against the provision of Section 28(3) of the Act which specifically provides that "arbitral tribunal shall decide in accordance with the terms of the contract". Further, where there is a specific usage of the trade that if the payment is made beyond a period of one month, then the party would be required to pay the said amount with interest at the rate of 15 per cent. Despite the evidence being produced on record for such usage, if the arbitrator refuses to grant such interest on the ground of equity, such award would also be in violation of sub-sections (2) and (3) of Section 28. Section 28(2) specifically provides that arbitrator shall decide *ex aequo et bono* [according to what is just and good] only if the parties have expressly authorized him to do so. Similarly, if the award is patently against the statutory provisions of substantive law which is in force in India or is passed without giving an opportunity of hearing to the parties as provided under Section 24 or without giving any reason in a case where parties have not agreed that no reasons are to be recorded, it would be against the statutory provisions. In all such cases, the award is required to be set aside on the ground of 'patent illegality'."

Another observation is : "What would constitute public policy is a matter dependant upon the nature of transaction and nature of statute. For the said purpose, the pleadings of the parties and the materials brought on record would be relevant to enable the court to judge what is in public good or public interest, and what would otherwise be injurious to the public good at the relevant point, as contradistinguished from the policy of a particular government."

The award which is patently illegal could be set aside if it is contrary to:

(a) Fundamental policy of Indian law; or
(b) The interest of India; or
(c) Justice or morality, or
(d) In addition, if it is patently illegal. Illegality must go to the root of the matter and if the illegality is of trivial nature it cannot be held that award is against the public policy. Award could also be set aside if it is so unfair and unreasonable that it shocks the conscience of the court. Such award is opposed to public policy and is required to be adjudged void."

The following issues which will defeat the arbitration process being against Public Policy are discussed below:

Fraud

Section 17 of the Indian Contract Act, 1872 defines fraud. However, 'fraud' has a wider meaning, far wider than the definition given under the Contract Act. Fraud is an act of deliberate deception with the design of securing something by taking unfair advantage of another. It is a deception in order to gain by other's loss. It is a cheating intended to get an undue advantage. Courts have held that "A litigant, who approaches the court, is bound to produce all documents executed by him, which are relevant to the litigation. If he withholds a vital document in order to gain advantage on the other side then he would be guilty of playing fraud on the court as well as on the opposite party". Section 17 defines fraud thus: "Fraud" means and includes any of the following acts committed by a party to a contract, or with his connivance, or by his agents, with intent to deceive another party thereto his agent, or to induce him to enter into the contract; (1) the suggestion as a fact, of that which is not true, by one who does not believe it to be true; (2) the active concealment of a fact by one having knowledge or belief of the fact; (3) a promise made without any intention of performing it; (4) any other act fitted to deceive; (5) any such act or omission as the law specially declares to be fraudulent.

Corruption

Corruption means bribery. It need not be in monetary terms. An improper relationship between an arbitrator and a party or a party's legal advisor may render the award open to attack also on this ground. Procurement of award by "Undue Means" is a ground for setting an award aside.

Accepting Hospitality

If an arbitrator accepts hospitality from one of the parties and the invitation was extended with the intention to induce the arbitrator to act unfairly or it has the affect of inducing the arbitrator to act unfairly, it may be said that the award was induced or affected by corruption. But mere dining or lunching with one of the parties or his witness or witnesses in the absence of the other party may not make him guilty. To influence the award making on such ground, there must be something more than mere suspicion.

Illegal Gratification

The arbitrator should always scrupulously avoid any course of action which even remotely bears the colour of his having put himself into a position where it might be said against him that he had received a pecuniary gain which might have had some effect on his adjudication process. An arbitrator ought to be an indifferent person between the disputants and should be incorrupt and impartial. If the arbitrator take bribe, the award would be liable to be set aside.

Confidentiality

Section 75 of the Act, 1996 pertaining to Conciliation provides that the Conciliator and the parties shall keep all matters relating to the conciliation proceedings Confidential. It further provides that confidentiality shall extend also to the settlement agreement except where its disclosure is necessary for the purpose of implementation and enforcement thereof. Thus, if an arbitral award is induced in violation of the provision contained in section 75, it shall be against the statutory provisions contained in Section 75 and as such, in conflict with the "Public Policy of India."

Not in Conflict with Public Policy of India

The following matter is not in conflict with public policy:

(i) "Mere error of law is not necessary a breach of 'Public Policy' within the meaning of section 34(2)(b)(ii)".

(ii) "Public Policy of India in no way stands in way of awarding interest.

(iii) "Award made and signed on earlier date by the Arbitrators and thereafter engrossed on Non-Judicial stamp papers furnished by the party at a later date cannot be said that the award was passed when non-judicial stamp papers were supplied and was ante-dated. No Violation of "Public Policy."

(iv) "Reference of disputes to foreign arbitration in accordance with arbitration clause adopted by the parties is not opposed to public policy"

Award in Conflict with "Public Policy of India"

(i) "Award not based on true construction of the terms and conditions of the contract between the parties and correct appreciation of the material in as much as he has ignored the certain important clauses of the agreement while arriving at the said findings is clearly in conflict with the "Public Policy of India."

(ii) "Where an Arbitrator or an Arbitral Tribunal ignores a well recognized principle of interpretation, such an award would be against public policy."

(iii) "If the award is found to be contrary to fundamental Policy of Indian law or Indian Interest or Justice or morality, the same could be held to be contrary to "Public Policy" of India" .

MISCONDUCT BY ARBITRATOR

The Act,1996 has no mention of misconduct. The word 'misconduct' does not necessarily comprehend or include misconduct of fraudulent or improper conduct or moral lapse but does comprehend and include actions on the part of the arbitrator, which on the face of the award, are opposed to all rational and reasonable principles resulting in excessive award or unjust result which tend to show non-application of the mind to the material facts placed before the arbitrator. In truth it points to fact that the arbitrator has passed his own judgment without having regard to evidences. Arbitrator had not applied his mind and not adjudicated upon the matter, although the award professes to determine them. Such situation would amount to misconduct. In other words, if the arbitrator is found to have not applied his mind to the matters in controversy and yet, has adjudicated upon those matters, there can be no adjudication made on them. In the act, 1996 at following places indirect reference to the conduct of arbitrator has been made:

S.12. *Grounds for challenge.* (1) *When a person is approached in connection with his possible appointment as an arbitrator, he shall disclose in writing any circumstances likely to give rise to justifiable doubts as to his independence or impartiality;.*

(2) An arbitrator, from the time of his appointment and throughout the arbitral proceedings, shall, without delay, disclose to the parties in writing any circumstances referred to in sub-section (1) unless they have already been informed of them by him.

(3) An arbitrator may be challenged only if—

(a) circumstances exist that give rise to justifiable doubts as to his independence or impartiality, or

S.16. *Competence of arbitral tribunal to rule on its jurisdiction—* (3) *A plea that the arbitral tribunal is exceeding the scope of its authority shall be raised as soon as the matter alleged to be beyond the scope of its authority is raised during the arbitral proceedings.*

S.18. *Equal treatment of parties— The parties shall be treated with equality and each party shall be given a full opportunity to present his case.*

S.24. *Hearings and written proceedings—(2) The parties shall be given sufficient advance notice of any hearing and of any meeting of the arbitral tribunal for the purposes of inspection of documents, goods or other property.*

(3) All statements, documents or other information supplied to, or applications made to, the arbitral tribunal by one party shall be communicated to the other party, and any expert report or evidentiary document on which the arbitral tribunal may rely in making its decision shall be communicated to the parties.

S.28. *Rules applicable to substance of dispute—(3) In all cases, the arbitral tribunal shall decide in accordance with the terms of the contract and shall take into account the usages of the trade applicable to the transaction.*

S.31. *Form and contents of arbitral award—(1) An arbitral award shall be made in writing and shall be signed by the members of the arbitral tribunal.*

(2) For the purposes of sub-section (1), in arbitral proceedings with more than one arbitrator, the signatures of the majority of all the members of the arbitral tribunal shall be sufficient so long as the reason for any omitted signature is stated.

(3) The arbitral award shall state the reasons upon which it is based, unless—

(a) the parties have agreed that no reasons are to be given, or
(b) the award is an arbitral award on agreed terms under section 30.

(4) The arbitral award shall state its date and the place of arbitration as determined in accordance with section 20 and the award shall be deemed to have been made at that place.

(5) After the arbitral award is made, a signed copy shall be delivered to each party.

S.34. *Application for setting aside arbitral award. (1) Recourse to a Court against an arbitral award may be made only by an application for setting aside such award in accordance with sub-section (2) and sub-section (3).*

(2) An arbitral award may be set aside by the Court only if—

(ii) the arbitration agreement is not valid under the law to which the parties have subjected it or, failing any indication thereon, under the law for the time being in force; or

(iii) the party making the application was not given proper notice of the appointment of an arbitrator or of the arbitral proceedings or was otherwise unable to present his case; or

(iv) the arbitral award deals with a dispute not contemplated by or not falling within the terms of the submission to arbitration, or it contains decisions on matter beyond the scope of the submission to arbitration:

Thus, the parameters of conduct of arbitrator has been laid down indirectly, any departure or non-compliance of these parameters would attract adverse inference for setting aside of award or removal of arbitrator himself. Besides, chapter on duties of arbitrator also touches upon the conduct of arbitrator.

Misconduct are of three types:

(i) Legal misconduct;
(ii) Personal misconduct; and
(iii) Misconducting proceedings.

What is a legal misconduct has to be considered on the facts of each case. Where the arbitrator hold talk with the counsel for the plaintiff on the back of the defendant, the arbitrator would be deemed to have misconducted himself. A positive act of the arbitrator to communicate with the other side is a conduct which would tantamount to violation of the principles of natural justice and would materially affect the award and would be a legal misconduct of arbitrator. Likewise when an award can be said to be improperly procured is again a question of fact in each case. If the arbitrator solicits and actually take the assistance of the plaintiff in the matter of getting his seat reserved by a train and for their return journey by air, it can safely be concluded that the arbitrators have misconducted themselves and the award would be deemed to have been improperly procured. It would not be accepted that such a conduct of the arbitrator was a mere indiscretion and was not a form of procurement. Ceaser's wife should be above "suspicion" and so should be the arbitrator. It would be imperative for the arbitrators that they scrupulously avoid any course of action which would even remotely suggest to bear the complexion of their having put themselves into a position where it could be said against them that they had received a pecuniary inducement which might have had some effect on their determination of the matter in arbitration. On the existence of this situation the arbitrators would be deemed to have misconducted themselves and the award would be deemed to have been improperly procured.

It is generally accepted that a Final Arbitral Award can be set aside by a Court if the Arbitrator has misconducted the proceedings. Misconduct, in this case, refers to legal misconduct which arises if the Arbitrator on the face of the award arrives at a decision ignoring material documents.

A party challenging an award must establish, not only that there is no evidence on which a reasonable man would have made it, but also that the lack of evidence is so glaring that misconduct on the part of the arbitrator can be inferred. The term "*misconduct*" does not refer to moral turpitude and "*gross irregularity in the conduct of the arbitration proceedings*" relate to the conduct of, and not the result of the arbitration. The irregularity must have been so serious that it resulted in the aggrieved party not having his case heard.

The arbitrator cannot act arbitrarily, irrationally, capriciously or independent of the contract. His sole function is to arbitrate in terms of the contract. He has no power other than what the parties have conferred upon him in the contract. An arbitrator cannot go beyond the terms of the contract between the parties. In the guise of doing justice, he cannot award contrary to the terms of the contract. If he does so, he will have misconducted himself.

It is settled law that arbitrator derives authority from the contract and if he acts in manifest disregard of the contract, the award given by him would be arbitrary. The deliberate departure from the contract terms amounts not only to manifest disregard of the authority or misconduct on his part, but it may tantamount to mala-fide action.

It is also settled that the administrative instructions which have no statutory authority, do not give rise to any legal right in favour of the aggrieved Party and cannot be enforced in any court of law against the administration. Therefore, these should not be considered unless these have been made part of contract.

While reviewing the conduct of arbitrator it should be seen that he has not :

- Committed misconduct in relation to his/her arbitration duties;
- Committed a gross irregularity in the conduct of the arbitration proceedings; and
- Exceeded his/her powers; or made the award improperly.

The above criteria refers to misconduct and irregularities, including, but not limited to:

- Taking into account evidence that was not put before the arbitrator;
- Refusing to allow valid and relevant evidence to be brought;
- Ignoring statutory requirements or legal principles;
- Unduly assisting one or other party with his/her case;
- Delivering a biased award;
- Taking a bribe;
- Failure to apply his/her mind to the facts in evidence;
- Using improper language;
- Not maintaining confidentiality;
- Not affording full opportunity to both the parties to present their case;
- Parties not being treated equally; and
- Gross-irregularity in conducting proceedings.

But in order to constitute legal misconduct, it is not necessary that there should be proof of any dishonesty or partiality on the part of the arbitrator. Any act amounts to a legal misconduct if it would give rise to a reasonable probability that the arbitrator would be subjected to any improper influence.

The rights of an arbitrator as regards the payment of his fee are well settled. After making his award he is entitled to retain the award until he has received his fee either from one party or the other. But that is a wholly different matter from taking a fee from one of the parties before he has actually made his award. The section 38 & 39 of Act, 1996 are very much relevant here. The tribunal may ask the parties to deposit the amount as an advance of court. Where one party does not pay, other party may be requested to pay the share of the other party and later on arbitrator may adjust the cost in award.

Arbitration in India is governed by the Arbitration and Conciliation Act, 1996. No provision under the Act of 1996 explicitly defines either 'serious misconduct' or 'biases' though misconduct was the basis for challenge to arbitrators under the Act of 1940. However, its implication can be inferred from a reading of sections 12, 13, 14, 15 and 34 of the Act. Though there is no direct provision or case law on arbitral immunity in India, a combined reading of these provisions and relevant case law, gives us a clearer picture of the extent of this protection. Under these sections suspicion by itself could not be made a ground for conclusion that the arbitrator would not act impartially or fairly. Hence, termination of the mandate is not allowed only on the apprehension of bias. To apply for a termination of a mandate, there must be actual bias. The apprehension must be judged from a healthy, reasonable and average point of view and not on mere apprehension of any whimsical person. However, the remedies against misconduct are the removal of the arbitrator, setting aside the arbitral award or the non-payment or partial payment of the arbitrator's fees. Reasonable apprehension or likelihood of bias of the arbitrator is sufficient ground for the removal of the arbitrator while actual bias must be proved for the setting aside of the award.

SUMMARY

1. Arbitrator is expected to conduct himself with dignity, fairness and impartiality.
2. Though no definition has been coined for Public Policy of India, but it connotes conduct of persons which is not injurious to others. It should be devoid of mischief, fraud, corruption, etc. Public policy indicates public good and public interest.
3. An award which is against public policy of India can be set aside.
4. Public Policy is not static. It is evolutionary in nature. At a given point of time it may vary from place to place.
5. The word 'misconduct' does not appear in the Act, 1996 except in the form of 'Public Policy of India'.
6. Dealings of arbitrator should be fair and unbiased in all respect with both the parties.
7. He should not conduct proceedings in slip-shod manner and give full opportunity to both the parties to present their case.

8. Arbitrator should remain within his domain which is carved out by Contract.
9. He should pass a reasoned award based on the evidence led before him. He should not use his personal knowledge or opinion except of specialised nature.
10. In case arbitrator's conduct is found to be non-complaint or there is justifiable doubt about his independence or impartiality, the objection should be raised without losing time.

5 Claim for Interest

Traditionally, the courts have held the view that interest should not be awarded as compensation for the late payment of a debt. This was originally based on a hostility to usury. Damages are awarded on the basis of the restoration of the plaintiff to the position he would have been in but for the defendant's wrong, subject to questions of remoteness and the duty to mitigate losses. The plaintiff suffers an economic loss if damages are not paid promptly, either in terms of expenditure incurred, (needing to borrow money on interest), or investment lost, not being able to put the money in the bank. Incurred expenditure and opportunity cost are much more than the late payment of damages. They are pecuniary losses suffered by the plaintiff as a result of the defendant's wrong. This kind of loss is not too remote and it is foreseeable. The plaintiff's loss is compensated by ordering interest to be paid on the amount due. The plaintiff's loss is best calculated by the use of interest.

Damages are usually calculated as at the date of the wrong. This rule is not universally applicable and another date may be chosen if it is necessary to give appropriate compensation. Interest is subject to different meanings. In a financial context, interest is the money paid by someone else for the use of a person's money, as on a loan or debt, on a checking account in a bank, on a certificate of deposit, or the amount due on a judgment. Traditional hostility is to the award of *interest to be paid on damages.* This thinking should go since world has changed from non-materialistic to materialistic. This is to be distinguished from the cases where interest is awarded as part of the compensation for the damage suffered by the plaintiff due to breach of payment conditions.

In contractual matters the payment of interest is a matter of debate. The reason could be delayed payment for work done and withholding of amount wrongfully. In railways so far as Stores purchase is concerned, the arbitration agreement does not put any restriction on payment of interest. The payment of interest is governed by the Act, 1996 and the contract conditions. In works contract, however, there are number of restrictive clause which deny interest for anything and everything. Even if railway is on the wrong side, no compensation would be paid. One could instead ask for Extension Of Time. No interest is payable for delayed payment or illogical withholding of amount. Together with contract agreement, the Act, 1996 and judicial decisions have created a situation of perplexity.

The life blood of contracts is cash flow. When payment obligations are not met on time, the contractor either has to finance expenditure from his own resources, or borrow, or both. The contractor loses the use of money due under the contract, but paid late.

Payment of interest arises in different circumstances. It can be the consideration paid by a borrower to a lender for use of the money lent. It can be the return given by a bank or financial institution invested with them by a customer. It can be the compensation paid by a person who withholds or defaults in paying an amount or in discharging a liability, when it is due and payable. Interest may be payable in pursuance of a contract, or a provision in a statute, or the fiat of a court. It is usually quantified in terms of a percentage of the 'principal' amount. Interest unless otherwise specified, refers to simple interest that is the interest paid on the 'principal' and not on any accrued interest.

In contract matters interest is payable for the pre-reference period, pendete lite and future interest. It is admissible under Act, 1996 as well as under Interest act provided parties to the agreement have not decided otherwise.

In a case "The authorities noticed in the working of the Provident Fund Act and the Scheme that an employer could delay payment of provident fund dues without any additional financial liability; amended the Act for recovery of damages on the amount of arrears, the object and purpose being to authorise the Commissioner to impose exemplary punitive damages and thereby to prevent the employers from making the defaults. This, however, did not prove sufficiently deterrent and the employers were still making defaults in making contributions to the provident fund and in the meanwhile utilising both their own contribution as well as the employees' contributions. It was held that it was a fit case for imposition of punitive damages to ensure due compliance of the provisions of the Act. There are powers to recover damages and the damages imposed must have co-relation with the loss suffered as a result of delayed payment." Thus payment of interest should not be treated as abhorrent.

In another case "the appellants did not dispute their liability to pay interest. They however contended that Section 31(7) of the Act, 1996 does not contemplate award of interest on interest; that an arbitral tribunal can award future interest only on the 'principal' amount but not on the interest thereon which had accrued up to the date of award.

Section 3 of the Interest Act, 1978 enables the courts and arbitral tribunals to award interest from the date of cause of action to the date of institution of legal proceedings or initiation of arbitration proceedings. Sub-section (3)(c) of section 3 of the Interest Act, 1978 makes it clear that nothing in the said section shall empower the Court or arbitrator to award interest upon interest. It should be noted that section 3 of Interest Act does not deal with either pendente lite or future interest. Courts have held that award of interest on interest is not opposed to the 'public policy' of India, but could be awarded only if authorized by contract or statute. Should it not be construed that when award of interest upon interest is not opposed to public policy then non-payment of interest should be against the public policy? The Act, 1996, on the other hand, contains a specific provision dealing with the power of the arbitral tribunal to award interest. The said Sub-section (7) of S. 31 is extracted below:

"Unless otherwise agreed by the parties, where and insofar as an arbitral award is for the payment of money, the arbitral tribunal may include in the sum for which the award is made, interest, at such rate as it deems reasonable, on the whole or any part of the money, for the whole or any part of the period between the date on which the cause of action arose and the date on which the award is made. **(Here it may be cautioned that no substantive changes can be made in original arbitration agreement during proceedings.)**

(b) A sum directed to be paid by an arbitral award shall, unless the award otherwise directs, carry interest at the rate of eighteen per cent per annum from the date of the award to the date of payment".

Courts have been maintaining that "Section 31(7) makes no reference to payment of compound interest or payment of interest upon interest. Nor does it require the interest which accrues till the date of the award, to be treated as part of the principal from the date of award for calculating the post-award interest. The use of the words "where and in so far as an arbitral award is for the payment of money"; and use of the words "the arbitral tribunal may include in the sum for which the award is made, interest...... on the whole or any part of the money" in clause (a) and use of the words "a sum directed to be paid by an arbitral award shall carry interest". In clause (b) of sub-section (7) of section 31 clearly indicate that the section contemplates award of only simple interest and not compound interest or interest upon interest. 'A sum directed to be paid by an arbitral award' refers to the award of sums on the **substantive claims** and does not refer to interest awarded on the 'sum directed to be paid by the award'. In the absence of any provision for interest upon interest in the contract, the arbitral tribunals do not have the power to award interest upon interest, or compound interest, either for the pre-award period or for the post-award period."

Courts have noted that "Some Arbitral Tribunals have misconstrued clause (b) of section 31(7) of the Act and assumed that the said provision requires the rate of post-award interest in all arbitral awards should be 18% per annum, and that they do not have any discretion in regard to post-award interest. Some have misconstrued it further to infer the rate of interest mentioned therein as an indication that invariably the rate of interest in arbitrations, either pre-award or post-award, should be 18% per annum. Both these assumptions are baseless and erroneous. If that was the legislative intention, there would have been no need for vesting discretion in Arbitral Tribunals, in the matter of interest, under section 31(7)(a). A comparatively high rate of post-award interest is provided in section 31(7)(b) of the Act, not because 18% is the normal rate of interest to be awarded in arbitrations, but purely as a deterrent to award-debtors from avoiding payment or using delaying tactics."

The difference between clauses (a) and (b) of section 31(7) of the Act may conveniently be noted at this stage. The difference is :

(i) Clause (a) relates to pre-award period and clause (b) relates to post-award period. The contract binds and prevails in regard to interest during the pre-award period. The contract has no application in regard to interest during the post-award period.

(ii) Clause (a) gives discretion to the Arbitral Tribunal in regard to the rate, the period, the quantum (principal which is to be subjected to interest) when awarding interest. But such discretion is always subject to the contract between the parties. Clause (b) also gives discretion to the Arbitral Tribunal to award interest for the post-award period but that discretion is not subject to any contract; and if that discretion is not exercised by the arbitral Tribunal, then the statute steps in and mandates payment of interest, at the specified rate of 18% per annum for the post-award period.

(iii) While clause (a) gives the parties an option to contract out of interest, no such option is available in regard to the post-award period.

In nutshell, in regard to pre-award period, interest has to be awarded as specified in the contract and in the absence of contract as per discretion of the Arbitral Tribunal. On the other hand, in regard to the post-award period, interest is payable as per the discretion of the Arbitral Tribunal and in the absence of exercise of such discretion, at a mandatory statutory rate of 18% per annum.

Clause (b) of Section 31(7) is intended to ensure prompt payment by the award-debtor once the award is made. The said clause provides that the sum directed to be paid by an arbitral award shall carry interest at the rate of 18% per annum from the date of award to the date of payment if the award does not provide otherwise in regard to the interest from the date of the award. But if the award is silent in regard to the interest from the date of award, or does not specify the rate of interest from the date of award, then the party in whose favour an award for money has been made, will be entitled to interest at 18% per annum from the date of award. Even if the pre-award interest is at much lower rate, if the award is silent in regard to post-award interest, the claimant will be entitled to post-award interest at the higher rate of 18% per annum. The higher rate of interest is provided in clause (b) with the deliberate intent of discouraging award-debtors from adopting dilatory tactics and to persuade them to comply with the award.

The job of judiciary is to interpret the intent of legislature. As rightly analysed by judiciary, the intent of legislature in prescribing 18% interest is to act as deterrent so as to seek compliance of implementation of award. The intention conveys to arbitrator that the post award interest should be high enough so as to act as deterrent in nature. When this be the case, it is improper for courts to interpret the intention of legislature in one way and apply it the other way. The intention of legislature is negated by tempering with the awarded interest in the name of reasonableness. Reasons have already been explained by judiciary and any more attempts to redefine the reasonableness will run counter to its own analysis. It would be proper if it is left to arbitrator without questioning his discretion. Ultimately, the interest rate is to ensure speedy enforcement which is not possible at low rates.

The court in (1994 Supp.(1) SCC 644) have held that award of interest on interest is not opposed to the public policy of India, but could be awarded only if authorised by contract or statute. Therefore, when payment of interest is not against 'Public Policy', the contractual restrictions cannot be given priority over provisions made in Act, 1996. The restrictive clauses are not only against "Public Policy" but they lead to unjust enrichment of one party at the cost of other.

"*The Supreme Court in (Indian Hume Pipe Co. Ltd.* v. *State of Rajasthan & Ors.*) has summarized the law relating to the powers of the Arbitrator to award interest. While recapitulating the legal position on the aspect the Supreme Court has held that the Arbitrator has the power to award interest for the period from the award to the date of payment, as also for pre-reference, pendente lite and post-award. The relevant extracts from the aforesaid judgment are reproduced herein below. The only caveat is that the amount of interest so awarded should be reasonable and agreement between the parties should not prohibit grant of such interest."

"The matter was also considered by constitutional bench in 1992(1) SCC 508. It will appear from what the constitution bench stated to be the legal position, that ordinarily a person who is deprived of his money to which he is legitimately entitled as of right is entitled to be compensated in deprivation thereof. This would be in terms of the principle laid down in section 34 of the Code of Civil Procedure. Their lordships pointed out that there was no reason or principle to hold otherwise in the case of an arbitrator. In other words, according to their, Lordship the arbitrator is expected to act and make his award in accordance with general law of the land but subject to an agreement, provided, the agreement is valid and legal. (*The Board of Trustees for the Port* v. *Engineers-De-Space*)".

(i) A person deprived of the use of money to which he is legitimately entitled has a right to be compensated for the deprivation, call it by any name. It may be called interest, compensation or damages. This basic consideration is as valid for the period the dispute is pending before the arbitrator as it is for the period prior to the arbitrator entering upon the reference. This is the principle of Section 34, Civil Procedure Code and there is no reason or principle to hold otherwise in the case of arbitrator.

(ii) An arbitrator is the creature of an agreement. It is open to the parties to confer upon him such powers and prescribe such procedure for him to follow, as they think fit, so long as they are not opposed to law. (The proviso to Section 41 and Section 3 of the Arbitration Act illustrate this point.) All the same, the agreement must be in conformity with law. The arbitrator must also act and make his award in accordance with the general law of the land and the agreement.

(iii) Interest pendente lite is not a matter of substantive law, like interest for the period anterior to reference (pre-reference period). For doing complete justice between the parties, such power has always been inferred.

SCI in (*Mcdermott International Inc.* v. *Burn Standard Co. Ltd. & Ors.*) while delving on the Public Policy of India has observed: "What would constitute public policy is a matter dependent upon the nature of transaction and nature of statute. For the said purpose, the pleadings of the parties and the materials brought on record would be relevant to enable the court to judge what is in public good or public interest, and what would otherwise be injurious to the public good at the relevant point, as contradistinguished from the policy of a particular government." [See *State of Rajasthan* v. *Basant Nahata*, (2005) 12 SCC 77].

In ONGC (2003)5 SCC 705 this Court observed:" Therefore, in our view, the phrase "public policy of India" used in Section 34 in context is required to be given a wider meaning. It can be stated that the concept of public policy connotes some matter which concerns public good and the public interest. What is for public good or in public interest or what would be injurious or harmful to the public good or public interest has varied from time to time. However, the award which is, on the face of it, patently in violation of statutory provisions cannot be said to be in public interest. Such award/judgment/decision is likely to adversely affect the administration of justice. Hence, in our view in addition to narrower meaning given to the term "public policy" in Renusagar case it is required to be held that the award could be set aside if it is patently illegal."

Whether interest is payable or not a party should always make claim for it and leave it for arbitrator to decide. Further it is advisable to satisfy the award immediately to the extent possible, to escape the burden of interest and rest of the award challenged. Besides, future interest should be given high enough and only on substantive award amount.

There appears to be some amount of conflict between statute, public policy and the party agreement. Statute is meant to serve the country in its betterment. Public policy also guides citizens for their good. Interest payment is not against public policy. Then, how the agreement between the parties can be against statute and public policy. However, for the present the rule made by SCI in the law that has to be followed.

The government contracts have payment terms somewhat similar to as mentioned below:

"On-Account" Payments: The Contractor shall be entitled to be paid from time, to time by way of "On-Account" payment only for such works as he has executed in terms of the contract. All payments due shall be subject to any deductions which may be made under these presents.

Final Payment: shall be made for total quantity of work executed by the Contractor up to the date of completion and on the accepted schedule or rates and subject always to any deduction which may be made under these presents and further subject to the Contractor having delivered to the Engineer either a full account in detail of all claims he may have on the Railway in respect of the works or having delivered "No Claim" Certificate.

The purport of the above payment clause is that the payment shall be released in reasonable time and money shall not be withheld for flimsy ground. If payment is not released in time and money is withheld without valid reasons which would be determined by arbitrator or court, in that event the act of owner should be treated as breach of condition and not only contractor would claim the payment of amount but compensation for delayed payment due to breach of contract. This plea should be raised forcefully before arbitral tribunal or court. Because the remedy for breach is compensation and in case of payment damages can be assessed based on rate of interest. Obviously, the payments are to be made in reasonable time.

It is noteworthy, that the Supreme Court has on more than one occasion held the finding by the court that a direction to pay interest on the awarded amount is not mandatory and it is erroneous. It has been held that if a person is deprived of use of money, he is legitimately entitled, as of right, to be compensated for such deprivation by granting monies by whatever name it may be called whether interest or compensation or damages. Supreme Court has reiterated the power of the arbitrators to grant pendente lite and future interest till realization. The statute has clearly empowered the arbitrator under Section 31(1)(a) to award pre-reference and pendente lite interest. Despite this ideology, the incongruous clauses in contract about interest payment are given primacy. A right cannot be waived and therefore clause which put bar on payment of interest are one sided and unconscionable.

Courts have been maintaining that "Constitutional provisions enjoin upon state not to act arbitrarily. In the matter of government contracts there is no parity of status between the individual contractor and the state; the individual parties are illiterate, poor or not political conscious of their rights. And individuals agreeing with the state are perforce made to agree to contractual terms which are unfair, unjust and inequitable. Sweeping discretionary and discriminatory powers are conferred upon state officials under the contract. State is exempted from non-performance or negligence in reciprocal contractual obligation. Mutuality of bargaining power between the state and a citizen is the casualty". Thus, the clause like, "No claim for compensation on account of delay to the work from any cause whatsoever shall be, except as hereafter defined" should be struck down being unconscionable.

Thus, the provisions in contract regarding payment of interest are against the principle of natural justice. These are unconscionable being completely favourable to establishment and detrimental to contractor. Such clause should be struck down for equity. Time has come to review them in new perspective.

Further, contracts have reciprocal promises. The contractor will perform on one side and owner will make payment. If the payment is not made in reasonable time or delayed badly or withheld for unsound reasons, breach of contact conditions takes place. The breach occurs at the stage of final bill when performance has been completed. At that stage there is no question of rescinding contract. Breach of contract leads to claims for damages. The interest being claimed by injured parties is not the interest on damages but the compensation for loss due to breach of payment condition. Besides, it is important that arbitration for claim of interest is contested on compensation ground.

We are living in a materialistic world where purchasing power counts a lot. The economy world over is highly fragile. Stoppage of payment due for few days can upset the balance sheets of big houses. Whereas the fact is that in contractual matters, the payments are delayed on unreasonable grounds. If interest is denied, then there is no incentive to officials to clear the payments. This is the prime reason that large sums are withheld on flimsy grounds for long periods or the matter is unnecessarily put in dispute. Certainly there is urgent need to review this aspect by concerned agencies. While for future interest the legislation has shown great concern, it has left the matter to master for pre-award period as if the bargain is on equal footing. A clause denying interest, whosoever puts it into contract, should be declared unconscionable and against public policy.

SUMMARY

1. Payment of interest and payment of interest on interest is not against public policy;
2. Damages can be levied for delayed payments;
3. Act permits payment of interest for pre-reference, pendente lite and after award period;
4. Interest before award is regulated by contract conditions whereas future award is not;
5. Future award is payable only on substantive award;
6. Claim for interest should be raised, let it be decided by arbitrator; and
7. Contract clause for payment of interest is not compatible with public policy and Natural justice.

6 Waiver of Breach and Mistakes in Contracts

WAIVER

A *breach of contract* is a failure to perform the contract in the manner called for by the contract. A party is entitled to contractual remedies if the other party breaches a contract. A breach does not always mean the end of a contract. One party may be willing to waive or ignore the breach. A *waiver* can be made by words or by conduct. Accepting a late payment would be an example of a waiver by conduct. It is possible to make a waiver by silence. For example, failure to object to the manner of performance in a timely manner would be a waiver by silence.

Waiver is abandonment or relinquishment of right. It signifies an intention not to insist upon the right. One who waives his rights, generally, cannot insist on them afterwards. There are cases where no withdrawal from waiver is possible. Withdrawal cannot be done without injustice to the other party. He will not be allowed to revert to his legal rights which he has already waived.

A party who waives a breach gives up the right to damages regarding such breach unless expressed otherwise. A waiver may be express or implied. A waiver only applies to the specific matter waived. A party is entitled to require the other party to strictly perform all other contractual obligations set forth in the contract. A party may retain the right to recover damages caused by another party's breach if the party expressly reserves the right to damages at the time the party accepts a defective performance.

In the following case the principle of 'waiver' was used very appropriately.

"A work of Communication was awarded in the year 2006. It was to be completed in 12 months. The completion period was extended six times, last being up to Sept., 2009. All extensions were granted without penalty. The work contained mainly purchasing and fixing "Electrical Point Detectors (EPDs) and supply & laying cables".

All works were completed within extended period. The Final bill was entered into MB. Claimant had signed the M.B. and the final bill. There was no recovery proposed in the bill. It is after the preparation of deviation statement for passing final bill that the issue of recovery was raised by respondent in the year 2012 for non-supply of two items. This matter which was lying dormant was not an issue and suddenly became active after competent authority for approval of deviation statement took objection to the proposal for deletion of these two items. The supply of the said two items was not made at all yet the works were completed.

Respondent too, did not make 'earnest attempt' to chase up the matter with claimant. During the entire currency of contract neither any correspondence was made with claimant contractor, nor mention was made in site order book, nor was any initiative taken to terminate the contract for failure to perform. The work was carried on by issuing cables in small quantity to official staff by department on need basis. Through and through cable was not replaced. Same was the situation with EPDs. All correspondence with claimant was made after the work came to close and currency of contract expired.

The work was completed in Sept., 2009 in all respect. Throughout the progress of work, the respondent did not press for supply of these two vital items. Not even once the claimant was cautioned that non-supply would be treated as breach of contract. Neither any step was taken to terminate the contract. It is because of the proposed recovery for two items and delay in making final payment that the dispute had arisen between the parties and it was referred to arbitration for adjudication. The claimant had disputed proposed recovery. The issue was if there was breach of contract?

Respondent had claimed that the claimant did not supply two items. Both the items were vital for commencing the work whereas claimant kept silent throughout the duration of work about supply of these items. However, work was taken up without obtaining supply of both items. In fact, entire work had been completed without 'reasonably insisting' for supplies. The claimant's version is that he was advised by Government officials not to buy these items since existing materials had enough of residual life. And in case little quantity was required here and there, the same would be used from departmental stock. The respondent too had stated that cables were used in patches depending upon the necessity of replacement/ extension. Through and through work was not required. Same was the case with EPDs. Arbitrator had no reason to disbelieve the claimant's version as seen from the conduct of respondent that all through the period of nearly 3 years he had maintained absolute silence. If the existing material had sufficient residual life not warranting replacement then the decision not to buy should be applauded as it had avoided wastage of national resources. There is no gainsaying in the fact that claimant had performed partially, but at the instance of respondent. And since these components were not required to be replaced, no loss has been sustained by respondent by not performing the two items. There appears to be honest and faithful performance by the contractor. There is no willful departure from essential points of the contract.

Another view could be that the contract had breached due to non supply of materials. But then the contract should have been terminated following breach. The fact of non termination of contract and not making any correspondence with claimant contractor conveys that the respondent had waived off the breach by his conduct. He did not make reasonable efforts to secure supply of materials, nor any steps were initiated to terminate the contract for failure of performance. Even while granting extensions, the right to recovery was not kept reserved.

This could have been treated as partial breach of contract. And for partial breach respondent would have been entitled for damages to the extent of limited breach. Even if for a moment we treat it as partial breach then the respondent by his very conduct has waived-off the breach. He had the option to rescind the contract or at least retain the right to recover damages.

The respondent's assertion that departmental material was used is not denied because these were used in patches through departmental labour. These two supply items were not operated at all. Thus, the claimant's version that no material was used for the reason mentioned earlier is reliable and logical. This situation cannot be called 'Breach of Contract'. Thus, the recovery proposed in the form of damages is unjustified, unreasonable and liable for rejection. Similarly, withholding of payment of final bill for this sake is also without valid ground and should be released immediately. The rest of the arguments are of no use since the issue of proposed recovery gets fully settled here and therefore it is not discussed any longer."

Section 63 of Indian Contract Act, 1872 which is relevant to this case is reproduced below:

> "*Every promise may dispense with or remit, wholly or in part, the performance of the promise made to him, or may extend the time for such performance or may accept instead of it any satisfaction which he thinks fit.*"

In another case A entered into contract with B for supply of match boxes. The contract was not performed fully. Subsequently, A placed another order on B for supply of another consignment of match boxes. While placing the order A did not mention at all about the poor performance of the first contract and claims/damages. Neither any separate correspondence was made. It was inferred that A had waived off the performance of the first contract.

A coal mine was leased to a company duly fixing lease charges and the time schedule for payment by entering into a contract. The company made defaults in payment of royalty and lease charges. The owner issued notices calling upon the company to pay the dues within sixty days from the receipt of the notices and intimating that if the dues were not paid within that period the lease would be terminated. In all six such notices were issued. As regards the first five notices, the company in each case paid the dues beyond sixty days from the receipt of the notice. As regards the sixth notice, the company fully complied with its terms and deposited all the dues within sixty days. In the meantime by an order the owner cancelled the lease and forfeited the security deposit on the ground that the earlier notices were not complied with in time. Under the Law it is well settled that if the lessor wants to take advantage of any breach of any term or condition so as to enforce his right to forfeit the lease he must not do anything after the breach which amounts to an acknowledgment of the continuance of the lease. Any act on the part of the lessor showing an intention to treat the lease as subsisting, amounts to waiver of forfeiture or more appropriately waiver of the breach which had the lessor so elected, would have enabled him to forfeit the lease.

During arbitration hearings the principle of waiver can be employed effectively to negative the claims of opposite party. While framing claims also this concept can be made use of. Had it been realized by respondent that substantial time has lapsed without cautioning contractor for fulfillment of the promise in sequential manner, perhaps dispute must not have arisen.

Mistakes

A "mistake" is a *"belief that is not in accord with the facts"*. If both parties have the same mistaken belief, the mistake is said to be *"mutual."* By contrast, if only one party has the mistaken belief, the mistake is *"unilateral"*. The doctrines applicable to mistake apply only to a mistaken belief about an *existing fact*, and *not* an erroneous belief about *what will happen in the future*.

The law believes that contracts are made to be performed. The whole structure of business depends on this as the businessmen depend on the validity of contracts. Accordingly, the law does not aid anyone to evade consequences on the plea that he was mistaken. On the other hand, the law also realises that mistakes do occur, and that these mistakes are so fundamental that there may be no contract at all. If the law recognizes mistake in contract, the mistake may render the contract *void*. Mistake affects contracts in two ways. Firstly, it may defeat the consent that the parties are supposed to have given. The consent is rendered as unreal. Secondly, the mistake may mislead the parties as to the purpose which they have contemplated. The situation where consent is defeated or there is no real consent between parties is covered under Sec.13 according to which, " two or more persons are said to consent when they agree upon the same thing in same sense". For creation of a valid contract it is essential that both parties should agree to the same thing in the same sense.

When mistake does not affect consent, but only misleads the parties, section 20 come into play which provides:

Sec. 20. Agreement void where both parties are under mistake as to matter of fact : Where both the parties to an agreement are under a mistake as to a matter of fact essential to the agreement, the agreement is void.

Explanation : An erroneous opinion as to the value of the things which forms the subject-matter of the agreement, is not be deemed a mistake as to a matter of fact.

Section 20 operates : (i) When both the parties to an agreement are mistaken, (ii) Their mistake is as to a matter of fact, and (iii) The fact about which they are mistaken is essential to the agreement. These points are further supplemented by Section 21 and 22 reproduced below:

Sec. 21. Effect of mistake as to law.

A contract is not voidable because it was caused by a mistake as to any law in force in India; but mistake as to a law not in force in India has the same effect as a mistake of fact.

Sec. 22. Contract caused by mistake of one party as to matter of fact.

A contract is not voidable merely because it was caused by one of the parties to it being under a mistake as to a matter of fact.

Mistakes can be classified as : (1) Mistake of Law, and (2) Mistake of Fact.

Mistake of law: when a party enters into a contract, without the knowledge of the law in the country, the contract is affected by such mistakes but it is not void. A contract is not voidable because it was caused by a mistake as to any law in force in India. The reason here is that ignorance of law is not an excuse at all. However, if a party is *induced* to enter into a contract by the mistake of law then such a contract is not valid. Mistake of law is a legal principle referring to one or more errors that were made by a person in understanding how the applicable law applied to their past activity that is under analysis. It is differentiated from mistake of fact.

Mistake of Fact: An error that is not caused by the neglect of a legal duty on the part of the person committing the error but rather consists of an unconscious ignorance of a past or present material event. Mistake of fact can be a factor in reducing or eliminating liability. A mistake of fact is of little consequence if it is born of unconscious ignorance or forgetfulness. A person cannot escape liability for intentional mistakes.

In contract law a mistake of fact may be raised as a defence by a party seeking to avoid liability under the contract. Also, a mistake of fact can be used affirmatively to cancel, rescind, or reform a contract. A mistake of fact can affect a contract only if the mistaken fact was material, or important to the agreement. To raise as a defence the mistake should be 'vital operative mistake'.

Operative mistake: For a mistake to affect the validity of a contract it must be an "operative mistake", i.e. a mistake which operates to make the contract void.

The effect of a mistake is: when the mistake is operative the contract is usually void *ab initio*, i.e. from the beginning. Therefore, no obligations can arise under it. Even if the contract is valid, the contract may be voidable on the ground of mistake. Obligations will arise unless and until the contract is avoided. However, the right to rescission may be lost.

Mistake is an erroneous belief, *at contracting*, that certain assumptions are true. It can be argued as a defence, and if raised successfully can lead to the agreement in question being found void *ab initio* or voidable, or alternatively a remedy may be provided by the courts. Three different types of mistakes have been identified in contracts: the 'unilateral mistake', the 'mutual mistake' and the 'common mistake'. It is important to note the distinction between the 'common mistake' and the 'mutual mistake'.

A Mutual Mistake

Contractors may obtain relief where they encounter extreme difficulties in carrying out performance due to mutual mistake. The mutual mistake doctrine arises when both parties assume a fact which is nonexistent or substantially different than reality. When a court finds that the risk was not assumed by either party, it may declare a mutual mistake and decide that additional costs are to be borne equally by the Government and the contractor. Several scenarios would warrant a mutual mistake determination when differing site conditions are encountered. Even though each party may have made reasonable attempts to investigate the existing conditions at the site or made reasonable assumptions that there was nothing unusual about the site that required investigation, a problem may still arise.

A mutual mistake occurs when both parties are mistaken but about different things; this has arisen rarely in practice and the legal position is unclear—often where such mistakes exists the agreement might be too vague or uncertain to be enforceable without the need to rely on mistake as a separate cause of action.

A **common mistake** occurs when both parties are mistaken about the same thing it is very rare for a common mistake to give rise to remedies although in equity remedies of rescission or rectification will sometimes be available.

Unilateral Mistake

Unilateral mistake occurs where only one party is mistaken as to the facts. It will only operate where the mistake is about the terms of the contract. It is well established that rectification is a remedy solely designed to correct such mistakes if the other party knew about it and omitted to point it out. Rectification only applies to a written contract in order to correct it to reflect the parties' true agreement.

Unilateral mistake is more common; it occurs when one party is mistaken about some aspect of the contract but the other is not. It is rare for the common law to provide a remedy for unilateral mistake. Often where this is the case there will be some misleading conduct involved which will provide separate—and superior—remedies. The relevant remedy where an actionable mistake exists is rescission or rectification.

In Modern view it is more difficult for the mistaken party to avoid the contract than in the mutual mistake situation. The mistaken party must show *either* that:

(i) The mistake is such that enforcement of the contract would be *unconscionable.* The mistaken contractor will succeed in showing unconscionability only if he shows that he will be *severely harmed* if forced to perform, or
(ii) The other party had *reason to know* of the mistake, or the other party's *fault* caused the mistake. The mistaken party may try to show that the other party either *knew* or had *reason to know* of the error.

The mistake is not only unilateral but one which the other party actually knew about it and consciously decided not to draw to the attention of the mistaken party. There will be a deliberate failure to disclose information which is relevant to the other party's decision to contract, in the knowledge that the other party was making a mistake.

The general rule is that if one party has made a mistake *as to the terms of the contract* and that mistake is known to the other party, then the contract is not binding. The reasoning is that although the parties appear, objectively, to have agreed terms, it is clear that they are not in agreement. Therefore, the normal rule of looking only at the objective agreement of the parties is displaced and the court admits evidence to show what each side subjectively intended to agree by way of terms. If it is clear from such evidence that there was no consensus, then there can be no contract, because the parties have not truly agreed on the terms. Some people talk of such a contract being "void", but others think it was never a contract at all.

Situation where all parties to a contract misunderstand one another:

> Mistake is a complex area of contract law. As a general rule, being mistaken about some aspect of a contract will not provide a party with a right to escape contractual obligations - even if that mistake is fundamental.

Unfortunately, there is no general doctrine of mistake—the rules are contained in a disparate group of cases. This is also an area of confusing terminology. No two authorities seem to agree on a common classification, and often the same terminology is used to cover different forms of mistake.

For a unilateral mistake to be operative, the mistake by one party must be as to a fundamental term of the contract itself, rather than an error of judgment as to the quality of subject matter. In other words, the mistake should be as to a term of the contract, and not as to the quality of the subject matter. Such a mistake would negative the consent.

Mistakes have relevance in the law of contract in different ways. They may prevent the mutuality of contract that is necessary for the formation of a contract. In order for two parties to conclude a contract binding in law each must agree with the other on the terms of the contract. Whether two parties have entered into contract in this way must be judged objectively, having regard to all material facts.

Contract caused by mistake of one party as to matter of fact: A contract is not voidable merely because it was caused by one of the parties to it being under mistake as to a matter of fact.

The term merely in the section implies that certain remedies are available under law under certain circumstances. As a general rule, being mistaken about some aspect of a contract will not provide a party with a right to escape contractual obligations—even if that mistake is fundamental. In the event of a unilateral mistake, only one party to the agreement is mistaken about a material fact. In such a case, the party adversely affected by the mistake will not be able to void the contract unless the other party knew or should have known the mistake, or unless the other party had a duty to disclose the mistaken fact. If a contract can be reformed, a court may not allow a party to rescind a contract on account of mistake of fact. The court reforms a contract to reflect the true intent of the parties.

WHEN MISTAKE OF BOTH PARTIES MAKE A CONTRACT VOIDABLE

Where a mistake of both parties at the time of contract was made as to a basic assumption on which the contract was made has a material effect on the agreed exchange of performances, the contract is voidable by the adversely affected party unless he bears the risk of the mistake under the rule.

WHEN MISTAKE OF ONE PARTY MAKES A CONTRACT VOIDABLE

Where a mistake of one party at the time a contract was made as to a basic assumption on which he made the contract has a material effect on the agreed exchange of performances that is adverse to him, the contract is voidable by him if he does not bear the risk of the mistake under the rule :

(a) the effect of the mistake is such that enforcement of the contract would be unconscionable, or

(b) the other party had reason to know of the mistake or his fault caused the mistake

Where the Parties are at Cross Purposes

In cases where the parties misunderstand each other's intentions and are at cross purposes, the court will apply an objective test and consider whether a 'reasonable man' would take the agreement to mean what one party understood it to mean or what the other party understood it to mean:

If the test leads to the conclusion that the contract could be understood in one sense only, both parties will be bound by the contract in this sense.

If the transaction is totally ambiguous under this objective test then there will be no consensus *ad idem* (agreement as to the same thing) and the contract will be void.

Remedy

If the contract is void at law on the ground of mistake, equity "follows the law" and specific performance will be refused and, in appropriate circumstances, the contract will be rescinded. However, even where the contract is valid at law, specific performance will be refused if to grant it would cause hardship.

Rectification for unilateral mistake will apply subject to the application of four principles:

1. That Party A erroneously believed that the contract contained or did not contain a particular provision which, mistakenly, it did contain;
2. That Party B was aware of the omission or the inclusion and that it was due to Party A's mistake;
3. That Party B failed to draw the mistake to Party A's attention; and

4. That the mistake must be one calculated to benefit Party B.

It is simply not fair to allow a party knowingly to take advantage of the other's mistake in such a case. Such conduct of other party is not in good faith. Law generally does not impose duty of disclosure. Non- disclosure does not cause the other party to make a mistake. At the most it fails to correct the mistake. Similarly, there is no general duty of good faith. Each party is entitled to act in his own interest as long as he does not mislead the other. Remedy for unilateral mistake would require some improper conduct on the part of the unmistaken party whereby that party seeks to prevent the other becoming aware of the mistake. The above decisions are based upon the provision of section 72 of Indian Contract Act, 1872 which reads as under: **"Liability of persons to whom money is paid, or thing delivered by mistake or under coercion:** *A person to whom money has been paid, or anything delivered by mistake or under coercion , must repay or return it.* A tender was invited through electronic process for purchase. It was very prominently displayed by respondent on the tender document that manual offers would not be considered.In the electronic offer submitted by claimant 'NIL' value was mentioned under PVC column. To correct his mistake he submitted the manual copy of PVC clause directly to office along with the tender fee. The hard copy was submitted despite knowing well that manual offer would not be considered. In turn he received LOA with PVC clause as mentioned by him. Rather he took a chance. The respondent submits that manual offer should have made no difference in finalization of tender. The PVC clause, however, got included mistakenly which was known to claimant. However, he did not point out because it benefited him. Respondent mentions that manual offers are not acceptable in e-tendering. The fact is well known to vendors. Therefore, mention of PVC clause in LOA is nothing but a mistake. The claimant vehemently deposed that the condition of manual offer was made by respondent. Respondent is dealing with e-tenders day in and day out in large numbers. Therefore, how can he afford to forget such an important clause. There can be no situation where a committee of senior officers can gloss over it and look for the PVC clause elsewhere in the file. The moment the committee touched the paper it should have become untouchable and accordingly not considered. It was further mentioned that the firm had submitted FIRM offer all inclusive rates and without PVC. It is also submitted that despite the fact that claimant had quoted 'NIL' PVC, the LOA got issued with

PVC by mistake. For the mistaken act undue advantage should not be allowed to claimant.

Discussions—It is a fact that the manual offers were not to be entertained in e-tendering. This fact was known to claimant as well as to respondent. The clause was designed by Respondent. Claimant submitted his offer electronically without PVC clause. However, he thought to revise the same with PVC and submitted the PVC provision through manual letter. In e-tendering all documents required for finalization of tender are generated through computer using a specially designed soft ware. Clearly, it is mentioned in the tabulation statement that claimant had quoted NIL PVC.

It is also a fact that tender committee had two offers before them from claimant for consideration out of which electronic offer was cheaper and beneficial to the organization. Ignoring lowest acceptable offer would invite problem for TC members. The act of TC in moving from e-offer to a manually submitted letter is certainly a conscious decision and firm application of mind. In no case this letter was to be entertained. The facts and circumstances are in favour of application of mind by TC in choosing this letter and giving cognizance.

The claimant was well aware that manual offer would not be considered. Despite that he did not inform respondent about the mistake in LOA. He did not inform this because he was beneficiary of the mistake.

Respondent observed that the mistake here is made out to be unilateral but one which the other party actually knew about it and consciously decided not to draw to the attention of the mistaken party. There has been a deliberate failure to disclose information which was relevant to the other party's decision to contract, in the knowledge that the other party was making a mistake.

The general rule is that if one party has made a mistake *as to the terms of the contract* and that mistake is known to the other party, then the contract is not binding. The reasoning is that although the parties appear, objectively, to have agreed to terms, it is clear that they are not in agreement. There is no common intention. If it is clear from such evidence that there was no consensus, then there can be no contract, because the parties have not truly agreed on the terms. Some people call such contracts being "void", but some think that there was never a contract at all.

For an agreement to be avoided on the basis of unilateral mistake, it must be shown that: (i) one party erroneously believed the truthfulness of the document sought to be rectified, (ii) the second party was aware of the omission that it was due to a mistake on the part of party, (iii) the party who was aware of the mistake omitted to draw the mistake to the notice of the other party, and (iv) that mistake must benefit the one party. The matter explained above clearly establishes that all these conditions should be satisfied in unilateral mistake. Here the respondent was not in error in believing the letter. He was aware that separate letter given manually was not to be entertained. The respondent was absolutely confident that his letter has been evaluated by respondent since the clause in to-to had appeared in LOA. Since it was conscious decision of TC, there is nothing to draw their attention to. On the whole, the PVC clause was approved by TC being in full senses. Hence, the case does not qualifies for 'unilateral mistake'. Since contract has already been performed fully the question of avoiding does not arise neither it is the requirement of law. Thus, LOA and PO reflects the true intention of respondent and insertion of the clause was not a mistake or over sight.

SUMMARY

1. The remedy of mutual mistake is that the contract is void.
2. Unilateral mistake has no remedy except in certain circumstances where it can be voided or rectified.
3. There is no remedy for mistake of law in contracts.
4. The mistake should be as to the term of contract.

7 Adverse Inference and Unconscionability

The edifice of justice dispensing system rests upon evidence. Be it oral evidence or documentary proof or circumstantial evidence, truth of the matter under dispute cannot be established in the absence of credible evidence. Some thinker has said that, "(P)roof must rest upon evidence and not upon its absence". Evidence is very vital and indispensable ingredient of dispute resolution mechanism whether it is at household level or dispute of contractual matters or adjudication of civil/criminal litigations. Therefore, preservation and production of evidence before trier of facts gains immense importance. However, strangely no sooner than the dispute appears, the evidence begins disappearing from them who are expected to be in its possession.

As the society is expanding, the litigation is also on the rise. The tendency to destroy the evidence by litigants is also growing since this step appears as an easy option to escape the noose of law. Therefore, effective control is required to be exercised to curb this tendency. However, instead of drawing adverse inference from spoliation of evidence, easier options are considered to be advantageous and lawful.

Spoliation has been defined as the destruction or significant alteration of evidence, or the failure to preserve property for another's use as evidence in pending or reasonably foreseeable litigation. The spoliation inference permits the trier of fact to infer therefrom that the spoliated evidence would have been unfavorable to the spoliator's cases.

Even if the burden of proof does not lie on a party, an adverse inference may be drawn if he withholds important documents in his possession which can throw light on the facts at issue. However, this is not sound practice for those desiring to rely upon a certain state of facts to withhold from the trier the evidence which is in their possession and which could throw light upon the issues in controversy.

It is nevertheless open to a litigant to refrain from producing any documents that he considers irrelevant; if the other litigant is dissatisfied it is for him to apply for an affidavit of documents and he can obtain inspection and production of all that appears to him in such affidavit to be relevant and proper. If he fails to do so, no inference will be drawn.

The scope of the adverse inference that may be drawn and its potential impact upon the ultimate outcome at trial will depend upon the nature of the spoliated evidence and its perceived relevance to the claims and defence at issue.

Adverse inference is based on commonsense approach that a party which destroys or fails to preserve evidence which it knows is relevant to existing or reasonably foreseeable litigation is more likely than not to have done so out of fear that the evidence is harmful to its cases.

There is general agreement that a party's bad faith destruction of evidence constitutes blameworthiness or a culpable state of mind sufficient to support the spoliation inference. Bad faith, for the purposes of inference, usually requires a showing that the party's actions were motivated by a desire to hide or suppress evidence.

For some, the crucial element for the spoliation inference is not that evidence was destroyed or lost, but rather the reason for its destruction or loss.

A litigant's suppression, alteration, fabrication, mutilation or destruction of evidence poses a serious threat to the integrity of system of adjudication. The law cannot and should not afford to ignore such mischief. A critically important question is what to do about such mischief when it is detected. This Article discusses one piece of incident under the existing system together with remedy for tampering with evidence.

If you should find that a party willfully *suppressed/hid/destroyed* evidence in order to prevent its being presented in the trial, you may consider such *suppression/hiding/destruction* in determining what inferences to draw from the evidence or facts in the case. If a party fails to produce evidence which is under that party's control and reasonably available to that party and not reasonably available to the opposite party, then you may infer that the evidence is unfavorable to the party who could have produced it but did not. It is a deliberate attempt to suffocate the justice system, and deny the other party of his right which have been trampled upon.

Adverse inferences have been drawn by justice dispensing institutions in reaction to evidence of tampering and arguments made by pleaders to elicit such inferences. The judicial agencies have been drawing adverse inference in relation to evidence of tampering and destruction. This response has obvious appeal. The inference does not apply to any specific fact but operates against the whole mass of alleged facts constituting the cause.

The adverse inference response perhaps became part of law at a time when very few tools of discovery were available. In such a system of litigation, there was little control over evidence tampering other than a party's ability to point to the misconduct at trial and ask the trier of fact to take it into account. This response continues to have, an obvious appeal.

It has often been understood that adverse inference, indeed, is one of the simplest in human experience—that a party's falsehood or other fraud in the preparation and presentation of his cause, his fabrication or suppression of evidence by bribery or spoliation, is receivable against him as an indication of his consciousness that his case is a weak one; and from that consciousness may be inferred the fact that his case lacks truth and merit.

However, this approach does not always lead to establishment of truth. It has its own weaknesses. For instance, abscondance of a person on the basis of which *adverse inference* could be drawn against him. The legal position in such cases is that in case a person is absconding after commission of offence of which he may not even be the author, such a circumstance alone may not be enough to draw an adverse inference against him as it would go against the doctrine of innocence, i.e. *"Innocent until proven guilty"*. It is quite possible that he may be running away merely being suspected, out of fear of police arrest and harassment. Thus, mere abscondance of a person cannot be taken as a circumstance which gives rise to draw an adverse inference against him.

Conviction can be established based solely on circumstantial evidence. However, the courts do bear in mind while deciding the case involving the commission of serious offence based on circumstantial evidence that the prosecution case must stand or fall on its own legs and should not derive any strength from the weakness of the defence case. The circumstances should be of conclusive nature.

The courts however take the view that when a party wants an adverse inference instruction based on spoliation, it has to establish the following:

1. That the party having control over the evidence had an obligation to preserve it at the time it was destroyed;
2. That the records were destroyed "with a culpable state of mind"; and
3. That the destroyed evidence was "relevant" to the party's claim or defence such that a reasonable trier of fact could find that it would support that claim or defence."

This is where things become dicey; destroyed evidence that cannot be produced must be shown to be "relevant" to the requesting party's claim in order for an adverse inference instruction to be granted. How can a party show evidence is relevant or not if they can't get their hands on it? The court bring up the opposite argument, questioning how a party can be sanctioned for the purposeful or negligent destruction of evidence without a showing that the evidence was even "minimally relevant" to the case.

The courts ultimately hold that **"no matter how inadequate a party's efforts at preservation may be... sanctions are not warranted unless there is proof that some information of significance has been lost".**

In a case "it was contended that though from time to time, time was granted to the State to produce the result of the interview along with the grounds for which the petitioner was considered unfit for absorption but the State failed to produce those documents before the Court so there may be scope to draw *adverse inference* against the State in view of the provisions. Despite such observations, the State Government did not choose to file counter-affidavit or took any steps in respect of which *adverse inference* was drawn on the petition.

In another case assessment proceedings were taken up by the trade Tax assessing authority of a client. As against the 19 transactions, client furnished the evidences relating to 10 transactions to establish that the goods had gone outside the State and Form-34 was surrendered at the exit check post. In respect of 9 transactions, client claimed that such transaction did not relate to it and requested that Form-34 and other documents may be confronted but the same could not be confronted and the assessing authority drew adverse inference and assessed the applicant in respect of the said transactions.

In a recent arbitration matter the issue of drawing adverse inference was pressed by claimant. The work entrusted to claimant was labour intensive one. According to guidelines, the claimant was called upon to maintain the details of labour employed together with wages paid to them as enjoined by Labour Laws. These vital details were admittedly not maintained by claimant. Instead, he claimed firmly that these details were being maintained by respondent or his representative at site in 'site order book'. He repeatedly insisted for production of site order book, the availability of which was repeatedly denied by respondent. Claimant requested tribunal to direct respondent for production of site order book. Since the site order book is the relevant document, the arbitral tribunal did direct the respondent to produce it for the satisfaction of claimant. In this regard, it was clarified by respondent that not only the site order book was not available but it was also not relevant to the matter for which it was being demanded. Respondent referred to relevant paragraph of Code which states that *"for all important works an order book should be opened and all instructions issued to the executive subordinate or the contractor, as the case may be should be duly entered therein with the replies opposite"*.

It is therefore established that the site order book was not relevant for the purpose of labour details since details of labour are not maintained in it. Thus, the claimant's submission that labour details were maintained in site order book as also demand of production of site order book for this purpose was unreasonable and unjustified.

The request to tribunal to direct the other party for supplying documents sought must establish the relevance of each document sought in such a way that the other party and arbitral tribunal are able to refer to factual allegation in the submission filed by the party.

The arbitral tribunal would normally order the production of documents or records to other party if they exist and are within the possession, custody or control of the other party. If this is contested, the requesting party will have to satisfy the arbitral tribunal that the document is indeed within the possession, custody or control of the other party. This, however, could not be proved by claimant. Claimant was referring to respondent's counter statement where it had been committed that the site order book would be produced during hearings which appear to be a mention made in good faith. The matter is nearly 15 year old. Admittedly, neither respondent stands to gain by concealing it nor claimant stands to lose anything from its production as the site order book is not meant for recording labour details. Keeping labour details was the primary responsibility of claimant.

Clearly, the details of labour employed by claimant were not available with either of the party. Therefore, wherever necessity of labour details would be felt in determination of claims, the tribunal would be guided by circumstantial evidence or the evidence tendered by parties.

The claimant alleged a criminal conspiracy by certain railway officials against him in not providing site order book as evidence before tribunal. That the officials have concealed and destroyed the important document to harm the claimant and pressed for invoking doctrine of inverse inference.

It has been observed earlier, that maintaining labour details was the primary responsibility of claimant. Tribunal had no hesitation in recording that Respondent had made *"reasonable and sincere efforts"* in locating the site order book. *There was no malafide apparent or malice toward claimant* as apprehended by other side.

In view of the aforesaid, the tribunal held that it had sufficient evidence before it, available in the form of statement and counter statement of facts, and recorded notes of minutes for making an award. Considering sufficiency of evidence, irrelevancy of site order book as evidence and failure of the claimant in proving that some information of significance has been lost, the need for drawing adverse inference against respondent was not justified.

Differently put, the requesting party must make it clear with reasonable particularity what facts or allegations each document sought is intended to establish. Only then the tribunal may issue direction to other party for production of desired documents to be used as evidence.

UNCONSCIONABILITY

It is not uncommon to hear a construction contractor at government site cribbing that the contract conditions are unfair, one sided and loaded against construction agency as if government department can do no wrong. The contracts are drawn on pre-printed formats designed several decades ago and have not been altered to absorb the societal and technological changes. They are nothing but fossils of old ideas. The extent of unequal bargain is that for every and any slip up of contractor there is penalty and for every wrong doing of department there is extension of time as if EOT mitigates and compensates undue hardship suffered by contractor. Some examples of biasness in contract conditions can be noticed from the following conditions:

(i) If in the opinion of the Engineer the progress of work has any time been delayed by any act or neglect of deptt or by other contractor employed by the deptt or in consequences of the contractor not having received in due time necessary instructions from the deptt then upon happening of any such event causing delay, the contractor shall nevertheless make constantly his best endeavours to bring down or make good the delay. The contractor may also indicate the period for which the work is likely to be delayed and shall be bound to ask for necessary extension of time. No other compensation shall be payable for works so carried forward to the extended period of time, the same rates, terms and conditions of contract being applicable as if such extended period of time was originally provided in the original contract itself.

(ii) In the event of any failure or delay by the deptt to hand over the Contractor possession of the lands necessary for the execution of the works or to provide the necessary drawings or instructions or any other delay caused by the deptt. due to any other cause whatsoever, then such failure or delay shall in no way affect or vitiate the contract or alter the character thereof or entitle the contractor to damages or compensation therefore but in any such case, the deptt. may grant such extension of the completion date as may be considered reasonable.

(iii) The time for the execution of the work or part of the works specified in the contract documents shall be deemed to be the essence of the contract and the works must be completed not later than the date(s) as specified in the contract. If the contractor fails to complete the works within the time as specified in the contract the department may, if satisfied that the works can be completed by the contractor within reasonable short time thereafter, allow the contractor for further extension of time. On such extension the deptt. will be entitled without prejudice to any other right and remedy available on that behalf, to recover from the contractor as agreed damages and not by

> way of penalty a sum equivalent to 1/2 of 1% of the contract value of the works for each week or part of the week.

One may be tempted to argue that why contractors should accept such unbalanced conditions. Well, if they do not, departments would not get construction agencies and agencies would not get business. This is a symbiotic dependence. Often they are deceived or matter is misrepresented to them. And it goes on and on. However, such double standard and biasness appears prominently unfair, repulsive and against the conscience of a common man. A question would immediately arise if EOT compensates all sorts of losses which arise due to failure of departments. Then why not go for EOT option again when delay is on the part of contractor.

Doctrine of Unconscionability is a concept designed as a contract defence in cases in which there is a combination of unfair contract terms and deficient bargaining. It provides relief to the party who is sufferer of gross imbalance in contract conditions.

WHAT IS UNCONSCIONABLE?

Unusually harsh and shocking to the conscience; that which is so grossly unfair that a court will condemn it.

When a court uses the word *unconscionable* to describe conduct, it means that the conduct does not conform to the dictates of conscience. In addition, when something is judged unconscionable, a court will refuse to allow the perpetrator of the conduct to benefit from it.

Unconscionability also means unequal bargaining power or disparity of economic strength in context of contracts. The principle is that courts will strike down an unfair and unreasonable contract or an unfair and unreasonable clause in a contract entered into between parties who are not equal in bargaining power. This principle will apply where the inequality of bargaining power is the result of the great disparity in the economic strength of contracting parties. It will apply where a man has no choice but to give his assent to a contract or sign on the dotted line in a standard format, howsoever, unfair, unreasonable and unconscionable a clause in that contract may be. At times parties are so unequal where one is so strong in bargaining power and other so weak that as a matter of common fairness, it is not right that the strong should be allowed to push the weak to wall. One who is in extreme need may knowingly consent to a most improvident bargain, solely to relieve the straits in which he finds himself.

The determination that a contract is not unconscionable is made in the light of its setting, purpose and effect. Relevant factors include weakness in the contracting process like contracting capacity, fraud, and other invalidating causes. A bargain is not unconscionable merely because the parties to it are unequal in bargaining position, not because inequality apportions risk on weaker party. But gross inequality of bargaining power together with highly unfavourable terms to the weak party may confirm the indications of deception or compulsion in the transaction.

In contract law an unconscionable contract is one that is unjust or extremely one-sided in favour of the person who has the superior bargaining power. An unconscionable contract is one that no person who is mentally competent would enter into and that no fair and honest person would accept. Courts find that unconscionable contracts usually result from the exploitation of consumers who are often poorly educated, impoverished, and unable to find the best price available in the competitive marketplace.

Contractual provisions that indicate gross one-sidedness in favour of the seller include provisions that limit damages against the seller, limit the rights of the purchaser to seek court relief against the seller, or disclaim a Warranty. Unconscionability is determined by examining the circumstances of the parties when the contract was made; these circumstances include, for example, the bargaining power, age, and mental capacity of the parties. The doctrine is applied only where it would be an affront to the integrity of the judicial system to enforce such contracts.

Unconscionable conduct is also found in acts of Fraud and deceit, where the deliberate misrepresentation of facts deprives someone of a valuable possession. Whenever someone takes unconscionable advantage of another person, the action may be treated as criminal fraud or the civil action of deceit.

No standardized criteria exist for measuring whether an action is unconscionable. A court of law applies its conscience, or moral sense, to the facts before it and makes a subjective judgment. In one case the Court ruled that pumping the stomach of a criminal suspect in search of drugs offends "those canons of decency and fairness which express the notions of justice of peoples." The Court relied on these general historical and moral traditions as the basis for ruling unconstitutional an unconscionable act.

Unconscionable refers to a contract or bargain which is so unfair to a party that no reasonable or informed person would agree to it. In a suit for breach of contract, a court will not enforce an unconscionable contract against the person unfairly treated on the theory that he/she was misled, lacked information, or signed under duress or misunderstanding. It is similar to an "adhesion contract," in which one party has taken advantage of a person dealing from weakness.

Unconscionability is a term used in contract law to describe a defence against the enforcement of a contract based on the presence of terms that are excessively unfair to one party. Typically, such a contract is held to be unenforceable because the consideration offered is lacking or is so obviously inadequate that to enforce the contract would be unfair to the party seeking to escape the contract.

Inadequate consideration is likely not enough to make a contract unenforceable. However, a court of law will consider evidence that one party to the contract took advantage of its superior bargaining power to insert provisions that make the agreement overwhelmingly favour the interests of that party. Usually for a court to find a contract unconscionable the party claiming unconscionability will have to prove both that there was a problem with the substance of the contract and the process through which that contract was formed. The substantive problem will usually be the consideration, but could also be the terms, interest payments, or other obligations the court finds unfair. Procedural issues that a court could consider include a party's lack of choice, superior bargaining position or knowledge, and other circumstances surrounding the bargaining process.

Upon finding unconscionability, a court has a great deal of flexibility on how it remedies the situation. It may refuse to enforce the contract, refuse to enforce the offending clause, or take other measures it deems necessary to have a fair outcome. Damages are usually not awarded.

UNCONSCIONABLE CONTRACTS

An agreement that is grossly unjust, unfair, or dishonest may be deemed an unconscionable contract. Determining whether or not an agreement is unconscionable usually raises questions of competency, fairness, and honesty. If it is found that these things have been manipulated in such a way that an agreement is shocking to the conscience of a normal person, judiciary will not allow the contract to be enforced.

The unconscionability of a contract usually arises as a defence. When one party contests a case for breach of contract before arbitrator the other party might sympathetically claim it did not fulfill its obligations because it was an unconscionable contract. It is important to understand that an agreement is not likely to be deemed unconscionable simply because one party's terms are unfavorable.

For a contract to be deemed unconscionable, it needs to be grossly unfair or unjust. This is purely subjective. The terms and potential benefit of the contract should be generally shocking to a normal person's conscience. A court's role in determining whether a contract is unconscionable is to prevent one party from benefiting from the exploitation of another.

Competency is one of the factors usually considered in such a case. An unconscionable contract is one that a competent person would not enter. When competency is taken into account, age is also commonly considered. An example could be an adolescent singer who signs a contract with a music executive that is unjustly in favor of the music company. A judge may find it is an unconscionable contract due to the knowledge and experience of the music executive compared to the youth and incompetence of the singer.

People usually have a great deal of liberty with regards to entering and drafting contracts. A court, however, may have the authority to assess the fairness of those contracts. The judicial system is based on a high level of integrity. To allow the judicial system to be used to enforce agreements that are grossly imbalanced is not generally viewed as serving the best interest of society.

Honesty is also considered when there are questions of conscionability. A court does not generally allow one party to benefit from an agreement where the facts have been intentionally and grossly misrepresented to another. Honesty is also considered with regards to the benefits to be received. Courts do not generally enforce contracts that are so one-sided that an honest person would disagree to the benefits.

There exists no clear definition of unconscionability. However, the purpose is to prevent oppressive and unfair surprise. This has been interpreted to entail procedural as well as substantive factors. Procedural unconscionability involves deficiencies in how the contract came to be, especially exploitation of difference in status and sophistication of the parties, deceptive appearance or language of the contract and questionable bargaining. Substantive unconscionability refers to the contract terms *per se*; it is often a matter of an excessively one-sided contract or a particularly offensive term.

STATUS AND BARGAINING POWER OF THE PARTIES

In the unfair contractual terms , a reasonable starting point is to ask who the parties are, especially with regard to education, experience and other factors related to their status. The relative position of the parties in the bargaining process is what is important, It is the difference between the parties which are most important and not each party's position *per se*. It is therefore precarious to try to describe characteristics which might support a finding of procedural unconscionability without taking into account the other party.

Lack of education is a factor which is very vital in this regard. Illiteracy or an inability to understand the language of the contract is also a matter for consideration. At the same time it is generally harder for poor people to negotiate and understand a contract.

Article 14 of constitution enjoins upon the state not to act arbitrarily since there is no parity of status between the state and the individual. The individual party to contract are either illiterate, poor or not aware of their political rights. Individuals enter into agreement with state perforce and are made to agree to contractual conditions which are unfair, unjust, and inequitable. State machinery is conferred with sweeping discretionary and discriminatory power and is exempted from responsibility and liability. The state normally takes the plea that the doctrine of equitable estoppels and waiver comes into play in as much as the contractor had voluntarily signed on the contract. Such explanations are rejected by judicial authorities stating that fundamental rights cannot be waived. In a bilateral relationship between the state and the citizen, the party is inherently unequal. There is no mutuality of bargaining power.

It is often consumers who are using unconscionability concept to defend themselves against big companies, but the doctrine is not limited to consumers. Franchisees, gas station and fueling station operators who are often in the hands of relatively large corporations have successfully invoked unconscionability. A relative lack of sophistication and education may not be a requirement for a finding of unconscionability:

Bargaining Procedure

Bargaining procedure involves the process leading up to contract formation. When the parties are on equal footing, it is often a matter of fair haggling with each party understanding the agreement, and agreeing after adequate reflection and with due care. One part of this is whether harsh and unusual clauses were called to the attention of the signer, so that he could make an informed choice.

Adhesion contracts are commonly identified as being particularly scrutinized by courts, not least within the realm of unconscionability. The reason is that such contracts, designed by one party and offered on a take it or leave it basis, are especially prone to one-sidedness. On the other hand, virtually everyone seems to recognize that form contracts serve an important purpose in today's society. An adhesion contract *per se* does not therefore precipitate an unconscionability ruling, but it will usually work in that direction; and it can support such a ruling if the contract is substantively unconscionable.

THE APPEARANCE AND LANGUAGE OF THE CONTRACT

The physical appearance of the contract as well as the language used plays a role in determining whether it is procedurally unconscionable. It is often a question of the appearance of principal terms, e.g., has an important term been "hidden in fine print." Some agreements appear to be designed to suppress attempts to read them by using fine print and other tactics that discourage reading, practices which courts tend to shun. There are also attempts to deceive using unnecessarily complex or confusing language as well as misleading headings. Courts usually consider what the reasonable expectations of a party are; if an unusual and tough clause has been effectively hidden, there will be a good case for procedural unconscionability.

APPROACH OF JUDICIARY TO UNCONSCIONABLE CONTRACTS

In order to ensure the requirement of mutuality, free consent and equal bargaining power, the judiciary has been playing a very significant role for contacting parties. The view adopted by it can be explained as under:

(1) If the court as a matter of law finds the contract or any clause of the contract to have been unconscionable at the time it was made the court may refuse to enforce the contract, or it may enforce the remainder of the contract

without the unconscionable clause, or it may so limit the application of any unconscionable clause as to avoid any unconscionable result.

(2) When it is claimed or appears to the court that the contract or any clause thereof may be unconscionable the parties shall be afforded a reasonable opportunity to present evidence as to its commercial setting, purpose and effect to aid the court in making the determination. Thus, the tool of arbitration can be used in solving disputes arising due to unconscionability of contracts. The parties to arbitration must prepare well before contesting on the platform of arbitration to ward-off damages in case of breach.

GAIL challenged the action of the ONGC for incorporating clause, in contract, to pay transportation charges of the gas. The stand of GAIL is that they are not liable to pay transportation charges as it transports the gas to its plant, through its own pipeline from the ONGC Metering Station and that the clause for payment of transportation charges incorporated in the contract is unfair, unreasonable, unconscionable and opposed to the public policy. It is contended by GAIL that they had no option but to fall prey to the unreasonably, arbitrary, unfair term of contract and, therefore, such terms were incorporated in the contract. ONGC is enjoying a monopoly so far as supply of the natural gas is concerned. Looking to the facts and circumstances of the case , it was held that the clause of term of contract, which compels petitioners to pay transportation charges, is unfair, unconscionable, arbitrary and against the public policy and is quashed and set aside.

The Awas Vikas Sansthan (AVS) was registered as a Society and brought into existence to achieve certain objectives. The objects of the society were to collect information regarding low cost technology for construction of houses, undertake studies for development of low cost building materials, undertake construction works, impart practical training in the State of Rajasthan.

The Rajasthan Housing Board sanctioned funds for setting up of some such centres in Rajasthan. The State Government or the Rajasthan Housing Board did not have any control over the AVS. The AVS started functioning in the year 1989, but in the year 1997, it began to incur heavy losses and could not pay its employees their salaries. The Rajasthan Government decided that, in view of the financial and administrative conditions of the AVS, it should be dissolved. The State Government directed the Rajasthan Housing Board to take immediate steps to liquidate the AVS. The State Government also directed that the employees of the AVS would be adjusted on priority against the vacant posts of Municipal Boards, Municipal Councils, Jaipur Development Authority. The condition of appointment was that no benefit of past service would be given. They were given employment on the lowest post of pay drawn in AVS. Benefit of 5th pay commission was denied on the plea that they were not government employee. At no point of time, the employees did claim that the terms of settlement were not fair. Court in this case held that the contract was unconscionable under section 23 of the contract Act. The principle deducible in this case is in consonance with securing social and economic justice and conforms to the mandate of the great equality clause in Article 14.

8 Substantial Performance and Termination of Contracts

In construction and manufacturing industry achieving full performance under contract is almost unthinkable, at least in prescribed time. There are myriads of situations which affect the performance. For example, time run-over and consequently cost run-over are galore. The blame for less than full performance is shared by both parties to contract. As a remedial measure, sometimes contracts are terminated even though the work is at very advance stage. This measure complicates the matter further. However, there are contracts under which near completion progress is achieved allowing the project to be put to use. This near completion approach is often called as substantial progress.

It is the endeavour of every contractor or manufacturer to complete the task in least possible time. This well intentioned approach lessens uncertainties of future and improves his profitability. However despite making sincere efforts with good intention in mind and deployment of adequate resources, the scheme does not work as thought of. Failures do take place putting the project behind the schedule. Finally, a stage is reached where the project is nearly complete barring minor deficiencies.

At this stage if owner remains dissatisfied, he may decide to terminate the contract withholding payment of contractor. Such a choice is not appropriate considering the intention of the contractor and progress he has achieved. Such an approach is unfair. The contractor would feel strapped of his right to receive payment for his labour.

When a person fully performs the contract, subject to such minor defects that he can be said to have substantially performed his promise, it is regarded as just to allow him to recover the contract price reduced by the extent to which his breach of contract lessened the value of what was done, than to leave him with no right of recovery at all.

The concept of "substantial performance" saves a party who has largely fulfilled his obligations under a contract from suffering major loss merely because he has unintentionally fallen short in some particular area which does not affect the -essence of the contract.

Substantial performance is a legal principle which says that if a good faith attempt is made to perform the agreement even if it does not precisely meet the terms of the agreement the performance will still be considered complete if the essential purpose is accomplished. However, this is subject to claim of damages for shortfall. A defendant when sued for non-performance cannot avoid paying damages by showing the substantially performed or came near to performing the requirements of the contract.

In the nature of things it is impossible for a civil engineer to draft a contract with numerous plans and specifications which will be mathematically accurate. Drafting contracts has never been an exact science. During its performance slight omissions and inadvertences may occur innocently. There are several factors which influence the performance and such factors are not within his control. Therefore, these should be regarded indulgently.

It is often said that extreme of everything is bad, so is the case with law. Extreme of law is injustice. The saying is frequently true and for this reason legal rules have been framed only to be modified for the purpose of affording justice in the greatest number of cases. The doctrine of substantial performance is one such rule which has been designed to adjust itself in construction contracts.

Substantial performance occurs when actual performance falls not far short of the required performance and the cost of remedying the defect is small in comparison with the contract price. The doctrine of substantial performance is not available to a party when that party has made a wilful departure from the terms of an agreement or omitted essential points of performance.

It is a term used to mean that the contract has been completed or performed to an extent that performance should be considered adequate. The concept arose under contract law, which was put into place to ensure that if a contract had been almost completely performed, the absence of the completion of small or insignificant details should not give one party license to breach a contract. In other words, if a person completes most or all of his responsibilities under a contract, he is entitled to payment or whatever else he was promised under the terms of the contract.

Contracts are legally enforceable promises. Contracts may contain numerous terms or conditions that the parties to the contract must meet. Completing some of the provisions of a contract may be time consuming and may take years.

Under this rule, when one party completes the contract in such a manner that performance is substantially the same as complete performance, the other party is bound to pay. In other words, if, for example, a contractor is bound to complete a contract using one type of wood but the wood is unavailable so he uses a wood that is equivalent, substantial performance will protect that contractor. It permits the contractor to enforce the contract and demand payment, although he did not perform the duties listed under the contract to the exact specifications listed in the contract.

In order for a contract to be enforced when there is substantial performance but not a complete fulfilment of all contract duties, the party requesting the substantial performance must have been unable to perform the exact duties in the contract through no fault of his own. This means a party will not simply decide to perform differently and expect substantial performance. Something beyond his control must have necessitated that he makes an alteration.

Substantial performance is a term which represents a definite idea and which accordingly can be defined. It has been said that substantial performance exists "if there has been an honest and faithful performance of the contract in its material and substantial parts and no willful departure from or omission of the essential points of the contract. Substantial performance is said to exist "where there has been no willful departure from the terms of the contract and no omission in essential points and it has been honestly and faithfully performed in its material and substantial particulars", and the only variance from strict and literal performance consists of "technical or unimportant omissions or defects".

"The concept is intended for the protection and relief of those who have faithfully and honestly endeavoured to perform their contracts in all material and substantial particulars, so that their right to compensation may not be forfeited by reason of mere technical, inadvertent, or unimportant omissions or defects. It is incumbent on him who invokes this protection to present a case in which there has been no willful omission or departure from the terms of his contract.

When a contract has not been fully, but has been substantially, performed, in that it has been in good faith complied with in all essentials to the full accomplishment of that which was contracted for, such contractor is entitled to recover the contract price, less such deductions there from as will make good to the proprietor the imperfections in the work.

Substantial performance in a contract dispute is a doctrine that allows one party to require payment from the other even if their contract duties were only partially performed. The doctrine states that if the performance was "substantially" completed, or completed in a way that is actually satisfactory, it may require payment according to the contract terms.

Substantial performance is a helpful doctrine that may allow the parties to avoid a more costly and complex filing for breach of contract. However, the parties may still need to go to court if they need to determine whether the performance was substantial enough to warrant payment. This may require the presentation of various points of evidence in support of the performance. Substantial performance will not be an issue if the contract specifies that the work absolutely needs to be fully completed.

AMOUNT OF RECOVERY IN CASE OF SUBSTANTIAL PERFORMANCE

The theory of substantial performance is that there is performance which, on the one hand, is less than strict and literal performance, but on the other hand, is so close to strict and literal performance that it cannot be regarded as breach. The amount which the party who has performed substantially is entitled to recover should therefore be something less than he would have been entitled to recover in case of strict and literal performance; but on the other hand the consequences of breach ought not to attach to substantial performance. The party who has performed substantially is not entitled to recover the full contract price. The contract price with necessary deduction should be the basis for the amount of recovery and it is not proper to fix the amount of recovery at the value of the performance to the owner. A contractor may be excused from relatively minor deviations from a contract's terms, subject to a monetary adjustment where necessary, to give the parties the benefit of their bargains.

However, the requirement to comply exactly with the terms of a contract is subject to certain limitations. For example, contracting party's minimum failures will be excused if they have no real impact on the contract value. Under this doctrine, a party must pay for work that is performed substantially in compliance with the contract terms, subject to adjustments intended to compensate for any omissions or defects. The doctrine saves a party who has largely fulfilled his obligations under a contract from suffering major loss merely because he has unintentionally fallen short in some particular manner which does not affect the essence of the contract.

The rule implies that there has been no willful departure from the terms of the contract, and no omission of any of its essential parts, and that the contractor has in good faith performed all of its substantive terms. If so, he will not be held to have forfeited his right to a recovery by reason of trivial defects or imperfections in the work performed.

The concept of substantial performance is very important especial for those contractors who have almost completed the work, but to dissatisfaction of owner he terminates the contract with levy of damages. In such eventuality it could be argued strongly before the arbitral tribunal profitably.

TERMINATION OF CONTRACTS

As observed elsewhere in the book, all contracts do not end up as a success story. Problems do arise during execution stage which requires solution by association of both the parties. A great deal of understanding is must between the parties. Yet there are intractable problems which evade solution. For instance at the time of tender invitation it is presumed that the land acquisition would be completed by the time LOA is issued. But this is rarity. Handing over site is a major source of dispute and breach of contracts.

Termination of contract means the time when the contract comes to an end. This can be on completion of work or expiry of validity or termination before expiry. However generally, it is felt that termination means ending a contract sooner than it otherwise would have ended. The other dimension is that people feel termination and expiration are two different things. However, both the terms mean ending a contract.

Generally speaking the termination entails one or more parties' ending a contract sooner than it otherwise would have ended; in the case when the contract is coming to an end due to expiry of its validity the correct word to use would be 'expires'.

One can readily find in legal reference works instances of *termination* used to refer to any means by which a contract comes to an end. Consider, for example, the following, "A contract may be discharged by performance in accordance with its terms; in fact, this is the normal termination of every contract. A contract may also be terminated by the expiration of the time during which it is to remain operative." In this passage, expiration is considered a form of termination rather than something distinct from termination.

The definitions of *termination* and *terminate* in *Black's Law Dictionary* are consistent with the notion that termination includes expiration. *Termination* is defined as meaning "The act of ending something" and "The end of something in time or existence." In other words, termination is both something you do and something that can simply happen. To the same effect, *terminate* is defined as meaning "To put an end to; to bring to an end" and "To end; to conclude." The word 'termination' generally refers to an ending, usually before the end of the anticipated term of the contract.

Most of the litigation in contracts fall under the category of delay in performance, either by owner or contractor failing to fulfil their part of promise leading to termination of contract. The right to terminate arises from breach of contract by the defaulter or from the conduct of defaulter that shows that he is unable or unwilling to comply with the terms of contract.

The right to termination is the most dreaded and essential tool. The termination provisions in contract require careful consideration of the meaning of various terms used in it otherwise it may lead to post termination complications. Termination of a contract is usually achieved by full performance. However, often it is early termination. Termination is not rescission notwithstanding the fact that people sometime use these terms interchangeably. To rescind a contract means unwind it back to its initial stage. The contract is given its full effect up to the time of termination.

In order to determine whether a party deserves termination, it is necessary to have some guidelines. These guidelines should not be aimed at crushing the rights of parties but to encourage them to perform.

METHODS OF CONTRACT TERMINATION

Most contracts end when the validity period of the contract has expired, the contracts are renegotiated and brought to life. However, there are three distinct termination scenarios that may be specified in a contract. These are cancellation for default, cancellation by mutual consent and cancellation for convenience.

CANCELLATION FOR DEFAULT

This is used by a customer when the vendor has failed to abide by the terms of the contract. Depending on how the contract is worded, the termination can be triggered by failure to adhere to delivery dates, or a failure to provide items with the level of quality required. Whatever the cause, the customer should be able to provide evidence to substantiate the cancellation notice. Depending on the contract, the vendor may have a period in which to address the issues, or if they disagree with the reasons provided by the customer, they can take their case to a mediator.

CANCELLATION BY MUTUAL CONSENT

In many cases the contract is terminated by mutual consent without any instances that trigger a cause. Sometimes the vendor stops production of a part used by the customer and therefore the contract can no longer be fulfilled. In other cases, the customer may no longer produce finished goods that require parts fulfilled by the contract.

CANCELLATION FOR CONVENIENCE

Vendors have found that customers have cancelled contracts for convenience due to the fact that they are in financial difficulties and do not want to be tied to a contract. If this termination occurs the vendor should not suffer any financial loss because of the actions of the customer.

In addition to above there are following reasons for which a contract can be terminated:

- Frustration
- Repudiation
- Cancellation for breach of contract
- Failure of a condition
- Termination for a cause under a contractual termination provision
- Termination without cause under a term of the contract
- Discharge by agreement

Frustration

A contract is frustrated if unforeseen events occur after the contract is entered into which makes performance of the contract either impossible or impracticable. Frustration requires the occurrence of an unforeseen event which fundamentally alters the contractual relationship between the parties. In frustration the parties are relieved of their contractual obligation.

Repudiation

A party to a contract may cancel it either by words or conduct conveying that he does not intend to perform his obligation under the contract. It is an unequivocal assertion of an intention not to be bound by the contract. This refusal will give a right of cancellation.

Cancellation for Breach

Every major breach or fundamental breach calls for termination of contract with claim for damages. However, smaller breaches may be waived off by parties. The ICA provides remedies for every type of breach.

Failure of a Condition

A contract may come to an end or a party may avoid an obligation under the contract by reason of a failure of a condition in that contract. Traditionally the conditions are : (i) condition precedent, and (ii) condition subsequent. A condition precedent refers to an event which must take place before any binding contract takes place between the parties. A condition subsequent refers to an event which has the effect of discharging the contract. The parties are bound by their agreement prior to the fulfilment of the condition, but should the event on which the contract is conditional, do not occur, the contract will fail.

Termination for a Cause Pursuant to a Term of the Contract

In this the contract expressly provides for a remedy in respect of misrepresentation or repudiation or breach of contract or any other matter. Any pre-condition to termination should be properly fulfilled

Termination without Cause under a Term of the Contract

It is common for either party to terminate without cause. This can take several forms-termination at will (without any notice period); on notice or upon certain eventuality. Termination " without cause" provision in the agreement is in effect a form of termination by agreement

Discharge by Agreement

It is an elementary principle of contract law that an agreement can be extinguished by agreement. Contracting parties remain free to agree to modify or entirely discharge their own agreement. An agreement to modify or discharge an agreement is itself a new contract.

The nature of promise broken is one of the most important of the matter. It is a condition that is broken. It is an essential promise. The injured party when realises this development, he has the right either to treat himself as discharged from the contract and to recover damages for particular breach. Breach of a term goes to the root of the contract such as to deprive the injured party of a substantial part of the benefit to which he is entitled under the contract. On the other hand, if the contract has been in the large part performed, it is less likely that the breach will be substantial enough to warrant termination. Whether the tardy performance is the breach, it will depend upon the intention of defaulter with reference to the particular promise.

Breaches of contract are normally compensated by damages. A cautious approach is required while framing termination clause which confers right to terminate. Where a procedure is laid out, ensure it is followed to the letter. There should be no ambiguity.

In construction contracts it is not uncommon for works to be partially completed and the injured party weighs the consequences of termination or continuing the contract. This will involve another local agency at higher cost and delay in recovering the additional cost from the defaulter.

Wrongful Termination

Wrong termination of contract is in itself a serious breach and entitles the other party to terminate. The role reverses quickly and the party with the high moral ground can quickly find itself as defaulter. The other party then has to decide to accept repudiation and terminate the contract. Wrong termination exposes a party to substantial risks. The other party is legally empowered to terminate the contract and seek damages as an injured party.

For instance, a work of construction of boundary wall was awarded to a firm. LOA containing conditions was issued. The site was to be handed over in phases. It was the express condition of the LOA that time extension would be granted in case delay takes place in handing over site and that firm would have no right to claim on account of delay. There was indeed delay in making over site. One unfateful day the owner terminated the contractor at firm's risk. Firm was given notice to pay the extra amount. At that stage the firm sought arbitration. The termination was proved to be wrong. The work was delayed on account of owner. It was concluded that termination was not valid and legal. Since time was no longer the essence, the contract should not have been suddenly terminated without first granting extension then making the time essence of the contract. Owners' counter-claims were dismissed and firms claims were admitted. The claims included office over heads, loss of profit, site over heads, etc.

In yet another case, contract was given for extension of terminal of an airport. Since the first phase was not completed in time, the owner terminated the contract. The matter went to high court where the termination order was set aside and directed for granting EOT. Since progress continued to be slow contract was again terminated. The matter was referred for arbitration. There it was concluded that the owner was responsible for delay and therefore termination was wrongful and owner was responsible for the consequences arising out of wrongful termination.

It is essential that the right to terminate is exercised correctly. Getting it wrong (which happens all the time) can have disastrous consequences.

A party that purports to operate a contractual termination clause, when it is not entitled to do so, may repudiate its contract. This is because a party who acts on a contractual termination clause usually ceases to perform its own·obligations. Incorrect termination in itself may be a fundamental breach. If the termination was invalid, and the other side has accepted your repudiation by leaving the site, you may be liable to the other side for damages for wrongful termination. If a contract is wrongfully terminated, a party can be expected to receive the full contract value of any work done at that time, less sums previously paid, and possibly a sum for loss of profit on the remaining works. It is important to remember that if you subsequently discover your mistake, you cannot simply restore the contract without the agreement of the other side.

Grounds for Termination

It should be checked if the grounds for termination can be proved. The circumstances in which a right to terminate arises must be shown to exist for the notice to be valid to be given by the engineer, but the actual notice of termination is to be given by the terminating party itself. A related point is that the contract often provides for a preliminary or warning notice followed by a notice of termination if the default is not remedied. There must be a reasonable connection between the initial and subsequent notices. It is not possible for a preliminary notice to be served, followed by a notice of default some considerable time afterwards, in circumstances where the recipient might not reasonably connect the two notices as relating to the same matter. Thus, a preliminary notice was served requiring a default to be remedied. A notice of determination was given 11 months later. It was held that where a contract provides for two notices to be served, that termination will only be valid if an ordinary commercial businessman could see that there was a sensible connection between the two notices both in content and time. This test was not satisfied in this case.

EXERCISE THE RIGHT WITHIN REASONABLE PERIOD

It is important that the right to terminate is exercised within a reasonable period, otherwise you may waive your right to terminate by having "affirmed" the contract. The courts like certainty when it comes to resolving legal disputes. Accordingly, there is a point at which parties can be forced to draw a line under a breach and move on. To do otherwise could expose the opposite party to the continuous threat of termination for years after a breach. If you wait too long, therefore, to decide whether or not to pull the plug, you might find the decision has already been made for you. It seems even clauses in the contract that give you as long as you like to make up your mind will not help you.

Take the case which emphasises the importance of certainty when terminating a contract. Tele-2 committed a material breach of its contract. Nobody disputed the fact that this was a material breach but the Post Office waited 11 months before purporting to terminate the contract. Given the delay in seeking to terminate, Tele-2 argued that the Post Office had lost its right to end the agreement. Tele-2 relied on something called the doctrine of affirmation, which states that if you know about a breach that gives you the right to terminate, you must decide whether to do so before "the law takes the decision out of your hands". Tele-2 said that allowing the contract to run for another 11 months implied that the Post Office As far as the Post Office was concerned, it did not matter how long it waited, it could still terminate at any time. Indeed, the Post Office pointed to its "non-waiver" clause—a provision in many construction contracts that states delay in exercising a right will not prevent enforcement at a later date. However, the Court of Appeal did not agree. In its opinion, continuing with the contract for 11 months was more than just postponing the exercise of a right—it was such clear evidence of the Post Office's intention not to terminate, it said, and that the only possible conclusion was that the contract remained in force. What we learn from this case is that if a party does want to keep its options open in response to a breach, it must "protest" and "reserve its rights" in a way that the Post Office failed to do. Promptly notifying the other side of its potential breach and spelling out that you are reserving your rights would seem to be a step in the right direction.

In some contracts right to terminate the contract without assigning any reason is kept reserved with the employer. After a few days of awarding the work, the contract is terminated only to assign the work to someone else as a mark of favour. The termination is illegal.

Damages for wrongful termination: If you do get it wrong, and you terminate wrongfully, what are the potential consequences? A party that has been wrongfully terminated is entitled to be placed in the position it would have been in if the contract had been completed without breach. The normal measure of damages protects a party's expectations under the contract, which should entitle a party to receive payment under the contract for work done, together with loss of profit on work not done. Secondly, termination frequently involves seizure or use of plant. Where the termination turns out to be wrongful, the terminated party will naturally be entitled to damages for any plant seized by the other side.

Serving notice on contractor for termination is not necessary where no time limit for performance is prescribed, if the contractor has not performed within reasonable time.

9 Extension of Time in Contracts

A construction project has thousands of activities to be performed before it can be put to purposeful use. For instance, in a building construction there is masonry, excavation, concreting, shuttering, water supply, sewerage system approach road, electrical installations etc. Keeping track of so many items in estimate and tender schedule is next to impossible. Certain items would probably be left out of contract. Besides, new requirements will generate as experience is gained and new wisdom dawns upon owner. In addition, surprises will also be encountered especially during excavation. Inefficiency of contractor is another area to be catered for. For accommodating new requirements weather addition/alteration or surprises or inefficiencies, target dates would be shifted. This shifting of completion dates which is nothing but delay would be either on owners account or contractor's account or both. Time assessment for completion of project is a very demanding task as it cannot be exact science. Yet adequate care in this matter can save the contract from tragic end.

There are other factors too which call for additional time. Labour unrest, shortage of construction material into market, rain and accidents at site put the project behind the schedule. The net result is that project would take longer than thought of which will have to be permitted by owner at the request of contractor creating a new binding contract between them. Specifying completion date is very essential as in absence of it, monitoring of project becomes impossible.

If no date is specified a 'reasonable time for completion' will normally be implied, based on the circumstances of the particular project. Without a fixed completion date, liquidated damages or other penalty laid down in contract will not be chargeable. For this reason, construction contracts will include a fixed completion date which may be extended through EOT provisions. Clause for EOT in contracts have benefits for both parties.

From a contractor's perspective: (i) Extensions cover delays that are neither the fault nor the responsibility of the contractor, and (ii) a contractor will not normally be liable to pay damages for delay if completion time is validly extended.

From an employer's perspective: (i) Provision of extension provide certainty as to how the completion date is to be fixed, and under what circumstances it may be adjusted; and (ii) provision is designed to protect the right to claim liquidated damages for delay in relevant circumstances.

There are three categories of delays:

Compensable delay : Events that entitles the contractor to EOT and to loss and expenses for cost flowing from that event.

Excusable delay : Event that entitles the contractor to EOT but where the contractor bears the risk of additional cost that may flow from that event.

Culpable delay : Events that do not entitle the contractor to either EOT or money.

TIME AS ESSENCE OF CONTRACT

In construction contracts often time is the essence of the contract is one of the conditions. However, it should be noted that there are large number of factors which influence the construction. As a result the project spills over and time is without exception required to be extended. A separate condition for granting EOT is also incorporated in these contracts. Where there is provision for EOT, time cannot be said to be essence of contract. If the intention of the parties to contract is that time should be essence of contract, then a failure to perform at the agreed time renders the contract voidable at the option of the opposite party. Time is considered to be so : (i) where delay is treated as injury, (ii) where the parties express their desire to treat the time so, and (iii) where necessity of the contract requires it to be so. By nature, time is never essence of the contract in construction contracts. On the other hand, in commercial contracts time is ordinarily of the essence. This is so because business world requires certainty. However for delayed performance, owner may reserve right for recovery of compensation. If no notice is given while extending time without recovery, no compensation can be recovered afterwards. . EOT cannot be granted unilaterally.

Supreme court of India has held in *Hind Construction Contractors* v. *The State of Maharashtra* that the question whether or not time is essence of the contract would essentially be a question of the intentions of the parties to be gathered from the terms of the contract. Even where the parties have expressly provided that time is the essence of the contract, such stipulation would have to be read along with other provisions of the contract and such clause may exclude the inference that the completion of the work by a particular date was intended to be fundamental. If the contract includes clause providing EOT in certain contingencies when the work undertaken remains unfinished on expiry of time provided in the contract, such clause would be construed as rendering ineffective the express provision relating to time being of the essence of the contract.

Invariably all contracts have extension of time clause incorporated in them to facilitate the parties to extend the target date in case of failure of owner in fulfilling his obligation or contractor encountering genuine problems during execution. Normally, a nominated authority has the power to extend time provided following conditions are satisfied:

(1) The contractor must seek EOT by making a written application;
(2) Grounds for seeking EOT must be stated conspicuously; and
(3) Application should be made well in time and before expiry of validity.

Nominated authority will extend the time if he is satisfied with the reasons seeking extension. The clause also states that the nominated authority's decision shall be final. However, it should be clear that his decision on whatever period of extension granted by him is proper, is not final. There is no bar on the contractor approaching arbitrator with the question of adequacy of the period extended. Thus, the period of extension is not a non-arbitrable issue.

If the right to EOT is not exercised within permitted time, in certain rare cases, contract may restrict its exercise. The question weather nominated authority can extend the period *suo-motto*, the matter was examined by GOI, Ministry of law according to which authority can extend the time where adequate and proper ground exists. However, such an offer has to be accepted by other party to make it effective.

There is an erroneous understanding on the part of owner that contractor would not be entitled to claim anything extra once EOT is granted. It has been held by Delhi High Court in *N.D.R. Israni vs Delhi development Authority (1989)* that the plea of EOT granted to contractor would eliminate claim for damages was not tenable because the respondent could not be a judge of its own cause, and in any case, mere grant of EOT for completion of work is not a satisfaction for the claim of damages. A division bench of Delhi high court in *Metro Electric Company, New Delhi* v. *Delhi Development Authority* upheld the award of damages against DDA recognising the contractor's right to damages for breach of the contract. Mere extension of time cannot be taken as a substitute for claim of damages. The award of damages in this case was on account of the loss incurred by the contractor due to increase in the prices of materials and because of delay on the part of DDA.

The very purpose of keeping EOT clause is to keep the contract alive when the period is validly and properly extended. EOT must be made in time otherwise it will be set at large and operation of LD clause becomes ineffectual.

The EOT cannot be extended unilaterally. In situations where only other alternative is the cancellation of contract and retendering, which is likely to take considerable time, EOT should be sanctioned. While sanctioning EOT, intention of recovery of compensation or otherwise should be given due thought. Delay by itself does not put an end to the contract.

TIME AT LARGE

The power to grant an EOT exists for the benefit of the employer, enabling it to grant EOTs for events for which he is responsible and preserve its right to LDs for Culpable Delays. If the contract does not include this power, and the employer commits an act which prevents the contractor from meeting the completion date, the contractor cannot be held liable for failing and the employer can grant an EOT. In these circumstances, the contractual completion date falls away and time is said to be "at large". Time will also be at large if the contract does not state a completion date. Because there is no fixed completion date, the employer is not entitled to LDs.

Where extension of time is not granted/intimated to the contractor in time despite his request for extension of time, abandonment of work by him is justified *(State of Madhya Pradesh* v. *Khusiram & Co.).*

Continuing to work on a contract with no signed contract renewal :

> Most contractors are familiar with the situation. The contract is coming to a close and the client has promised a contract renewal but the client's internal 'bureaucracy' has not caught up and the contract has not been renewed. Or maybe the agent has sent through the new contract, but the contractor has not got round to negotiating some unpleasant clauses, but keeps turning up for work at the client's site every day. Whatever the reason, "Continuing to work without a signed contract, or contract extension, in place is potentially A Bad Idea." Busy contractors who have not bothered to sign and return their contract extension, and continue to work for the client beyond the original contract, may be asking for trouble.

If the contractor continues to work into the new contract period, for which a new contract has been sent, then even if the contractor hasn't signed the new contract, they may be deemed to have accepted it because they've continued working. Not responding to an unfavourable new contract can be a double-edged sword, and the lesson is that contractors should respond to and renegotiate with the client or agency well before the term of the original contract expires.

If the new contract is left unsigned, but not undisputed, and the contractor continues to work after the original contract period, then this may be considered 'affirmation' of the new contract's terms and, should the contractor later stop working, they might be in breach of contract.

EXTENSIONS OF TIME

Building projects often cost more and take longer than originally planned. Delays may occur for example because the contractor was working inefficiently, which is its own fault, or because the employer instructed additional work, for which the contractor will be entitled to additional payment. If delays impacted upon the critical path rather than merely taking up available float, such that the contractor failed to meet the contractual completion date the contract will generally entitle the contractor to an extension of time to the completion date for delaying events which under the contract are the responsibility of the employer. The contractor may also be entitled to losses and expenses.

Contract regulates the relationship between the parties and apportions risk. It should list those events for which the contractor is entitled to an EOT if there is delay, which will be at the employer's risk. Events that are not listed will be at the contractor's risk. The typical events include: acts of default by the employer, such as failure to grant possession of the site by the start date, perfectly valid actions, such as instructing variations or additional work; and neutral events which the parties agree will be at the employer's risk, such as unforeseen ground conditions and exceptionally adverse weather.

When a contract contains reciprocal promises and one party to the contract prevents the other from performing his promise, the contract becomes voidable at the option of the party. If, in case of a contract being voidable on account of the promisor's failure to perform his promise at the time agreed, the promisee accepts performance of such promise at any time other than agreed, the promisee cannot claim compensation of any loss occasioned by the non-performance of the promise at the time agreed, unless, at the time of acceptance, he gives notice to the promisor of his intention to do so.

EOT for completion of work: The EOT shall be granted by owner without LD, if the work is delayed owing to :

(i) Force majeure;
(ii) Reason of exceptionally inclement weather;
(iii) Reason of dispute of owner with neighbour or authority having effect on work;
(iv) Delay caused by other contractors employed by owner for the same work;
(v) Delay in giving instruction to contractor in time; and
(vi) Reason of civil commotion, earthquake, strike, lock out, etc. affecting the performance of contract.

In case contractor's performance of the contract is delayed or prevented due to :

(i) A cause beyond reasonable control, reasonably unforeseeable and without the fault of contractor;
(ii) An act of God, strike, flood, neglect of owner, epidemic, war earthquake, etc;

(iii) Inability on account of a cause beyond the reasonable control of contractor to obtain necessary materials.

With respect to such delays, EOT shall be the remedy, except that in the event of when contractor's performance is delayed by act of owner, the contractor shall be entitled to actual cost in respect of such delay. Actual cost may include:

(a) Cost of all sub-contractors to the main contract;
(b) Labour and material escalation cost;
(c) Standby cost during period of suspension of work;
(d) Cost associated with mobilisation and demobilisation cost; and
(e) Extended overhead cost such as extended supervision, site supervision, home office overheads and site cost, etc.

Section 55 of ICA deals with performance of contracts related to time which is reproduced as under: **Effect of failure to perform a fixed time, in contract in which time is essential :** *"When a party to a contract promises to do a certain thing at or before a specified time, or certain things at or before a specified time and fails to do such things at or before a specified time, the contract or so much of it as has not been performed, becomes voidable at the option of the promisee, if the intention of the parties was that time should be of essence of the contract.*

Effect of such failure when time is not essential: If it was not the intention of the parties that time should be of the essence of the contract, the contract does not become voidable by the failure to do such things at or before the specified time; but the promisee is entitled to compensation from the promisor for any loss occasioned to him by such failure.

Effect of acceptance of performance at time other than agreed upon: *"If, in case of a contract voidable on account of the promisor's failure to perform his promise at the time agreed, the promisee accepts performance of such promise at any time other than agreed, the promisee cannot claim compensation of any loss occasioned by the non-performance of the promise at the time agreed, unless, at the time of acceptance, he gives notice to the promisor of his intention to do so."*

DELAY IN SUPPLIES FOR WHICH SUPPLIER IS NOT RESPONSIBLE

Normally, in the following circumstances, the contractual

delivery period needs to be re-fixed to take care of the lost period, without imposing any penalty to the supplier.

(i) Cases where the manufacture of stores is dependent on the approval of the advance sample and delay occurs in approving the sample though submitted by the supplier in time.
(ii) Where extension in delivery period is granted on account of some omission on the part of the purchaser which affects the due performance of the contract by the supplier.
(iii) Cases where the purchaser controls the entire production.

The delivery cannot be re-fixed to make a contract a 'severable' contract without the specific agreement of the supplier, if the delivery originally stipulated in the contract was in the form of an 'entire' contract.

REMEDIES TO PURCHASER FOR DELAY IN SUPPLY/ NON-SUPPLY FOR WHICH SUPPLIER IS RESPONSIBLE

The purchaser has the following options depending upon the circumstances of the case:

(i) Extend the delivery period with imposition of liquidated damages and other denial clauses
(ii) Forfeit the performance security
(iii) Cancel the contract
(iv) Impose other available sanctions/penalties

EXTENSION OF DELIVERY PERIOD

If the supplier is unable to complete the supply within the stipulated delivery period for which the supplier is responsible, supplier is required to request for extension of delivery period. If the purchaser agrees to extend the contractual delivery schedule, the same may be done by issue of an amendment to the contract with suitable denial clauses and with imposition of liquidated damages for delay.

POINTS TO BE CONSIDERED FOR EXTENDING THE DELIVERY/OR TO CANCEL THE CONTRACT

Whether the extension of delivery date is to be granted as asked for by the supplier or the contract to be cancelled, would be decided on the merits of each case. The purchase officer has to balance time factor required for making repurchase and the needs of the indentor.

Extension should be granted only where the competent purchase officer is convinced that supplies would come forward during the extended period. Where purchase officer is convinced that there are no prospects of supplies forthcoming, particularly after granting one extension, it would be advisable to cancel the contract with a view to making repurchase as per the provisions of the Conditions of Contract.

Where under the terms of the supply order, the supplier has guaranteed delivery by stipulated date and he applies for extension, the case has to be examined on its merits. Whenever such extension is granted, the Purchaser should reserve its right to recover LD and make it clear that notwithstanding any stipulation as to 'Price Variation' Clause in terms of the original supply order, no such increase will be granted if it takes place during the extended period of delivery.

In case of difficult item or items for which sufficient capacity does not exist, the officer concerned shall have to use his discretion in deciding whether or not the order is to be cancelled.

If the execution of contract/supply order is delayed beyond the period stipulated in the contract/supply order as a result of force majeure, declaration of an embargo or blockage on the item, fire or flood due to act of God, then the management may allow such additional time by extending the delivery period as it considers to be justified by the circumstances of the contract. As a result of the above, the price variation clause may be agreed to during the extended period also.

If any modifications have been ordered which in the opinion of the Engineer have materially increased the magnitude of the work, then such extension of the contracted date of completion may be granted.

In the event of any failure or delay by the owner to hand over the Contractor possession of the land necessary for the execution of the works or to give the necessary notice to commence the works or to provide the necessary drawings or instructions or any other delay caused by the owner due to any other cause whatsoever, then such failure or delay shall in no way affect or vitiate the contract or alter the character thereof or entitle the contractor to damages or compensation therefore but in any such case, the owner may grant such extension or extensions of the completion date as may be considered reasonable.

In the event of any failure or delay by owner which may include following reasons for delay:

(i) To handover land
(ii) To give necessary notice to commence work
(iii) To provide necessary drawings or instructions

Then this failure will not violate the contract and contractor will not be entitled to damages or compensation there for but owner may grant extension of time.

Certain government departments provide similar condition in the contract as shown below:

Extension of Time for Delay due to Contractor

The time for the execution of the work specified in the contract documents shall be deemed to be the essence of the contract and the works must be completed not later than the date(s) as specified in the contract. If the contractor fails to complete the work within the time as specified in the contract for the reasons attributable to contractor, if department is satisfied that the works can be completed by the contractor within reasonable short time thereafter, allow the contractor for further extension of reasonable time. On such extension the owner will be entitled to recover from the contractor the agreed damages. Provided further, that if the owner is not satisfied that the works can be completed by the Contractor during extended period, the owner shall be entitled to appropriate the contractor's security deposit and rescind the contract.

Such clauses do not convey parity of bargain. For delay attributable to owner, he may grant EOT whereas for delay on account of contractor there is penalty. The compensation to contractor is EOT and to owner it is liquidated damages which are not comparable in severity.

SUMMARY

Disputes/differences do arise in construction contracts as well as in supply contracts as to who is responsible for slow/delayed progress. Reasons of delay should be logged carefully and category wise, namely: (i) delay on account of owner, (ii) delay due to unforeseen events, etc. EOT should be sought for adequate period and reasons for delay should be spelt out clearly in the application for EOT to avoid LD. Claims and counter-claims are raised before arbitral tribunal by both sides. The issue of extension of time especially where employer is at fault can be used as effective tool for compensation or to avoid recovery. Similarly, the concept of "time at large" and force majeure can be used as defence. In construction industry, time is never the essence of contract and therefore termination of contract without paying heed to this fact would make it wrongful termination.

10 Differing Site Conditions and Losses in Construction

Large and complicated construction projects have peculiar and unimaginable problems associated with them. Even engineer with rich experience cannot forecast as to the nature of problem that would be encountered during construction. The worrisome issue however is that how to allocate risk in such projects. Obviously the owner would like to shift entire risk on to contractors by inserting various exculpatory clauses in contract. One of the major area of concern is the below ground conditions that would be met with. Sometimes there may be minor variation than what has been shown in bid document. At other times conditions encountered may be entirely different than what is shown. These are called differing conditions. There are also occasion when problem encountered is never anticipated and not shown on documents. These are not accounted for in the bid. Thus the issue revolves around allocation of risk. Who will take it ?

A construction bid package typically contains plans, specifications and quantities and possibly a geotechnical report. When contractor bids based upon the information in the bid package, he have limited time to investigate site conditions and assume that the site information reflected in the bid package is by and large correct and that the project can be constructed pursuant to the plans and specifications. Everyone knows, however, that construction does not always proceed as planned. All too frequently contractors encounter subsurface conditions that differ from the information contained in the geotechnical report, or other conditions in the field that differ from what was expected or shown on the plans, in ways sometimes minor and sometimes significant.

Often, people keep guessing as to who will bear the risk of the additional cost associated with differing site conditions. In the context of fixed price contracts, the general expectation, with some exceptions, is that a contractor assumes the risk of additional costs associated with differing site conditions of which neither party is aware. It is an accepted norm that where "one agrees to do, for a fixed sum, a thing possible to be performed, he will not be excused or become entitled to additional compensation, because unforeseen difficulties are encountered." Faced with this barrier of differing site condition risk management, contractors tend to include a financial cushion to protect themselves from the possibility of having to address unforeseen site conditions.

Adding a differing site condition clause to a construction contract introduces some uncertainty for an owner regarding the ultimate cost of a project. However, this uncertainty may be offset by lower bids from contractors who will not have to account for unknown conditions by including contingencies in their bids. The inclusion of clause may also decrease the potential for project disputes and litigation.

The differing site conditions for which a contractor may be compensated generally fall into one of two types: (1) a "Type I" differing site condition, which is a site condition that is materially different from what is *shown or indicated in the contract documents;* or (2) a "Type II" differing site condition, which is an unknown physical condition, of an unusual nature, and which differs materially from those ordinarily encountered and generally recognized as inherent in the type of work encompassed by the contract.

A differing site condition exists if the contract documents substantially misrepresent a hidden physical site condition. Typically this involves a difference between the material indicated in the boring logs and what is actually encountered in construction. Obviously rock is substantially different than soil and causes not only increased excavation costs for the Contractor but a change in work operations. Subsurface differences that do not cause both documented increased costs and changes to Contractor's operations are not significant. Other differing site conditions could include a higher water table or change in site access shown in the plans.

Additionally, a differing site condition also exists if a hidden physical condition not included or described by contract documents differs substantially from what is normally encountered in the work. It is difficult for a Contractor to successfully tide over a differing site condition under this provision because it must be proved that the condition is very unusual. An example of this type of differing site condition could be encountering an artesian water source during excavation.

Once notice of a differing site condition has been given, the Engineer-in-Charge will determine whether a contract adjustment is warranted due to a differing site condition. An adjustment is appropriate if a differing site condition causes a change in both the Contractors unit costs and work operations.

Differing site conditions can be compensated by an increase or decrease in the unit prices for the work and a contract extension with time related costs for the extended period required to complete the contract. If a cost adjustment is requested by the Contractor, and the Engineer-in-Charge agrees, an agreed price should be negotiated as soon as possible to avert force accounting the work.

SITE INSPECTION CLAUSE

Owners of construction projects generally insert a clause in their bid document to put the risk of differing site conditions on contractors. The owner wants to escape the unestimable claims. Generally speaking, the site investigation should be with owner. He should have the geo-technical investigation done well in advance and provide the same information to bidders so that bidders do not unnecessarily account for risk and load the bid. By inserting the site inspection clause, the entire risk of an unanticipated site condition is attempted to be shifted to contractor which may be lethal.

Where the contract contains a differing site conditions clause, the site inspection clause may not successfully transfer to the contractor the risk of an unanticipated site condition. Nevertheless, in absence of a differing site conditions clause, this type of site inspection clause is particularly dangerous for the unsuspecting contractor. Courts have held that bidders are obligated only to discover conditions that would have been revealed by a "reasonable" pre-contract investigation. And, that "reasonableness" determination will be influenced by the amount of time allowed for the preparation of the bid, the accessibility of the site, and the cost of performing more than a "sight" investigation and the size of project.

The following practical suggestions are offered to owners and contractors struggling with the risks of differing site conditions.

For Owners

To avoid liability for unknown site conditions, it may be wise to:

(a) Disclose all known conditions prior to the submission of bids.

(b) Include a differing site conditions clause in the contract; impose strict notice requirements and consider limiting the reimbursable costs to only direct job site costs incurred by the contractor.

(c) Exculpatory (Excuse) clauses may not avoid liability when the contract documents make positive representations about the site or subsurface conditions. Avoid such representations within the contract documents or otherwise.

(e) Prior to letting out a project, be certain that you understand how the contract allocates the risk of unknown or differing site conditions.

For Contractors

Prior to bidding on a project it is wise to:

(a) Carefully review the contract and understand how it assigns the risk of differing site conditions.

(b) Search the contract for onerous exculpatory clauses or contract language disclaiming the accuracy of site information reflected in the bid documents.

(c) Perform a reasonable site inspection and make a written and photographic record of your site investigation. Notice the physical characteristics of the surrounding property.

(d) If a differing site condition is encountered, follow carefully the contract notice requirements and wait for instructions from the owner before disturbing the site conditions.

(e) Keep careful and separate cost records of your additional costs flowing from differing site conditions.

Claims for Concealed or Unknown Conditions: If conditions are encountered at the site which are : (1) subsurface or otherwise concealed physical conditions which differ materially from those indicated in the Contract Documents, or (2) unknown physical conditions of an unusual nature, which differ materially from those ordinarily found to exist and generally recognized as inherent in construction activities of the character provided for in the Contract Documents, then notice by the observing party shall be given to the other party promptly before conditions are disturbed. The engineer will promptly investigate such conditions and, if they differ materially and cause an increase or decrease in the Contractor's cost of, or time required for, performance of any part of the Work, will recommend an equitable adjustment in the Contract Sum or Contract Time, or both. If the conditions encountered are materially different, the Contract Sum and Contract Time shall be equitably adjusted, but if the Owner and Contractor cannot agree on an adjustment in the Contract Sum or Contract Time, the adjustment shall be referred to the engineer for initial determination.

Claims for Additional Time: If the Contractor wishes to make Claim for an increase in the Contract Time, written notice shall be given. The Contractor's Claim shall include an estimate of cost and of probable effect of delay on progress of the Work. In the case of a continuing delay only one Claim is necessary.

If adverse weather conditions are the basis for a Claim for additional time, such Claim shall be documented by data substantiating that weather conditions were abnormal for the period of time, and had an adverse effect on the scheduled construction.

Construction Losses

If one would ask which is the single most factor in construction industry which leads to cost overruns, strained relationship between owner and contractor, disputes, etc., the answer would be 'Delay'. Delay invariably leads to time overrun and cost overrun. In construction industry, delay may be defined as the time over run beyond completion date as specified in contract or beyond the date parties have agreed upon for delivery of project. Delay is slipping of project over planned schedule. Construction delay is common and universal across continents. The effect of delay can be country specific or region specific. However, for owners it is loss of revenue in the form of non-availability of rentable space, production facilities, etc.

The significant effect of delay, to contractor is higher overheads, because of longer work period, higher material cost through inflation, increase in labour cost, etc. Delay is a mark of inefficiency of performance. All that is owing to several variables and unpredictable factors which crop up from many sources on both sides. These could be performance of parties, resource availability, environmental conditions, contractual relations and involvement of outside agencies in various manners. Therefore, completion of project in time is chimera or rarity. In our country, although survey data are not at hand, hardly any project gets completed in time.

The prolongation of project is generally on three accounts attributable to owner:

(i) Not handing over site in time'.
(ii) Not issuing design and drawing in time.
(iii) Delay in issuing instructions by engineer in charge.

To give possession of site is obviously the prime duty of respondent to facilitate carrying out work by contractor as planned. Possession should be afforded unhindered and peaceful. It is the implied duty of employer to provide the contractor the right to occupy the site. No kind of misrepresentation should be attempted as the contractor is expected to quote his rates according to the status of site. If the employer fails to give possession of site or prevents the contractor from starting the work, this will mean repudiation by employer . Further, not to give possession of site will constitute breach of contract and entitle the contractor to damages.

Prolongation is the extended duration of the work during which additional costs are incurred such as general overheads, site overheads, loss of profit etc. Therefore contractor is right in claiming damages for prolongation. However, it is not a correct thinking that an entitlement to an EOT would automatically lead to an entitlement of compensation for prolongation cost during the period of EOT. The main effect of EOT is that the contractor is relieved of its liability for LD during the period of extension.

The prolongation of project gives rise to additional cost to contractor which have not been accounted for. These are : (i) General overhead, (ii) field overheads, (iii) idling of machinery, (iv) increase in cost of labour, (v) increase in prices of materials, and (vi) loss of profit. These parameters give rise to claims. In-order to effectively contend the claims before arbitration documentations of various activities and events should be properly chronicled to be used as evidence.

The biggest customer of the construction industry is the government. To the dislike of owners, contractors and consultants, many government projects experience extensive delays and thereby exceed the initial time and cost estimates. This problem is more prominent in the traditional type of contracts in which the contract is awarded to the lowest bidder. Studies have suggested that ensuring timely delivery of projects is one of the important needs of clients of the construction industry. Contractors are primarily concerned with quality, time and cost and yet the majority of construction projects are procured on the basis of only two of these parameters, namely, time and cost.

Many a problems can throw the project off the rails if not addressed properly and timely. One can never anticipate and plan for any and all problems. Still a formal review can assist in capturing some of them. A risk is a possible future event that may affect the project negatively. And as it impacts negatively, it has cost attached to it. Therefore, as a mitigating measure review should be done on a continuous basis.

Assessment of realistic 'construction time' has become increasingly difficult and important because it often serves as a crucial benchmark for assessing the performance of a project and the efficiency of the contractor.

WHO BEARS THE RISK?

As between an owner and a contractor, who bears the risk of the additional costs associated with differing site conditions? Generally, if the contract documents are ambiguous, the costs associated with the differing condition is assigned to the contractor. In the context of fixed price contracts, the general rule, is that a contractor assumes the risk of additional costs associated with differing site conditions of which neither party was aware. In some cases particularly with respect to publicly-owned projects, the traditional allocation of differing site conditions risks may be altered by an owner's misrepresentation of site conditions or concealment of site information from the contractor. In many construction contracts, attempts to alter the allocation of risks are made by a variety of contract terms by inserting exculpatory clauses as discussed below:

GEOTECHNICAL INFORMATION DISCLAIMER

Some owners attempt to avoid responsibility for unexpected site conditions by including in the contract exculpatory (excuse) clause disclaiming liability for the accuracy of site condition and sub-surface data presented in the contract documents. For example, a standard geotechnical disclaimer might read as follows:

"The accuracy of this information is not guaranteed and it is not to be understood as part of the plans governing construction of the project. It is the bidder's responsibility to make his own arrangements to review the same prior to bidding. He may conduct whatever site investigation or testing may be required, and make his own determinations as to all sub-surface conditions". Nevertheless, the contractor encountering such an evasive clause at least the following must be considered:

1. A possible contingency in its bid;
2. A pre-bid letter to the owner requesting all site information available to the owner; and
3. A site inspection which goes beyond the traditional "sight" inspection conducted by most contractors.

DIFFERING SITE CONDITION CLAUSE

A differing site condition is a physical condition other than weather, climate, or other act of God discovered on or affecting a construction site and differing in some material respect from what reasonably was anticipated. The condition must be physical. As a general matter, under the common law, a mere unanticipated condition which renders contract performance more difficult, burdensome, or more expensive provides no excuse for non-performance and no basis for modification of the contract. Where one agrees to do, for a fixed sum, a thing possible to be performed, he will not be excused or become entitled to additional compensation, because unforeseen difficulties are encountered. Thus one who undertakes to erect a structure upon a particular site, assumes ordinarily the risk of subsidence of the soil. In the absence of a differing site conditions or changed conditions clause, contractors must increase the amount of their bids or proposals to cover the contingency of encountering unexpected difficulties, make their own sub-surface investigation, bear the risk of uninvestigated, unknown conditions without price contingencies, or choose not to bid at all.

NOTICE REQUIREMENT

Changed condition clauses generally require the contractor to give the owner notice of the changed condition before the conditions are disturbed. The purpose is to provide the owner an opportunity to verify the conditions before it is disturbed, to have his own investigation and to negotiate time extension or change in cost.

SITE INSPECTION CLAUSE

Some contracts contain superficial provisions requiring the contractor to perform its own site inspection and satisfy itself that it has an understanding of the conditions to be encountered on the project. The clause in Indian Railways is:

> "*Care in Submission of Tenders:* (a) Before submitting a tender, the tenderer will be deemed to have satisfied himself by actual inspection of the site and locality of the works, that all conditions liable to be encountered during the execution of the works are taken into account and that the rates he enters in the tender forms are adequate and all inclusive to accord with the provisions in General Conditions of Contract for the completion of works to the entire satisfaction of the Engineer."
>
> ***Contractor's understanding:*** It is understood and agreed that the Contractor has, by careful examination, satisfied himself as to the nature and location of the work, the conformation of the ground, the character, quality and quantity of the materials to be encountered, the character of equipment and facilities needed preliminary to and during the progress of the works, the general and local conditions, the labour conditions prevailing therein and all other matters which can in any way affect the works under the contract. This is purely superficial as it does not afford any opportunity to know the sub-surface conditions.

Change Clause

The majority of construction contracts include a "change" clause giving the project owner the unilateral right to order changes in the contract work during the course of performance. In the absence of a change clause, a modification of the contract must be agreed to by both parties and cannot be done unilaterally. In exchange for the owner's right to order unilateral changes, the contractor is promised a price adjustment if the change increases the cost or time of performance. It is customary to provide such clauses for the contractor to be entitled to payment for the performance of such "extra work."

The four major purposes served by change clause are : (1) to provide flexibility by giving the owner the unilateral right to order changes in the work to accommodate advances in technology and changes in the owner's needs and requirements; (2) to provide the contractor a means of proposing changes to the work, thereby facilitating more efficient performance and improving the quality of contract end products; (3) to furnish procurement authority to the contracting officer to order additional work within the general scope of the contract; and (4) to provide legal means by which the contractor may process claims through the contract disputes process. Sample of a change clause on Indian Railways is as under:

> "*Alterations to be authorised:* No alterations in or additions to or omissions or abandonment of any part of the works shall be deemed authorised, except under instructions from the Engineer, and the Contractor shall be responsible to obtain such instructions in each and every case in writing from the Engineer."
>
> " *Rates for extra items of works:* Any item of work carried out by the Contractor on the instructions of the Engineer which is not included in the accepted schedules of rates shall be executed at the rates set forth in the "Schedule of Rates of ... Railway" modified by the tender percentage and such items are not contained in the latter, at the rate agreed upon between the Engineer and the Contractor before the execution of such items of work and ... need for the special item has come to the notice."

When delay in completion of the whole project results, a contractor will usually suffer:

(i) A loss owing to the fact that his off-site overheads, which will partly be independent of the actual site expenditure;

(ii) Loss of profit earning capacity of the particular contract organisation affected, due to it being retained longer on the contract in question without any corresponding increase in the monetary benefit earned and without being free to move elsewhere to earn the profit which it otherwise might do;

(iii) An increase of cost in his running on-site overheads, that is to say those elements, of cost directly attributable to the contract which are governed by time and which are independent of the amount of work carried out, for instance supervisory cost, costs of permanent plant such as site huts, and certain special plant needed throughout the work; and

(iv) In a contract without an applicable fluctuations clause, the inflationary increases in the cost of labour or materials which he would not have incurred but for the delay.

In awarding compensation for prolongation of contract period, some amount of guess work is inevitable and it cannot be contended that reasoning given is not proper. "The fact that damages are difficult to estimate, or could not be assessed with certainty or precision, cannot relieve the wrong doer of the necessity of paying the damages for breach. Lack of evidence in such matters would not be a sufficient ground for awarding only nominal damages."

Off-site overheads are usually known in the industry as "Head Office Overheads." It is convenient to deal with these together with profit, because it is the practice of most contractors of any substance in major contracts, after making their best estimate of the prime cost of the whole project, to add a single percentage thereto for both the above items.

Site overheads: These will include items like field supervision hutting, permanent gantries or hoists, certain types of pumping or dewatering arrangement in engineering contracts, and idle time of plant required to be retained on the site. Some of these will not necessarily be present for the whole period of delay.

Rises in cost of materials and labour: These call for little comments, except that it may be very difficult exercise, for which careful examination of the contractor's likely programme will be required, to decide when materials would have been ordered, or labour engaged, but for the delay.

Loss of productivity: As stated, this may not necessarily be associated with any overall delay. This damage is usually very hard to assess. In many cases where there has been delay, a delaying factor may cause little or no loss under this head, because if the extent and duration of the delay can be forecast with reasonable notice, the contractor can postpone engaging, or reduce, his plant and labour force during the period when the delaying factor is operating, so that they bear a similar ratio to output to that during periods when progress is more rapid. In assessing claims for loss of productivity of plant, such plant, if hired, will be paid for by the contractor at "standing" rates.

Prohibition on award of damages: If the arbitrator awards compensation when there is a specific bar in the contract then the arbitrator would be said to have travelled beyond the terms of the contract. A typical prohibition clause in railways is as under:

"In the event of any failure or delay by the Railway to hand over the Contractor possession of the lands necessary for the execution of the works or to give the necessary notice to commence the works or to provide the necessary drawings or instructions or any other delay caused by the Railway due to any other cause whatsoever, then such failure or delay shall in no way affect or vitiate the contract or alter the character thereof or entitle the contractor to damages or compensation therefore but in any such case, the Railway may grant such extension or extensions of the completion date as may be considered reasonable."

In *Asian Techs Ltd.* v. *Union of India*, the Supreme Court have held that:

" Apart from the above, it has been held by this Court in *Port of Calcutta* v. *Engineers-De-space-Age,* (1966)1 SCC 516, that a clause like Clause 11 only prohibits the Department from entertaining the claim, but it did not prohibit the *arbitrator* from entering it. This view has been followed by another Bench of SC in *Bharat Drilling & Treatment (P) Ltd.* v. *State of Jharkhand*, (2009) 16 SCC705."

A contract specifically provided that in the event of delay in completion of work, the contractor shall not be entitled for compensation. Work could not be completed within time and the EOT was allowed. Dispute arose between the parties and the contractor claimed compensation for prolongation of contract period. The arbitrator awarded compensation. It was held that award was contrary to stipulations of the contract and desired to be set aside.

Specifications in A.P. provide that no claim for compensation on account of any delay or hindrance to the work from any cause whatsoever shall lie, has been subjected to close judicial scrutiny and "held that the clause was totally inequitable and unreasonable."

The clause in contracts putting bar on payment of losses sustained due to prolongation of construction is unreasonable, unconscionable, imbalanced and indicative of unequal bargaining power. When delay in handing over site is significant, the contractor may treat the same as breach by owner and can repudiate the contract claiming damages.

11 Breach of Contract

The function of the law is to enable rights of the citizens to be vindicated and to provide remedies when duties have been breached. Vindication describes the making good of the claimant's legal right by the grant of an adequate remedy. Unless an infringed right is met with an adequate remedy, the right is devoid of force and contents. As society is becoming more rights-focused and law more rights-conscious, the vindicatory function is likely to become increasingly dominant. The courts have already recognised that their primary objective in awarding a remedy for breach of contract is the vindication of the claimant's rights under that contract. While the limited availability of specific relief and the preference for compensation as a substitute for performance suggest that contractual rights are vindicated only in a weak sense. Compensation is very much a means to an end. That end is the making good of the claimant's right to performance of the contract. Till sometime ago it was commonly accepted that damages for breach of contract were exclusively loss-based. The fundamental basis of contractual damages was to compensate 'for pecuniary loss naturally flowing from the breach'. But now damages may be measured by the gain made by the defendant or the better view is that these damages are vindicatory in nature.

The entire gamut of commercial activities world over is managed through contract system. It has become the chariot of economics. Much attention is paid by interested groups in drafting the contract agreements. Attempt is generally to allocate as much risk to promise or as possible. Form contracts have become order of the day. The buzz word is " take it or leave it". Competition is growing stiffer by the day. Howsoever fair a contract we may draw and cooperate with the contractor in performance of the contract, all contract do not end up with success story. Some end up with insignificant failure; some in material failure and some are disaster. The failures are commonly known as breach of contract.

Breach : Where two parties have made a contract which one of them have broken, it is breach of contract. When a party fails or refuses to perform his part of promise it is said to be breach. A breach of contract is a civil wrong. A breach of a duty is the infringement of a right. A Contract gives rise to primary right of performance.

Fundamental breach of contract : If a party actually informs the other that he intends not to perform the contract as a whole, or any part of it, either now or in future or where he acts in such a way as to render his own future performance impossible is known as fundamental breach. In fundamental breach the injured party may treat the contract as at an end. The aggrieved party must have been substantially deprived of what it was entitled to expect under the contract. In other words, as a consequence of the non-performance or incorrect performance of a contractual obligation of the other party, the aggrieved party must have mainly lost its interest in the contract.

An unjustified and continued failure to remedy defective work which requires rectification, will also be treated as fundamental breach. The breach could be on account of owner or contractor. The owners breach could be of two types from view points of damages. The employer can bring the work to an end or prevent it from starting, in which case the contractor will be deprived of the right to profit. This may also be classified as wrongful termination of contract committing fundamental breach bringing the contract to an end.

An **anticipatory breach of a contract** is when the non-breaching party realizes that the other party to the contract will fail to perform his part of the contract in the future or it has been declared so and can terminate the contract and claim for damages before the breach occurs.

Section 73 of the Indian Contract Act, 1872 covers this issue of damages which reads as under:

> "**73. Compensation for loss or damage caused by breach of Contract :** "*When a contract has been broken, the party who suffers by such breach is entitled to receive, from the party who has*

broken the contract, compensation for any loss or damage caused to him thereby, which naturally arose in the usual course of things from such breach, or which the parties knew, when they made the contract, to be likely to result from the breach of it. Such compensation is not to be given for any remote and indirect loss or damage sustained by reason of the breach. "

Explanation—In estimating the loss or damage arising from a breach of contract, the means which existed of remedying the inconvenience caused by non-performance of the contract must be taken into account.

Section 73 applies where a contract is broken by failure or refusal to perform it. There is no breach of the contract if the party has some justification for slow or non-performance. Failure to perform may be on any ground.

The term compensation signifies that which is given in recompense, an equivalent rendered. Damages on the other hand constitute the sum of money claimed or adjudicated to be paid in compensation for loss. A mere delay of short duration in performance would not give rise to any cause of action for claiming damages. However, if offending party seeks unreasonable time or there is an element of uncertainty as to when it would be possible to get the work commenced, it would give immediate cause of action to the injured party to claim damages for breach of contract.

Here the statute emphasizes on mitigation of losses of the party who is responsible for breach by the other party. The party claiming compensation must take every reasonable step so that the other party's loss come down. Although no such duty is cast upon the party claiming loss, yet while computing loss, amount proportionate to his neglect would be reduced under the doctrine of contributory negligence.

The other important aspect of the section is that the compensation should not be given for any remote losses. It is obvious that one loss would lead to another consequential loss and so on. We will have to draw a line beyond which it would not be entertained. Such loss will not be naturally arising. It becomes oppressive for the breaching party.

"The two principles on which damages in such cases are calculated are well-established. *The first is that, as far as possible, he who has proved a breach of a bargain to supply what he contracted to get is to be placed, as far as money can do it, in as good a situation as if the contract had been performed; but this principle is qualified by a second, which imposes on a plaintiff the duty of taking all reasonable steps to mitigate the loss consequent on the breach, and debars him from claiming any part of the damage which is due to his neglect to take such steps.*

The general rule is that the party which ought to receive compensation in respect of such breaches of contract should be fair and reasonable, arising naturally.

Difficulty however arises in measuring the amount of the monetary compensation. A general principle cannot be laid down for measuring it, and every case must to some extent depend upon its own circumstances. It is, however, clear that in the absence of any special circumstances the measure of damages cannot be the amount of the loss ultimately sustained by the representee. It can only be the difference between the price which he has paid and the price which he would have received if he had resold them in the market forthwith after the purchase provided of course that there was a fair market then.

In contracts for sale or purchase the rule for assessing damage is that : *"Where a contract to deliver goods at a certain price is broken, the proper measure of damage in general is the difference between the contract price and the market price of such goods at the time when the contract is broken, because the purchaser, having the money in his hands, may go into the market and buy".*

Non-performance of a contract will put the other party to loss and will call for payment of compensation to the injured party. Compensation is also understood as damages. The object of damages in contract is to compensate the victim of the breach for losses arising as a result of the breach. Damages in a commercial contract would therefore normally include loss of profit.

The basic principle, and the starting point for the assessment of damages for breach of contract, is that " . . . *we should as nearly as possible get at that sum of money which will put the party who has been injured, or who has suffered, in the same position as he would have been in if he had not sustained the breach for which he is now getting his compensation or reparation.*" Nevertheless, the difficulty lies in the application of the principle. The general principle of damages for breach of contract is:

1. Breach of contract is actionable *per se.*
2. The object of damages is to compensate.
3. There is a requirement to mitigate loss.

4. Damages can be recovered only for loss sustained.
5. The loss must be caused by the breach.

Types of damages: Damages are mainly of two types, namely: (i) General Damages, and (ii) Special Damages. Apart from these two categories, damages may also be classified as Liquidated and Un-liquidated. The later classification is limited to only contracts or agreements.

Liquidated Damages : are a fixed sum ascertained in advance by the parties to a contract as the amount to be paid in the event of a breach, or an amount of money specified in a contract to compensate a party for injury suffered because of a breach of contract by the other party to the agreement precluding any liability in excess of the amount stipulated in the contract. The fixed amounts are recoverable provided the sums fixed are a fair pre-estimate of the likely consequences of a breach, but not if they were thought to be imposed as a penalty.

Un liquidated damages: are damages, the amount of which is fixed by the courts. It is the court that determines how much is to be paid as damages. The court bases its decision on the testimony and facts before it.

General Damages: are damages that the law presumes to have resulted from the defendant's breach of contract. They are normally damages at large and can be nominal or substantial depending on the circumstances of each case.

Nominal Damages: When it is not possible to assess the actual loss in an accurate manner or reasonable manner or plaintiff is not able to prove the loss suffered, he will be entitled to recover nominal damages for breach. Nominal Damages will be awarded where the court decides in the light of all the facts that no actual damage has been sustained. The function of nominal damages is to mark the vindication, where no real damage has been suffered, of a right which is held to be so important that infringement of it is a wrong. This means that nominal damages are normally awarded in all wrongs that are actionable including breach of contract.

Measure of damages: In assessing the amount of damages the following guidelines should be followed:

(i) The amount of damage is to compensate for the loss and not to punish the defendant.
(ii) Damages are compensatory and not restitutionary.

In a contract for sale of goods where measure of damages is the difference between the market price as at the date of breach and the contract price so that only nominal damages will be awarded.

Assessment of losses : For centuries various principles have derived in order to standardise the measure of damages in given types of situations or under a given type of contract. One such principle is what might be termed the "available market principle". Derived from sale of goods law, this states that if there is an available market for the goods in question, the aggrieved party is deemed to have availed itself of that market for the purpose of assessing damages. To take a typical example: if a seller fails to deliver goods and the buyer terminates the contract, the measure of damages is the cost to the buyer of substitute goods at the time of the termination. The available market principle would yield to the general rule that an aggrieved party is entitled to recover its actual losses.

The issue is what the correct measure of damages is where there is no available market at the time of breach, but such a market subsequently emerged? The "available market" rule is not to be applied where an available market emerged after the breach. Damages, in such cases, should be assessed with reference to the actual loss of the owner.

In order to succeed in an action for damages the buyer has to prove the market price. The market prices is the buying price at which the buyer can obtain equivalent goods. It is the current price or the prevailing price at the contractual time of delivery when the buyer can obtain identical goods in an available market. The buyer is not to prove that he actually bought the goods after the seller had failed to deliver. Buying is not essential. All that has to be proved is the buying price at which he can obtain substitute goods.

Available market : The available market for any particular goods or service is the number of buyers who are both willing and able to purchase the products offered for sale. Generally, this share of the population are those who have some degree of interest in the products offered, and also have the financial resources to purchase those products as and when they are produced and released for sale.

As it relates to evaluating the potential of the marketplace, the available market is only one step in concentrating sales and marketing efforts to reach customers who ultimately will buy the goods and services offered. Generally, a potential market is made up of consumers who have some interest in products, whether or not they can actually afford to buy them. An available market is that portion of the potential market that not only has the interest, but also the means to pursue that interest all the way to a sale.

The market price rule : The market price rule is most usually invoked in respect of contracts for the sale of goods. The law provides that for non-acceptance and failure to deliver goods the *prima facie* measure of damages is the difference in market and contract prices at the time the goods ought to have been accepted or delivered, subject to the existence of an available market. In the sale of goods context, market price rule is straightforward. It crystallises damages as at the time of breach. It accords with the principle that the injured party is entitled to have his lost rights vindicated as at the date of the loss.

Principles for assessment of damages where contract is repudiated : There are only two legitimate purposes for the award of damages in a breach: one is compensation for loss or damage caused by wrongful conduct; the other is vindication of a right that has been violated by wrongful conduct. The breach of contract is a wrong, a failure to comply with legal obligations for which the innocent party has bargained for. The law responds to the deficiency of the performance by an award of damages. The measure of damages can differ according to the wrong but the ruling principle applies nonetheless, qualified by questions of remoteness and mitigation. It is contended that the principles that apply to an award of damages in such circumstances are settled.

1. The repudiation of a contract by one party, if accepted by the other, brings the contract to an end and releases both parties from their primary obligations under the contract.
2. The injured party thereby becomes entitled to vindicate the repudiator's failure to comply with his primary legal obligations by enforcing against the repudiator the secondary obligation to pay damages.
3. The damages recoverable by the injured party are such sum as will put him in the same financial position as if the contract had been performed.
4. The injured party is entitled to recover such damages as arise naturally, that is, according to the usual course of things, from the breach, or such as may reasonably be supposed to have been within the contemplation of both parties at the time they made the contract as the probable result of the breach.
5. The injured party is not entitled, by the award of damages

on breach, to be placed in a superior position to that which he would have been in had the contract been performed . The injured party recovers no more than the net benefit he would receive under the contract and the defendant acquires no right to profit by his breach.

6. Where there is an available market for the goods or services the subject of the contract, the normal measure of damages recoverable is the difference between the contract rate and the market rate for the goods or services; this is because the injured party has been wrongfully deprived of a marketable asset.
7. As a general rule, damages for breach of contract involving a marketable asset are assessed as at the date of breach; in the case of wrongful repudiation of a contract, this is the date on which the injured party accepts the repudiation and terminates the contract.
8. As the injured party suffers the loss at the time of the defendant's wrong, the task of a tribunal is, so far as money can do it, to put the injured party into the position he would have been in if the defendant had made immediate reparation, or reparation at the earliest time that the injured party could reasonable have made good his loss. Thus, the amount of the injured party's claim crystallises as at the date of the loss, or shortly thereafter, and subsequent delay will have an effect only on the interest component of the final award.
9. Specific performance is usually sought in cases where there is no available market. In such cases the injured party's legitimate interest in actual performance justifies his failure to seek a substitute in the market and so a later date may be used to value the remedy for breach.
10. It is permissible to take into account later events that are "predestined" or "inevitable" but not to discount for "vague possibilities" or the possibility of the contract being frustrated.

Damages for non-delivery : If the time for delivery is fixed by reference to the happening of an event, it is fixed within the meaning. On the other hand, if the contract provides for delivery within a reasonable time after a future date, it is not a contract for delivery at a fixed time within the meaning. In any event the damages are to be ascertained with reference to the market price at the time of the refusal to deliver does not apply to a case where the breach is an anticipatory breach. If, for instance, the seller repudiates the contract before the time at which the goods ought to have been delivered, the buyer, without buying against the seller, may bring his action at once, but if he does so, his damages must be assessed with reference to the market price of the goods at the time at which they ought to have been delivered under the contract. If the action comes on for trial before the contractual date for delivery has arrived, the court must arrive at the price as best it can. The buyer must, however, do what is reasonable to mitigate the damages, and if the seller can show that the buyer acted unreasonably in not buying against him, the date to be taken is the date at which the buyer ought to have gone into the market to mitigate the damages.

The advantage of this market-based approach is that it allows damages to be quantified relatively quickly after a repudiatory breach so that the dispute can be resolved within a reasonable time. Where there is no available market rate, then damages will be assessed on the basis of the owners' actual losses because there is no "like-for-like" basis for calculating the losses.

Law contains a rule for measuring damages for non-acceptance and for non-delivery where there is an "available market" for the goods. The measure is "*prima facie* to be ascertained by the difference between the contract price and the market or current price at the time when the goods ought to have been accepted or delivered in the case of non-delivery or if no such time was fixed, at the time of the refusal to accept or deliver.

Where there is an available market for the goods in question the measure of damages is *prima facie* to be ascertained by the difference between the contract price and the market or current price at the time or times when the goods ought to have been accepted or (if no time was fixed for acceptance) at the time of the refusal to accept."

Further, Section 74 does not say that the amount of liquidated damages shall be payable. It says "... *whether or not actual damage or loss is proved to have been caused thereby, to receive from the party who has broken the contract reasonable compensation not exceeding the amount so named or, as the case may be, the penalty stipulated for.*"

In a case the respondent failed to prove the market price of the product to be supplied. He is therefore not entitled to the amount claimed as damage. He may at best be entitled to nominal damages.

It has been held by court that "it is not necessary that on default by the seller to deliver, the plaintiff should have actually bought the goods elsewhere and only then claim the difference. The court said that damages could be claimed on market basis without actually purchasing the goods."

Discharge of the contract : A breach of contract does not, by itself, discharge the contract. A breach of condition gives rise to an election on the part of the victim to either affirm the contract and sue in damages or to treat the contract as having been repudiated by the other party, accept the repudiation, treat the contract as at an end and claim for losses in damages. The victim has a choice to elect. He may affirm the contract or accept the repudiatory breach and treat the contract as at an end. For contracts other than sale of goods, a victim, with full knowledge of the breach, is said to affirm the contract where he elects to go on with it. The right to repudiate in such a case is then lost. The victim may, of course, still bring an action in damages for the breach and repudiate the contract for all future breaches.

Where the contract is not discharged by the breach both parties remain liable to perform the contract. Where the victim accepts a repudiatory breach the contract comes to an end, both parties are released from their future obligations. Extant obligations remain binding and damages are payable by either party in respect of breach arising before termination.

"In an arbitration case, the respondent had submitted counter-claim. The item being procured was a special item being made only for respondent and hence it had no available market. In order to assess the loss suffered by respondent recourse was taken to the rate accepted for similar item (with variation in Drg. And chemical composition) nearly six months ago. It is therefore quite clear that the two items were dissimilar and non-comparable for the purpose of assessment of losses. Though it would discharge the same function yet these cannot be compared in this context. A plastic water tap and a chromium plated steel water tap discharge the same function but they are non-comparable.

Further, for assessment of losses '*available market principle*' or 'Market price principle' has been made use of by respondent. The respondent contended that the rate used for computation of loss represent the market rate for the contracted item and have been adopted for assessment of loss. Therefore, General Damages' computation as done by respondent was argued to be reasonable and realistic. Using a different material for managing day-to-day work is no justification to adopt its rate for assessment of general damages. Neither the argument has relevancy to 'available market'.

The normal measure of damage in case of breach is the difference between the market price of contracted goods on the day of breach and the contract price. This principle is universally accepted. In the case under dispute the market rate is not available with respondent on the day of breach. Rates are adopted from a different contract. This rate in no way can be termed as market rate on the day of breach. If the intention of the rule was to bring another running contract rate under its ambit, the phraseology of sentence would have been different and unambiguous. It is doubted, if 'available market' exists for such special items at all. These items are not sold in the market. Therefore, for special items 'available market' theory will not apply.

In this case the respondent could not prove the market rate at the date of breach. Being unsuccessful in proving the market rate, the respondent was not entitled to the amount claimed as damages. In order to succeed in an action for damages the buyer has to prove the market price. In case of special items, where market does not exist, it is better to go for risk and cost purchase or recover LD as provided in the contract and close the contract.

Proof of loss is necessary: While making claim for general damages, the plaintiff has to assert that he has suffered some loss but for the purpose of claiming special damages plaintiff will have to prove that he has sustained such special loss. It is necessary that some loss should be shown by evidence.

In case of works contracts generally a notice has to served upon contract for his failure and making good the progress before termination is done in order to be entitled for claim of damages. In *Bombay Housing Board* v. *Karbhase Naik and Co.* (1975) SC held, "it was provided in clause 15 that before the Engineer-in-charge could stop the work and get the work done by another contractor, he should give the. respondent a written notice and as such a notice was not given, the respondent was entitled to damage. We see no reason to think that observance of the condition as regards the written notice was not mandatory. We see no force in the argument that the written notice was not necessary as that was specifically provided for in the clause."

Where the employer prevents performance, for instance, not handing over site or drawings in time, the breach is on account of employer and contractor may claim damages. Termination of contract in such situation by employer will be wrongful. If the work is practically completed, the measure of damage is the contract price deducting from it what it would have cost to complete the work when it was stopped. This falls under substantial performance principle. Where, the owner owing to financial difficulty, spreads the work over longer period duly informing the contractor and contractor demands extra payment due to increase in wages and cost of material, the owner does not communicate anything but work continues, it was held that contractor was entitled to receive extra payment.

When breach of a works contract takes place, damages must be established with reasonable accuracy. However it is very difficult to do so. Calculating losses is not an exact mathematical exercise. Certain guess work will be involved. The fact that damages cannot be ascertained with certainty does not relieve the wrongdoer of the necessity of paying damages. In case of failure to assess, at least nominal damages shall be recovered for breach of contract. Under the term of section 73, the compensation is only for the loss actually suffered and such compensation is not to be given for any remote or indirect loss by reason of breach. However, section 74 of the contract act provides solution for difficult situation where assessment is difficult.

"In order to succeed in its claim for damages the plaintiff must establish that the cancellation of agreement before the expiry of the period was wrongful." *G.L. Kilikar* v. *State of Kerala* (1971).

Whether actual damage or loss is proved or not, the court is competent to award reasonable damages not exceeding the stipulated amount. Generally for works contracts following remedies are provided in the contract in case of breach:

(a) Wherever a contract is rescinded, the security deposit shall be forfeited.

(b) Performance Guarantee encashed and the balance work shall be got done independently without risk and cost of the failed contractor, the failed contractor shall be debarred from participating in the tender for executing the balance work.

(c) To measure up or the whole or part of the work from which the contractor has been removed and get it completed by another contractor, the manner and method in which such work is completed but without risk and cost of the failed contractor shall be decided.

It has however been held that where employer did not suffer any damage in consequence of breach, he was not entitled to forfeit Security deposit which amounted to imposition of penalty. In a case between *State of U.P.* v. *Chandra Gupta & Co. (1977)* the contract had to be terminated in which the agreement had the following clause:

> "Time is the essence of the contract. The contractor shall complete the work within the period specified in the tender. If the contractor fails to comply with this condition he shall be liable to pay as compensation an amount equal to one per cent or such smaller amount as the Executive Engineer may decide on the said estimated cost of the whole work for every day that the quantity of work remains incomplete. Provided always that the entire amount of compensation to be paid under the provision of this Clause shall not exceed ten per cent on the estimated cost of the work as shown in the tender."

It appears from the Conditions of the Contract that the defendant at the time of making the payment for the work done under the contract had deducted 10% amount from the amount payable to contractor, in exercise of the power given by Clause 1. The amount deducted was kept by it by way of security. The deduction was justified by the State Government on the ground that the plaintiff having not done the work within time and having left the same unfinished, was liable to forfeiture. The submission made by the respondent was that as the defendant had debited the plaintiff with the actual cost which was spent in getting the remaining work done, therefore, he was not entitled to forfeit the amount of security left with him. The submission is well founded. The State of U. P. having deducted the excess amount which it had to pay to the debiting agency for getting the unfinished work done and completed, it is not entitled to forfeit the security deposit as it would result in conferring double benefit to the State.

The plaintiff urged that as no damage was suffered by the State Government it could not forfeit the security deposit made by the plaintiff. Reference was made by him in this connection to Section 74 of the Contract Act, which reads as under:

> "When a contract has been broken, if a sum is named in the contract as the amount to be paid in case of such breach, or if the contract contains any other stipulation by way of penalty, the party complaining of the breach is entitled, whether or not

actual damage or loss is proved to have been caused thereby, to receive from the party who has broken the contract reasonable compensation not exceeding the amount so named or, as the case may be, the penalty stipulated for."

The submission made was disputed by the State on the ground that the security deposit having been taken from the respondent in order to ensure the due performance of the contract and the respondent having defaulted the entire amount was liable to be forfeited.

The court held that Section 74 of the Indian Contract Act entitles a person to get reasonable compensation and does not entitle him to realise anything by way of penalty. If a contract is not duly performed but still no damage is suffered on account of non-performance, the promisee would not be entitled to get damages.

A similar question regarding the right of the Union of India to forfeit the security came up for consideration before the Supreme Court in *Maula Bux* v. *Union of India*, (AIR 1970 SC 1955), in that case, Maula Bux had entered into a contract with the Government of India for the supply of certain goods and had deposited certain amount of security for the due performance of the contract. It was stipulated in the contract that the amount of security was to stand forfeited in case the appellant neglected to perform his part of the contract. On Maula Bux committing default in the supply, the Government did not only rescind the contract but also forfeit the security deposit. The Supreme Court held that under Section 74 only reasonable amount can be forfeited if a contract is not performed. But, where under the terms of the contract the party in breach has undertaken to pay a sum of money or to forfeit a sum of money which he has already paid to the party complaining of a breach of contract, the undertaking is of the nature of penalty. Applying the law to the facts of the present case, the court held in the case of *State of U.P.* v. *Chandra Gupta* that state government did not suffer any damage and it was not entitled to forfeit the security deposit, inasmuch as forfeiture of security would amount to imposition of penalty.

In order to complete the unexecuted work left by the previous agency whose contract was terminated, the employer has to engage a new agency. The amount which will be required to be paid to new agency for completion of work shall be recovered from the terminated agency. This is another way of arriving at actual losses.

12 Mitigation of Losses and Doctrine of Frustration

Contract is an instrument of free bargaining between parties on the basis of equality. The basic object of Contract is to avoid litigation, to establish set of rules for compliance and to penalize defaulters. Contracts are not entered into with the purpose of breaking them. These are to be performed/worked together to get successful results. Without the co-operation of both sides, the outcome could be disastrous. In our country, contracts are governed by the Indian Contract Act, 1872. Any breach of Contract leads to, rectification, cancellation/termination of contract, and claim for damages or injunction (temporary or permanent).

The measure of compensation that a claimant is entitled to recover is the loss naturally flowing from the legal wrong. This measure of damage is offset by a duty to mitigate—or minimize—losses suffered by them by taking all reasonable steps to mitigate the loss consequent on the breach.

The liability of compensation is regulated by section 73 of contract act, 1872 which is reproduced below:

73. Compensation of loss or damage caused by breach of contract.

When a contract has been broken, the party who suffers by such breach is entitled to receive, form the party who has broken the contract, compensation for any loss or damage caused to him thereby, which naturally arose in the usual course of things from such breach, or which the parties knew, when they made the contract, to be likely to result from the breach of it.

Such compensation is not to be given for any remote and indirect loss of damage sustained by reason óf the breach.

Explanation : In estimating the loss or damage arising from a breach of contract, the means which existed of remedying the inconvenience caused by non-performance of the contract must be taken into account.

Thus, simply because a defendant breaches a contract does not mean that a claimant is entitled to recover endless damages or compensation for breach. Every breach will have endless consequences flowing from one another. There would be no limit of compensation if the remotest consequence is also taken care of. A line will therefore have to be drawn which is known as 'losses in usual course of things'.

For instances, a supplier of goods or services fails to deliver, the buyer is not entitled to sit back on a rising market or wait until a contract for onward supply has fallen through, and then claim the loss from the defendant. They must approach the market with reasonable haste and buy equivalent goods or services or obtain market prices and assess the compensation.

Under the mitigation of damages doctrine, a person who has suffered an injury or loss should take reasonable steps, where possible, to avoid additional injury or loss to defendant. The failure of a plaintiff to take protective steps after suffering an injury or loss can reduce the amount of the plaintiff's recovery. The mitigation of damages doctrine is sometimes called minimization of damages or the doctrine of Avoidable Consequences.

In contract law the non-breaching party should mitigate damages or risk, a reduction in recovery for the breach. For example, assume that a property owner and home builder contract for the construction of a home in exchange for payment. Assume further that the builder begins constructing the home but that the owner wrongfully cancels the contract before the builder has finished construction. If the builder must sue the owner to recover the unpaid portion of the contract price, a court may reduce the amount of money that the builder would like to claim by minimizing losses by way of selling the materials already purchased for the job or use the materials in another job. The savings that the builder realizes will be deducted from the loss incurred on the contract in computing the builder's net recovery.

The claimant has certain duty in case of breach: Failure to mitigate loss may prevent the innocent party from recovering damages for avoidable loss. Defendants often assert that claimants have failed to mitigate their loss in an effort to reduce the level of damages.

Generally, courts are sympathetic to the efforts made by a claimant seeking to deal with a breach of contract. The requirement to take 'reasonable steps' is not a high standard. In particular, the courts will typically reject criticism of a claimant seeking to do its best to mitigate its loss when faced with a breach of contract, particularly when decisions have to be made—often quickly—by a claimant with imperfect knowledge. It is, after all, the defendant that has put the claimant in the position of having to deal with a breach of contract.

However, the courts will penalize a claimant in damages where it has demonstrably and unreasonably failed to take any steps to mitigate its loss, or where the steps that it has taken are clearly inadequate. In circumstances where a claimant could, for example, potentially mitigate its loss by selling goods in the market, the court will usually expect to see evidence of meaningful attempts to do so. That should not be difficult if such attempts are genuine. A claimant that gives the impression that it is more concerned with enhancing a claim than mitigating loss should expect deductions in the damages awarded to it. Under the doctrine of contributory negligence, his claim would be reduced by some percentage depending upon the circumstances.

Burden of proof on defendant : It is the defendant who has the burden of proving that the claimant has failed in its duty to mitigate loss. What exactly the claimant is required to do with respect to mitigation is an issue of fact. The Court, for instance, will not expect the claimant to adopt some dangerous or futile method or where the likelihood of a successful outcome is uncertain. While the plaintiff has the burden of proving the breach of contract, the defendant must prove that the plaintiff could have and should have mitigated the loss.

Following a breach of contract, the innocent party has a duty to mitigate the loss it has suffered. This duty requires reasonable steps to be taken to limit the losses that are incurred (and also to avoid incurring unnecessary expenditure seeking to remedy the breach). A claimant cannot simply sit on its hands watching losses accumulate with the intention of recovering them in full from the defendant. However, a claimant need not take unusual steps that would be outside the normal course of business, or even incur undue costs. The reasonable costs of mitigation are recoverable from the defendant.

The duty to mitigate the damages has been recognized and laid down in the explanation attached to Sec. 73 ICA which reads:

"In estimating the loss or damage arising from a breach of contract, the means which existed of remedying the inconvenience caused by non-performance of the contract must be taken into account.

The expression 'the means which existed of remedying the inconvenience' has been interpreted to mean that it lays a duty upon a person complaining of a breach of contract, to use common intelligence and guidance, and take all natural and obvious steps available to diminish the loss arising from the breach. However, the rule in the explanation to Sec. 73 must be applied with caution: a party, who has already put himself in the wrong by breaking his contract, has no right to impose new and extraordinary duties on the aggrieved party. The latter can be only expected to use ordinary and reasonable diligence. It must be noted that a person is under no obligation to take any steps to minimise the damages until a breach of the contract has actually accrued. The amount of damages should not, therefore, be reduced on the ground that he did not try to minimise the same before the date on which the defendant actually committed the breach.

Expenses arising from a contract are a loss or damage arising naturally from the contract. The test of reasonableness under the circumstances is whether a prudent man would have acted in the same way, as he did if the original wrongful act had been the result of his own default.

Where a party to a contract refuses to perform the contract the other party has a right to decide whether he accepts the repudiation at once, or refuse to accept the repudiation and wait till the date of performance of the contract. In the case of an anticipatory breach of contract the duty to mitigate the damages arises immediately on the acceptance of the repudiation. On the other hand if the repudiation is not accepted and the promisee waits till the due date and still the promisor refuses to perform the contract the duty to mitigate arises only on the contractual date for performance. Sec. 73 postulates a valid and binding contract between the parties and deals with one of the remedies for breach of the contract in the nature of the claim for compensation for loss or damages. Therefore if an agreement is void, the forfeiture clause of such void agreement cannot be enforced and earnest money cannot be forfeited on the ground of breach of contract.

Interpretation of the doctrine : There is a fundamental principle of the law of damages, i.e., the plaintiff entitled to claim damages on the breach of contract must take reasonable steps to mitigate the loss arising from such breach. According to explanation of sec. 73, "In estimating the loss or damage arising from a breach of contract, the means which existed of remedying the inconvenience caused by the non-performance of the contract must be taken into account."

It means that whether the plaintiff has taken steps to mitigate the loss or not is a factor which has to be taken into account in assessing damages. If the plaintiff has not availed of the duty to mitigate the loss the damages claimed by him cannot be said to have arisen 'naturally' in the usual course of things. Whether the plaintiff has discharged his duty of taking reasonable steps to mitigate the loss is a question of facts which depends upon circumstances and facts of a particular case.

The concept of the principle is that the person who has broken the contract should not suffer the burden of additional damages which could be prevented if the plaintiff had acted upon in time to mitigate the damage. This principle ensures that plaintiff should not get anything more than the loss suffered after acting reasonably in order to mitigate damages. The rule also allows for the defendant for efficient breach as he may break his contractual obligation if he gets higher profit from a new contract and profit even after paying the damages.

The doctrine of mitigation is governed by three rules:

1. The plaintiff cannot recover the loss consequent upon the default of the defendant if the plaintiff could have avoided the loss by taking reasonable steps.
2. If the plaintiff avoids or mitigates the loss consequent upon default, he cannot recover for such avoided loss even if he takes steps which are more than what was reasonably required of him.
3. Where the plaintiff suffers loss or incurs expense by taking reasonable steps to avoid or mitigate the loss resulting from the defendant's default, he may recover this further loss or expense from the defendant.

However the plaintiff can recover expenses or further loss incurred by him in taking reasonable steps to mitigate his loss resulting from the defendant's breach, even when the mitigation steps were unsuccessful or had led to greater loss. The plaintiff may claim damages to place him in position of breach. This does not disallow him from getting remedial damages from breach of contract.

The duty to mitigate damages is present in Art. 77 CISG, which reads:

> *"A party who relies on a breach of contract must take such measures as are reasonable in the circumstances to mitigate the loss, including loss of profit,, resulting from the breach. If he fails to take such measures, the party in breach may claim a reduction in the damages in the amount by which the loss should have been mitigated."*

When the contract is avoided, damages generally amount to the difference between the contract price and the market price. The market price must be obtained within a reasonable time after avoidance. This is in keeping with the duty to mitigate damages in Art. 77 CISG.

The thrust of Article 77 is to deny recovery of damages that could have been reasonably avoided. The judiciary interpreted Article 77 CISG as requiring mitigation and allowing consequential damages for costs incurred in the mitigation process. This interpretation is in accordance with Indian law but it is doubtful if this is the correct interpretation of the provision.

It is often a point of debate not only amongst contracting parties but even in judicial circles as to why there should a duty for non-breaching party to mitigate losses in the face of liquidated damages clause. Liquidated damages clause constitute agreement by the parties as to the appropriate compensation for breach of contract and are awarded in lieu of actual damages. These clauses are favoured when damages are uncertain in nature and there is no market standard or other objective value to measure the actual loss in the event of breach. The justification for LD is derived from two elements: (a) the difficulty of proof of loss, and (b) the reasonableness of the predetermined amount in relation to actual or anticipated damages.

On the other hand the doctrine of avoidable consequences, the mitigation doctrine simply states that "damages are not recoverable for loss that the injured party could have avoided without undue risk,." The mitigation doctrine imposes both negative and positive obligations on the non-breaching party. First, the non-breaching party must avoid any activity that increases the loss. Second, a non-breaching party must take affirmative actions to minimize loss. The doctrine does not, however, require the non-breaching party to be successful in this effort to mitigate. The doctrine is simply to encourage a party to make "reasonable efforts" to minimize loss. Mitigation of liquidated damages can promote efficiency and avoid economic waste. Second, mitigating liquidated damages prevents the non-breaching party from earning double profits. Third, mitigation prevents penalizing the defendant for his breach and thus effects the purposes of the law of damages by limiting the damages award to compensation only. Additionally good business sense dictates that the non-breaching party work to make up its loss, even if it is entitled to damages.

Mitigation prevents wastage by disallowing the non-breaching party from taking actions that increase its damages. If there is no duty to mitigate, a defendant may be forced to accept goods that he does not want, thereby denying the market of such goods where they may be in greater demand. In sale of goods cases, there is likely to be another person in the free market who wants and is willing to pay for such goods, encouraging sellers to mitigate their damages by entering into Without mitigation, some plaintiffs would allow avoidable losses to mount, knowing that full damages would be recoverable in court.

The, damages in breach of contract cases aim to put the non-breaching party in as good a position [financially] as he would have been in had the contract been performed. If a party successfully mitigates its damages, but is allowed to recover the same amount as if it did not mitigate its damages it is obtaining a greater benefit than it deserves under strict compensation and may in fact be receiving "double profits". In fact, if a plaintiff avoids any loss, "allowing recovery for the avoided loss would leave him in a position better than the one he would have been in if the contract had been performed".

It is a long-held, and well-settled, principle of contract law that contract remedies are to be compensatory, and not punitive. Liquidated damages provisions are not immune to this rule. Thus, mitigation disallows the non-breaching party from gaining more than he has lost as a result of the breach.

Damages on repudiation of the contract before due date : Where either party to a contract of sale repudiates the contract before the date of delivery, the other party may either treat the contract as subsisting and wait till the date of delivery, or he may treat the contract as rescinded and sue for damages for breach of contract. The term "repudiation" may be taken to be a refusal to perform the contract. What constitutes repudiation is to be inferred from the circumstances of the case and the conduct of the party. If he brings an action for damages after treating the contract as rescinded (akin to "avoided") he will be entitled to such damages as would have arisen from the non-performance of the contract at the appointed time.

Measure of damages by applying Sec. 73 ICA : The most important question in the case of anticipatory breach is with reference to what date is the market price to be calculated, whether on the date of breach or on the date fixed for performance.

As per the first rule in Sec. 73 ICA, the rule is that in estimating damage in the case of anticipatory breach the value of the performance at the date fixed for performance must be taken and not the value at the date when the refusal to perform was made. The reasoning is that "since the value of a contract would normally be determined by the benefit which its performance would confer, the exact measure of damages upon an anticipatory breach is ... precisely the same as it would be, if the repudiation were not accepted as a breach and the injured party brought a suit, after the time of performance, for the non-performance at the time set".

Duty to mitigate : Where a party to a contract refuses to perform the contract the other party has a right to decide whether he accepts the repudiation at once, or refuse to accept the repudiation and wait till the date of performance of the contract. In the case of an anticipatory breach of contract the duty to mitigate the damages arises immediately on the acceptance of the repudiation. On the other hand if the repudiation is not accepted and the promisee waits till the due date and still the promisor refuses to perform the contract the duty to mitigate arises only on the contractual date for performance.

Duty to mitigate in case of anticipatory breach: A claimant must take reasonable steps to mitigate loss. Claimants are not entitled to recover those damages represented by sums that are avoidable by taking reasonable steps. If the claimant has failed to take reasonable steps to avoid particular losses, the claimant is not entitled in law to recover them, as they are not entitled to profit from their own neglect. This neglect may take the form of either failing to take action reasonable steps or allowing an act to continue that would have increases loss.

A claimant is not entitled to recover sums or for actions taken that were unreasonably spent or steps that were unreasonably taken. The claimant will only be entitled to recover those expenses that were reasonably incurred.

Where a claimant takes measures to mitigate loss, the defendant is entitled to the benefit of those steps, such that the defendant is required to pay the reduced measures of damages resulting from the steps made in mitigation. In this way, the claimant must hand over the benefit of the steps made in mitigation to the defendant. This applies even if the claimant would have been entitled to recover the losses if the particular steps made in mitigation had not been made.

WHAT CAN BE REASONABLE?

Although the claimant is not required to nurse the interests of the defendant as if they were his own. A claimant does not need to act with perfect knowledge or with ideal wisdom. However, the law will protect against wanton, needless or careless conduct.

The parties must act reasonably between themselves having regard for the turn of events between them. The claimant is not required to take unusual steps outside the ordinary course of business; indeed if they do so, they will not be entitled to recover the sums expended.

Guidelines useful for determining claimant's duty to mitigate loss:

1. The time that the claimant came into the knowledge that a breach had taken place may be relevant to determining when it would be reasonable for them to take action to mitigate loss.
2. Where damage may be caused in the natural course of events to the claimant's property, they may be required to make their own repairs rather than allowing their damage to exacerbate by not acting.
3. Allowing time to pass to acquire alternate goods or services in order to deliver on a contract, a claim that the claimant has failed to mitigate is more likely to be successful.
4. Where sale of property may be made to minimize loss in a buoyant market and is not made, there may have been a failure to mitigate.

On the other hand, the claimant may not be required to mitigate:

1. When the claimant does not need to undertake undue risk in expending resources to mitigate loss.
2. Commencing action against another defendant, where a cause of action lies against other parties who are liable to them, where a case with reasonable prospects of success cannot be shown.

3. In circumstances that would require the insured party to surrender, dispose of or destroy their own property rights to mitigate the loss of defendant.
4. A claimant will not be required to act against the interests of innocent parties to reduce recoverable loss.
5. The claimant is not required to sacrifice their commercial reputation in order to avoid losses suffered by a breach of contract.
6. To allocate resources, including personnel and finances that they do not have to take steps to mitigate their loss. Note that this would need to be proved with sworn evidence.

Recovering sums spent in mitigation : When a Claimant takes steps to mitigate its loss, the cost incurred by the claimant as a result of taking those steps is recoverable from the defendant. This remains the case if the steps taken incur greater expense or loss than would have been incurred if these actions had not been taken.

In conclusion there is a fundamental principle of the law of damages, i.e., a party who relies on a breach of contract must take such measures as are reasonable in the circumstances to mitigate the loss, including loss of profit, resulting from the breach. Thus the plaintiff entitled to claim damages on the breach of contract must take reasonable steps to mitigate the loss arising from such breach. It means that whether the plaintiff has taken steps to mitigate the loss or not is a factor which has to be taken into account in assessing damages. If he fails to take such measures, the party in breach may claim a reduction in the damages in the amount by which the loss should have been mitigated. This principle must be made use of in arbitration if defendant can prove that claimant took no reasonable steps to mitigate the losses.

DOCTRINE OF FRUSTRATION

Frustration of performance of contract may occur in many ways, some of which are destruction of the subject matter of the contract, death of the promisor, outbreak of war, change of law, etc. This doctrine does not, however, normally, cover : (a) difficulty in performance, (b) impossibility caused by the behaviour of a third person, and (c) temporary impossibility. Strike, lockout and civil disturbances are also normally outside the scope of the concept of supervening impossibility or the task becomes onerous due to hike in prices of commodities. In the contract, however, some of the contingencies mentioned above which render performance of the contract impossible either totally or over a period, are generally provided for in the shape of a 'Force Majure Clause'. If the whole work substantially becomes impossible of performance or impracticable due to some subsequent cause for which neither party is responsible, is known as frustration of performance. Frustration depends on what has actually happened and its effect on the performance of contract.

If the performance of a contract becomes impracticable then it must be held that the performance has become impossible. The essential principle on which the doctrine of frustration is based is the impossibility or rather impracticability of the performance of contract brought about by unforeseen circumstances

The doctrine stems from the theory of absolute obligation whereby a person is absolutely bound to perform any obligation which he has undertaken. In a case it was explained that, When the party by his own contract creates a duty upon himself, he is bound to make it good, if he may, notwithstanding any accident because he might have provided against it by his contract. And therefore if the lessee promises to repair a house, though it be burnt by lightning, or thrown down by enemies, yet he ought to repair it.

The above ideology has been made milder by doctrine of frustration. It has been held that if the contract is brought to a halt by some unavoidable and extraneous cause for which neither party is responsible, the contract terminates forthwith and the parties are discharged from further performance of their obligations.

In another case a contractor entered into a building contract to build a number of homes for a local authority for a fixed sum within eight months. Owing to unexpected circumstances, and without the fault of either party, adequate supplies of labour were not available and the work took twenty-two months to complete. The plaintiff claimed that the contract had been frustrated. It was held that in these circumstances there was no frustration with the observation that, "It appears that frustration depends, at least in most cases, not on adding any implied term, but on the true construction of the terms which are in the contract and the relevant surrounding circumstances when the contract was made."

In matter of business, a thing is said to be impossible when it is not practicable, and a thing is impracticable when it can only be done at an excessive or unreasonable cost.

Elsewhere it was stated that, "perhaps it would be simpler to say that frustration occurs whenever the law recognises that without default of either party a contractual obligation has become incapable of being performed because the circumstances in which performance is called for would render it a thing radically different from that which was undertaken by the contract.

An Indefinite Stoppage of Work has been held to be Sufficient cause for Frustration

It has also been observed that: "The theory of frustration belongs to the law of contract and it is represented by a rule which the courts will apply in certain limited circumstances for the purpose of deciding that contractual obligations, ex facie binding, are no longer enforceable against the parties. The description of the circumstances that justify the application of the rule, and consequently, the decision whether in a particular case those circumstances exist is, the questions of law." Thus it remains for the Court to determine in each particular situation whether the doctrine applies.

The doctrine of frustration only applies if the unsettling cause goes to the extent of substantially preventing the performance of the whole contract.

Consequences Resulting from the Application of the Doctrine of Frustration

The contract is discharged the moment the frustrating event occurs. The parties are released from performing any obligations that accrued after the time of discharge; but any obligations that accrued prior to the frustrating event remains in force. Therefore, the contract is valid and binding for the period before the frustration. Under the principle of unjust enrichment, where a party has paid money to another party for the performance of an obligation under a contract but no part of the performance has taken place and the contract is discharged, the party is entitled to reimbursement of his money as the consideration for his payment has completely failed. If substantially the whole contract becomes impossible of performance or impracticable due to some reason, the parties shall be excused. Frustration actually depends on what has actually happened and its effect on the performance of contract.

Events that Occur after Frustration

A party may well do acts or incur expenses after what the law regards as the time of discharge either because he does not know of the frustrating event or because he does know of it but does not know of their legal quality. While he may recover his loss in the first instance he would not in the second because it is a mistake of law.

Section 56 of Indian Contract Act, 1872 lays down the simple principle that "an agreement to do an act impossible in itself is void". For example, an agreement to build a house at moon being impossible of performance, is void. The second paragraph of Section 56 lays down the effect of subsequent impossibility of performance. Sometimes the performance of a contract is quite possible when it is made, but some event subsequently happen which renders its performance impossible or unlawful. In either case the contract becomes void. Where, for example, after making a contract of marriage, one of the parties goes mad, or where a contract is made for the import of goods and the import is thereafter forbidden by a Government Order, the contract in each case becomes void.

Indian Contract Act, 1872 provides following Legal Provisions :

56. ***Agreement to do impossible act.***—An agreement to do an act impossible in itself is void.

> *Contract to do act afterwards becoming impossible or unlawful.— "A contract to do an act which, after the contract is made, becomes impossible, or, by reason of some event which the promisor could not prevent, unlawful, becomes void when the act becomes impossible or unlawful.*

Compensation for loss through non-performance of act known to be impossible or unlawful.—Where one person has promised to do something which he knew, or, with reasonable diligence, might have known, and which the promisee did not know, to be impossible or unlawful, such promisor must make compensation to such promisee for any loss which such promisee sustains through the non-performance of the promise."

(a) *A* and *B* contract to marry each other. Before the time fixed for the marriage, *A* goes mad. The contract becomes void.

(b) *A* contracts to take in cargo for *B* at a foreign port. *A's* Government afterwards declares war against the country in which the port is situated. The contract becomes void when war is declared.

Loss of Object or Frustration

In this case the performance of the contract had become physically impossible because of the disappearance of the subject-matter. But the principle is not confined to physical impossibilities. It extends to cases where the performance of the contract is physically possible, but the object the parties had in mind has failed to materialize Thus the doctrine of frustration comes into play in two types of situation, first, where the performance is physically cut-off, and, second, where the object has failed. The Supreme Court has held that Section 56 will apply to both kinds of frustration. The performance of an act may not be literally impossible but it may be impracticable and useless from the point of view of the object and purpose which the parties had in view; and if an untoward event or change of circumstances totally upsets the very foundation upon which the parties rested their bargain, it can very well be said that the promisor finds it impossible to do the act which he promised to do. Frustration means that a contract has ceased to bind the parties because the common basis of mutual understanding has failed.

Commercial Hardship

The alteration of circumstances must be "such as to upset altogether the purpose of the contract. Some delay or some change is very common in all human affairs, and it cannot be assumed that any bargain has been made on the tacit condition that such a thing will not happen in any degree". A situation like this has often been described as one of commercial hardship, which may make the performance unprofitable or more expensive or dilatory, but is not sufficient to excuse performance, as it does not bring about a fundamentally different situation which can frustrate the venture. Such cases may not fall within the purview of Section 56. In commercial business, a thing is said to be impossible when it is not practicable or can be done at an excessive or unreasonable cost.

Specific Grounds of Frustration

The principle of frustration of contract or of impossibility of performance is applicable to a great variety of contracts. It is not possible to lay down an exhaustive list of situations in which the doctrine is going to be applied so as to excuse performance. The law in this regard is an evolving process. Yet the following grounds of frustration have become well established.

Destruction of Subject-Matter

The doctrine of impossibility applies with full force where the actual and specific subject-matter of the contract has ceased to exist. A promise to let out a music hall was held to have frustrated on the destruction of the hall. Similarly, where the defendant contracted to sell a specified quantity of potatoes to be grown on his farms, but failed to supply them as the crop was destroyed by a disease, it was held that performance had become impossible. Where the parties can still perform their main obligation despite the fact that the subject-matter has gone out of their hand, frustration may not follow. Thus, an agency for dealing with the goods "manufactured or sold" by the principal was not frustrated when the principal's factory was destroyed, for the agent could still deal with the goods sold by the principal.

Change of Circumstances

A contract will frustrate "where circumstances arise which make the performance of the contract impossible in the manner and at the time contemplated". This happens when the change of circumstances has affected the performance of the contract to such an extent as to make it virtually impossible or even extremely difficult. "But there is no general liberty reserved to the courts to absolve a party from liability to perform his part of the contract, merely because on account of unexpected turn of events, the performance of the contract may become onerous. The parties to an executory contract are often faced, with a turn of events which they did not anticipate—a wholly abnormal rise or fall in price, a sudden depreciation of currency, an unexpected obstacle to execution, or such like. Yet this does not in itself affect the bargain they have made.

Escalation

Law has to adapt itself to economic changes. Marginal price rise may be ignored. But when prices escalate out of all proportion than could have been reasonably expected by the parties and make performance so crushing to the contractor as to border on impossibility, the law would have to offer relief to the contractor in terms of price revision. When an agreement is predicated upon an agreed fact situation, and that situation ceases to exist, the agreement, to that extent, becomes irrelevant. Once the rates became irrelevant on account of circumstances beyond the control of the contractor, it is open to him to make a claim for compensation.

Foreknown Chances of Alteration

Where the possibility of alteration of circumstances was within the contemplation of the parties at the time of the contract, they can hardly complain of any such alteration. Thus, where a railway company accepted goods for transport and happened to convey them to a wrong destination, which on account of partition fell in Pakistan and the railways could not bring them back into India, they were not permitted to plead frustration to their liability to pay for the loss of the goods.

Non-occurrence of Contemplated Event

Sometimes the performance of a contract remains entirely possible, but owing to the non-occurrence of an event contemplated by both parties, the value of the performance is destroyed. There, a contract to hire a room to view a proposed coronation procession was held to have frustrated when the procession was postponed. Therefore, it is necessary that the happening of the event should be the foundation of the contract.

Death or Incapacity of Party

A party to a contract is excused from performance if it depends upon the existence of a given person, if that person perishes or becomes too ill to perform. Where the nature or terms of a contract require personal performance by the promisor, his death or incapacity puts an end to the contract.

Government or Legislative Intervention

A contract will be dissolved when legislative or administrative intervention has so directly operated upon the fulfilment of the contract for a specific work as to transform the contemplated conditions of performance. Where a vendor of land could not execute the sale deed because he ceased to be the owner by operation of law, it was held that the contract had become impossible of performance.

Intervention of War

Intervention of war or warlike conditions in the performance of a contract has often created difficult questions. If there are more than one ways of performing a contract and the war cuts-off only one of them, the party is still bound to perform by the other way, however inconvenient or expensive it may be. The appellants claimed that the rails specified under the contract were to be rails manufactured by a German firm and by that firm only. On this they based their claim to be excused from their failure to deliver the goods because to do so would have involved a dealing with alien enemies due to the outbreak of World War II and hence the performance of the contract became impossible and illegal. Their Lordships held that it was not open to the supplier to invoke the doctrine of frustration. There was nothing in the contract which called for the rails to be obtained from Germany only. The reference did not indicate a source of supply, but merely a specification of the rails. There were many other sources of supply, and the contract left the supplier with a free hand in the matter.

Effects of Frustration

It is well-settled that if and when there is frustration the dissolution of the contract occurs automatically.

Frustration should not be Self-induced

It is universally accepted that frustration should not be self-induced. The essence of 'frustration' is that it should not be due to the act or election of the parties. Frustration should arise without blame or fault on either side. Reliance cannot be placed on a self-induced frustration.

Frustration Operates Automatically

Frustration operates automatically to discharge the contract irrespective of the individual's concerned, their temperaments and failings, their interest and circumstances. The legal effect of frustration does not depend on their intention or their opinions, or even knowledge, of the event. Section 56 of the Contract Act does not leave the matter to be determined according to the intention of the parties.

Adjustment of Rights (Restitution)

The rights of the parties are adjusted under Section 65. Where a contract has become void due to frustration, as a result of circumstances beyond the control of parties, the plaintiffs are not entitled to any damages but are entitled to be reimbursed only for so much of the benefit which the defendant had received from them.

S. 65. Obligation of person who has received advantage under void agreement or contract that becomes void :

> "When an agreement is discovered to be void, or when a contract becomes void, any person who has received any advantage under such agreement or contract is bound to restore it, or to make compensation to it, to the person from whom he received it".

Discovered to be Void

An Agreement is void *ab initio* if it does not qualify to be a contract. But the parties discovered this at a later stage. "The word 'discovered' connotes the pre-existence of that which is discovered." This will cover cases of "initial mistake". Where, for example, money is paid for the sale of goods, which, unknown to the parties, have already perished at the time, the money is refundable. The principle will apply whether the agreement is void by reason of law or by reason of fact. Where the contract has become void due to frustration, as a result of the circumstances, beyond the control of the parties, the plaintiffs are not entitle to any damages but are entitled to be reimbursed only for so much of the benefit which the defendant has received from them.

In case a contractor encounters any of the above situations, he should invoke section 56 of the contract act and terminate the same.

SUMMARY

1. Frustration should not be confused with initial impossibility which renders the contract void *ab initio.*
2. Frustration operates in situations where it is established that due to subsequent change in circumstances the contract is rendered impossible of performance.
3. Difficulty in performance is not covered by frustration.
4. The consequence of frustration is that the contract is discharged the moment frustrating event occurs and the parties are released from obligations.
5. Section 56 of Indian Contract Act, 1872 deal with this aspect of contract performance.
6. If there are more than one ways of performing a contract and one way is cut-off, the party is bound to perform by the other way.

13 Liquidated Damages

Despite the emergence of best construction methods and development of computerised critical path programming, many construction projects still overrun their original contract period. For an employer, a delay will mean that the asset being constructed will not be available for use when originally intended. This may mean the employer has to incur additional costs or suffer a delay in receiving income from the project. For the contractor, delay to the completion of the project may result in a liability for delay damages to the employer. The purpose for award of damages is compensation for loss or damages caused by wrongful conduct; and other is vindication of a right that has been violated by wrongful construction.

As a result of these risks, most construction contracts fix the damages in advance that will be payable to the employer for late completion. These are referred to as 'liquidated damages' (LD).

Extensive provisions are made in construction contracts for establishing the date by which a contractor must complete the work that it has agreed to perform. If no date is specified a 'reasonable time for completion' will normally be implied, based on the circumstances of the particular project. Without a fixed completion date, LD will not be chargeable. For this reason, construction contracts will include a fixed completion date which may be extended through extension of time provisions. Extensions of time benefits for both parties.

From a contractor's perspective:

- Extensions cover delays that are neither the fault nor the responsibility of the contractor; and

- a contractor will not normally be liable to pay damages for delay if completion time is validly extended.

From an employer's perspective, extensions of time:

- provide certainty as to how the completion date is to be fixed, and under what circumstances it may be adjusted; and
- extensions are designed to protect a right to claim LD for delay in relevant circumstances.

Requirements for a valid liquidated damages provision: **To succeed in a claim for damages, a party must establish:**

- that there has been a breach of contract;
- that it has suffered loss; and
- that there is a causal connection between the breach and the losses that party wants to recover.

The benefit of a valid LD clause from the employer's perspective is that it removes the need for the employer to prove its actual loss and to 'mitigate', that is to take reasonable steps to avoid or reduce, the loss covered by the LD clause under section 73 of ICA. From a contractor's perspective, LD effectively act as a upper limit on its liability for delay. Recovery of LD is also a good measure where special item is procured. For instance, railways buys draw bars with assembly from approved sources. If the supply fails, there is no way to calculate the damages since there is no available market. In such situation recovery of LD is prudent.

Although the court will uphold LD clause wherever possible, a risk still exists that a poorly drafted clause will be unenforceable. It is important to ensure that:

- the clause is a genuine pre-estimate of any loss likely to be sustained, rather than a penalty designed to deter a party from breaching the contract in the first place. If the clause amounts to a penalty it is likely that it will be unenforceable;
- there is a definitive date fixed by the contract from which damages can run;
- any specific contractual procedures, such as giving written notice within specified time limits, have been complied with;

- the employer has not waived the right to deduct or claim LD;
- if the contract is otherwise brought to an end, LDs will still be payable if appropriate.

Relevant Sections 73 and 74 of Contract Act which provide for compensation are as under:

- *73. **Compensation for loss or damage caused by breach of contract:** When a contract has been broken, the party who suffers by such breach is entitled to receive, from the party who has broken the contract, compensation for any loss or damage caused to him thereby, which naturally arose in the usual course of things from such breach, or which the parties knew, when they made the contract, to be likely to result from the breach of it.*

Such compensation is not to be given for any remote and indirect loss or damage sustained by reason of the breach.

- *74. **Compensation for breach of contract where penalty stipulated for.** When a contract has been broken, if a sum is named in the contract as the amount to be paid in case of such breach, or if the contract contains any other stipulation by way of penalty, the party complaining of the breach is entitled, whether or not actual damage or loss is **proved** to have been caused thereby, to receive from the party who has broken the contract reasonable compensation not exceeding the amount so named or, as the case may be, the penalty stipulated for.*
- *Explanation.* A stipulation for increased interest from the date of default may be a stipulation by way of penalty.

In case where Court arrives at the conclusion that the term contemplating damages is by way of penalty, the Court may grant reasonable compensation not exceeding the amount so named in the contract on proof of damages *(Oil & Natural Gas Corporation Ltd.* v. *Saw Pipes Ltd.)*

"In the same case Court refers to Section 74 of Contract Act and observed that Section 74 deals with the measure of damages in two classes of cases (i) where the contract names a sum to be paid in case of breach, and (ii) where the contract contains any other stipulation by way of penalty. The Court observed that "The measure of damages in case of breach of a stipulation by way of penalty is reasonable compensation not exceeding the penalty stipulated for".

In *Maula Bux* v. *Union of India* it was held that "where loss in terms of money can be determined, the party claiming compensation must prove the loss suffered by him."

> In the same case court observed that *"under the common law a genuine pre-estimate of damages by mutual agreement is regarded as a stipulation naming liquidated damages and binding between the parties : a stipulation in a contract in terrorem is a penalty and the Court refuses to enforce it, awarding to the aggrieved party only reasonable compensation".*

Penalty : When a contract contains a term which, not being an integral part of the contract, is introduced only for the purpose of securing the performance of the contract, that term is penal, and, as such, a penalty is a term which is extraneous and collateral to the actual contract. A penal clause, therefore, must be one which imposes, some penalty for the default, that is to say, which puts the defaulter in a worse position than he would occupy if there were no penal clause. *(Union of India* v. *Vasudeo Agarwal)*

Continuing the observations the court said in the same case that the whole principle of the law of penalty is this : If in making provision for breach of contract, the promisee puts in a stipulation not by way of reasonable compensation to the promisee on the breach of contract but in order that by reason of its burdensome or oppressive character it 'may operate in terrorem over the promisor so as to drive him to fulfil the contract, then the stipulation is one by way of penalty. The idea is very common that what is called a "penalty clause" in a contract is a mere agreement that neither party has any intention of enforcing at all to any extent. Such a penalty clause merely fixes a maximum limit for damages which would be difficult to estimate in terms of money and anyhow does not deprive the aggrieved party of his right to damages that can be so estimated.

Liquidated Damage : The parties to a contract may at the time of entering into it provide, that in case of breach the party in default will pay to the other a certain sum specified in, or ascertainable from, the contract. This sum may be either liquidated damages, in which case it is not to be interfered with by the Court, or a penalty, which covers the loss if proved but does not assess it. If it is a sum which can be regarded as a genuine pre-estimate by the parties of the loss which they contemplated would flow from the breach, it is liquidated damages.

If on the other hand the sum does not attempt to assess the loss, but is imposed as security for the due performance of the contract it is a penalty. A liquidated damage, therefore, is a damage agreed to between the parties.

The word "penalty" in Section 74 implies that there is a main contract and a subsidiary contract providing for some more drastic consequences in the event of the breach of the original contract. It is totally inapplicable to a term of the original contract or consequence of the original contract not owing to breach but owing to fulfilment.

> *"The effect of Section 74 is to disentitle the plaintiff to recover simply the penal sum named in the agreement as due and payable on a breach of contract, whether as penalty or liquidated damages, unless he proves the damages he has suffered".*

According to this provision, in the event of the breach of a contract whether actual damage or loss is proved to have been caused, the party complaining may still claim reasonable compensation not exceeding the amount named in the contract. The provision, therefore, contemplates that there must be a damage or loss in fact. It is only in the event of want of proof that a reasonable compensation can still be determined by the Court and be paid to the party complaining.

> "The effect of Section 74 is to disentitle the plaintiffs to recover simply the sum fixed in the contract whether penalty or liquidated damages. The plaintiffs must prove the damages they have suffered".
>
> "The provision of this section came up for interpretation in *S.A. Bhut* v. *V. N. Jamdar*, AIR 1959 Bom 452, Mudholkar J. (as he then was) observed: "No doubt, Section 74 says that where a" sum is stated in the contract as payable to a party if a breach thereof caused by the other party the Court has power to grant compensation to the firm even though actual loss or damage is not proved. But that does not mean that compensation can be awarded even though no loss whatsoever has been caused. For the very concept of award of compensation is bound up with loss or damage that results from a breach of contract.
>
> Where, as here, no loss or damage has ensued there can be no question of awarding compensation........"

The section undoubtedly says that the aggrieved party is entitled to receive compensation from the party who has broken the contract whether or not actual damage or loss is proved to have been caused by the breach. Thereby it merely dispenses with proof of "actual loss or damage"; it does not justify the award of compensation when in consequence of the breach no legal injury at all has resulted because compensation for breach of contract can be awarded to make good loss or damage which naturally arose in the usual course of things, or which the parties knew when they made the contract to be likely to result from the breach.

The same principle has been reiterated in another Supreme Court case, *Maula Bux* v. *Union of India*, AIR1970 SC 1955. According to these authorities, it is amply clear that if on account of breach of contract, the complaining party has not suffered any loss, he is not entitled to any compensation whatsoever even if the sum is named in the contract and is to be paid in the event of breach. As already noticed, what the section provides is that if the loss has in fact occurred but the complaining party has not been able to prove it, in that event, the Court has got a discretion to determine reasonable compensation and award the same to the complaining party. In the present case, the respondent has very clearly, and categorically stated that on account of the delay on the part of the contractor in completing the work, there occasioned, in fact, no loss to the Government.

The question whether the employer can recover the amount specified in the contract by way of liquidated damages without proving that there had been "legal injury" has been answered in some decided cases. In Fateh Chand Vs Balkishan Das , the Supreme Court of India has held that Section 74 of the Indian Contract Act doubtlessly says that the aggrieved party is entitled to receive compensation from the party who has broken the contract, whether or not actual damage or loss is proved to have been caused by the breach. Thereby it merely dispenses with proof of "actual loss or damage". However it does not justify the award of compensation when in consequence of the breach no legal injury at all has resulted, because compensation for breach of contract can be awarded to make good loss or damage which naturally arose in the usual course of things or which the parties knew when they made the contract, to be likely to result from the breach.

Section 74 of the Indian Contract Act, 1872 does not dispense with the basic condition of the breach resulting in any loss or damage which can be called "legal injury". The party complaining of breach of contract and claiming compensation is entitled to succeed only on proof of "legal injury" having been sustained on account of such breach. Thus, Section 74 deliberately states that what is to be awarded is a reasonable compensation. In a case where the party complaining has not suffered legal injury in the sense of sustaining loss or damage, there is nothing to compensate him, for there is nothing to recompensate, satisfy or make amends. Therefore, he will not be entitled to compensation.

Where the Chief Engineer has very categorically stated that on account of the delay on the part of the contractor in completing the work, there occasioned, in fact, no loss to the Government. compensation cannot be granted by the Courts even if a sum is named in the contract as payable in the event of breach of contract.

Liquidated damages cease to be payable where the employer has waived the right to insist upon them. e.g. where he has failed to deduct or retain them in cases where it is imperative on his part under the contract to do so.

"Where the parties name in a contract reduced to writing a sum of money to be paid as liquidated damages they must be deemed to exclude the right to claim an unascertained sum of money as damages. The right to claim liquidated damages is enforceable under section 74 of the Contract Act and where such a right is found to exist no question of ascertaining damages really arises. Where the parties have deliberately specified the amount of liquidated damages there can be no presumption that they at the same time intended to allow the party who has suffered by the breach to give a go by to the sum specified and claim instead a sum of money which was not ascertainable or ascertainable at the date of the breach."

The effect of section 74 of the Indian Contract Act is that a party cannot get the full amount mentioned in the contract as a matter of absolute right or as a matter of course. But if the party proves that he has suffered damage to the extent of the full amount or that the Court considers, even without any proof that the full amount is a reasonable compensation which can be awarded under the circumstances, the Court can award the full amount. One thing is however certain, that. the party is entitled to get some amount, not exceeding the sum named, which the Court considers as reasonable compensation, whether any actual loss or damage is proved to have been suffered by him.

Union of India v. *Rampur Distillery and Chemicals Limited* (AIR 1973 SC 1098) it was held that "the party to a contract taking security deposit from the other party to ensure due performance of the contract is not entitled to forfeit the security deposit on the ground of default, when no loss is caused to him in consequence of such default."

Another way to lose the protection of LD is to prevent the performance of contract—the most common and effective defence against LD. In short, a party cannot impose a contractual obligation on the other where it impedes the other party in the performance of that obligation. Given that construction contracts are complex, an employer needs to be wary to avoid falling into this trap.

Early use and partial possession : Partial possession is where an employer is allowed, with the consent of the contractor, to take possession of any part of the works. If the employer exercises this right then that part of the work is effectively deemed to be completed. Most standard forms of construction contract have clauses to reduce a contractor's liability for LD proportionately if any part of the works is certified as complete before the contract is completed in full.

Early use is where an employer is allowed, with the consent of the contractor, to use or occupy part of the works before that part is deemed to be completed. Early use will leave the risk and responsibility for the site and the works with the contractor, and therefore the contractor's full liability for LD as stated in the contract will continue. However if the employer delays or disrupts the contractor, the contractor may have a claim for loss and expense.

Sub-contracts and liquidated damages : To minimise exposure, many contractors will seek to enter into contracts with the sub-contractors on substantially the same terms as their contract up the chain. Stepping down the main contract terms works well for most obligations, however attempting to pass down liability for LD to subcontractors can be difficult.

The contractor's loss will have three main elements:

- its own costs of delay—site costs, overheads, financing etc;
- its liability for LD under the main contract;
- its other sub-contractors' loss and expense.

The first two are fairly easy to estimate, but the effect of one sub-contractor's delay on the progress and cost of the others is almost impossible to pre-estimate. A number of the standard forms therefore avoid LD clauses, instead providing that the subcontractor must pay the contractor for its loss and expense resulting from the subcontractor's failure to complete on time. This loss and expense may include all three elements outlined above.

Liquidated damages is a consolidated pre-estimate of the damages that can be levied by a party to the contract in case there is a breach by the other party. This provision is kept so that there cannot be an unlimited claim for damages and both parties are also aware what can be the amount of claim if there is a breach. On the other hand, compensation for delay is a provision in contract to pre-empt the possible amount that can be claimed in case there is a delay. It is a compensation for the losses suffered and not necessarily includes damages. Thus, if there is a delay due to breach of some provision of contract, a party can claim compensation for losses suffered under this clause. However, if both clauses are there in the contract, one cannot claim both and its normally either/or case. Rules of interpretation state that if there is a specific clause for delay compensation, one has to necessarily go under the same and LD clause may come in to effect in case of any other damage. In some cases, stand has been taken that LD clause acts as a upper limit to this compensation clause. However, there are varied opinions on this issue. If there is delay from Employer, and he has paid compensation for the same, he cannot levy LD in normal circumstances since it will mean taking advantage of his own default.

The purpose of damages is to restore an injured party to the position the party was in before being harmed. As a result, damages are generally regarded as remedial rather than preventive or punitive. However, Punitive Damages may be awarded for particular types of wrongful conduct. The law recognizes three major categories of damages: Compensatory Damages, which are intended to restore what a plaintiff has lost as a result of a defendant's wrongful conduct; nominal damages, which consist of a small sum awarded to a plaintiff who has suffered no substantial loss or injury but has nevertheless experienced an invasion of rights; and punitive damages, which are awarded not to compensate a plaintiff for injury suffered but to penalize a defendant for particularly wrongful conduct.

The principle behind award of damages is that an injured plaintiff is not entitled to be placed in a superior position to that which he would have been in had the contract been performed. Furhter the damages recoverable by injured party are such sum as will put him in the same financial position as if the contract had been performed.

SUMMARY

Where the respondent granted extension of time without levy of liquidated damages, it proves that they did not hold the claimant responsible for the delay in execution of work.

Compensation for delay caused in the completion of the work under a works contract will not be awarded in the absence of evidence to show that any loss was suffered consequent upon the delay.

Where a specified amount is mentioned as damages for breach of contract, the court can award reasonable compensation.

Where the contract abandons the work and the employer rescinds the contract, levy of liquidated damages by employer in terms of condition of contract is perfectly justified and cannot be interfered with.

Section 74 of ICA recognises the right to reasonable compensation on breach of contract, which must mean some compensation howsoever small. The mere use of word penalty cannot be said to be harsh if the amount to be recovered does not exceed 10% of the value of contract.

14 Law of Equity, Quantum Meruit, Estoppel, Discovery

LAW OF EQUITY

The concept of equity substantially developed in England where Common law was not practically adequate to provide relief in the matter relating to contract.

Equity connotes fairness and justice with three main ingredients, firstly, there is just and reasonable interpretation of law, secondly, there is proper application of law and thirdly, there is plugging of shortcomings of law. In India, there is no separate equity court, but in a number of substantive laws of the land provisions have been incorporated on the basis of principles of equity and justice.

In England during the 13th Century, equity was the part of customary and statutory law. On account of rigidity, narrowness and inadequacy, the relief sought by means of common law often gave insufficient remedy or sometimes it rendered no remedy at all. At that time, the administration of prevailing law caused inconvenience and provisions of law were not wholly based on principles of natural justice. The litigants were compelled to make petition to the King-in-Council to exercise his extra-judicial powers. Such petitions used to be referred to the Chancellor who was the Chief of the Secretaries of King. In such circumstances, the Chancellor dealt with the petition while performing judicial functions. As a result, the "Court of Chancery" was constituted besides the Court of Common Law. In absence of express provisions, the Chancellor acted in view of his own judicial conscience. In the Court of Chancery, the administration of justice was carried out on the basis of fairness and conscience which were called "equity", Notably, up to 1873 there remained two distinct judicial systems i.e.—Common Law Court; and Chancery Court. In latter part of 1873, these courts were amalgamated and the new Courts were created which were given the task of enforcing all the legal rights and remedies and also equitable rights and remedies.

In England, equity developed separately from the Common Law. The Court of Equity has a separate jurisdiction and it is administered by the Chancellor and guided by the principles of natural justice. Equity does not supersede the existing law, but it is supplementary to civil law.

In India, the history of equity is as old as in England. The root of equity is traceable in ancient Indian society and judicial system.

Under Indian Legal System there is no independent branch of equity. But, the concept of equity has its due place in the development of law under the Indian Legal system which has been statutorily recognized by its incorporation in various enactments.

Equity regards and treats that as done which in good conscience ought to be done. It regards that a person who had taken an obligation to do something, must have done the same. It will treat the subject-matter of agreement, as to consequences and incidents in the same manner as if the final acts agreed by the parties have been performed exactly as they ought to have been done.

Equity is commonly said to "mitigate the rigor of common law", allowing courts to use their discretion and apply justice in accordance with natural law. Equity is considered and estimated, as acts of parties. Thus, where a person is under an obligation to do a certain act, and he does some other act which is capable of being regarded as an act in fulfillment of his obligation, he is supposed to have fulfilled his obligation . In other words a person is presumed to do what he is bound to do.

Contracts are promises that the law will enforce. The law provides remedies if a promise is breached or recognizes the performance of a promise as a duty. To be legally binding as a contract, a promise must be exchanged for adequate consideration. Adequate consideration is a benefit or detriment which a party receives which reasonably and fairly induces them to make the promise/contract.

Common law is founded upon "common sense" which is often not written but it is based upon tradition and prior cases. Codification is the attempt to write down and interpret what the common law is in a particular area. Statutes are usually not based upon the common law in any form.

The modern law of contract has grown up around as action known as the action of assumpsit. The origin of action of assumpsit can be traced back into the 14th century, that it achieved as a remedy for broken agreements and it became the regular common law contractual actions. The Chancery in late medieval England expressed an extensive jurisdiction over contracts which went a considerable way in supplementing and correcting the deficiencies of common law.

Certain doctrines became firmly established within equity such as the defense of the unconscionability of contracts. At law, the parties are viewed as having freely negotiated the terms of a contract so that the contract *per se* cannot be seen as unfair. At equity, the court is free to take into consideration the fact that certain contracts, depending upon the bargaining positions of the parties, can be grossly unfair, in other words unconscionable.

The following were developed to give relief :

Equity follows the law;
Equity regards that as done which ought to be done;
One should not profit by intentional misdeeds;
Whoever seeks equity must be equity;
Where there is equal equity, the law must prevail;
Equity will not suffer a wrong to be without a remedy;
Equity regards substance rather than form;
Equity aids the vigilant, not those who rest on their rights; and
Equity is equity.

These maxims of equity are reflected in various provisions of Indian Contract Act and are referred to, for example, in giving relief in the contract made under undue influence, fraud and mistake, Equitable maxims, were further developed by the courts and used to arrive at decisions in equitable cases.

Discovery : An arbitrator may permit such discovery as he think is appropriate in the circumstances, taking into account the needs of the parties and relevance of the documents to the arbitration proceeding and the desirability of making the proceeding fair, expeditious and effective. An arbitrator may issue order to prevent the disclosure of privileged information, confidential information, trade secrets and other information protected from disclosure. In the absence of proper evidence, the outcome may be frustrating. In such a logjam situation, party may request arbitrator for issuing directions to the other party for discovery which will issue suitable direction.

Before a litigation begins and things are fine, the papers are in the custody of different people in the firm. After eruption of dispute, the two sides take different and non-cooperative position. Documents required by one party and same being in the possession of other party are difficult to come by. In such situation not only filing claims becomes difficult but to sustain them through litigation process is equally difficult.

The discovery process allows the parties to obtain facts and information from other parties to the arbitration in order to support their own case and prepare for the hearing. The fair conduct requires parties to cooperate with each other to the fullest extent practicable in the voluntary exchange of documents and information to expedite the arbitration process. However, no duty is cast upon the parties to exchange vital information. Proper discovery requests should be made, other party should respond to such requests, objection to discovery requests if any should be made, and arbitrator should use his authority to issue sanctions against parties for discovery abuses.

If the parties cannot agree on their own to resolve any discovery dispute, then the party who still wants more documents or information may make a motion to arbitrator to compel the reluctant party to produce the requested documents. In the motion, the requesting party should explain to the arbitrator(s) why the discovery is relevant and necessary to the case and ask the panel to issue an order compelling production. The arbitrator(s) may schedule a hearing before deciding the motion.

If a party fails to produce documents or information required by a discovery order, the arbitrators may draw adverse inference against the party; and can even dismiss a claim, defence, or even the entire case.

In a case the claimant was unable to file the claim before the Arbitrator because of non-availability of balance-sheet, copies of bank statements, income expenditure accounts for the financial year. Directions were given to the petitioner by the Arbitrator from time to time, but the petitioner had not been furnishing full documents to him. Respondent placed on record that in view of non-giving of details by the petitioner, the respondent had not been able to file the statement of claim.

The plea of holding back of documents by the petitioner or non-discovery of documents by the petitioner is concerned, the plea could have succeeded only if the respondent had filed his claim before the Arbitrator and asked the Arbitrator to pass necessary orders for discovery of documents from the petitioner.

Contributory Negligence : Hardly do we come across in our lives, where in a contract whether for purchase and supply or construction mistakes are not committed by both the parties to the contract. Ultimately breach of contract may be on any party's account but the underlying point is that every party contributes in some measure to the failure. If the events from beginning of contract are properly and honestly recorded one could easily discern the share of negligence of each party although these might have been waived off. Where any person suffers damages the result partly of his own fault and partly of the fault of any other person or persons, a claim in respect of that damage shall not be defeated by reason of a fault of the person suffering the damage, but the damages recoverable in respect thereof, shall be reduced to such extent that the court thinks just and equitable having regard to the claimant's share in responsibility for the damages provided that:

The doctrine provides that if the claimant (plaintiff) suffers damages partly as the result of the claimant's failure to take reasonable care (contributory negligence) and partly as a result of the wrong of another person, the claim is not thereby defeated but damages recoverable in respect of the wrong are to be reduced or apportioned.

In a construction project, adequate data was not given in the bid document, Besides the contractor was asked to execute extra work. Both the facts contributed in delaying the completion of the project. Contractor too was negligent in execution. Court decided the dispute by observing that it was case of contributory negligence where both parties were responsible for the delay.

In another case NHAI awarded a contract of four laning to one firm. Dispute arose which was referred to arbitration. The tribunal inferred that the contract could not be performed due to contributory negligence where compensation was reduced proportionately.

Superior knowledge: Superior knowledge is defined as vital knowledge or information not possessed by the other party which is necessary to the successful performance of the contract; it is generally a significant factor in determining allocation of risk. The Government has a duty to disclose information which is "vital" to the performance of the contract, and may affect a contractor's performance. The duty applies to any special information unknown or unavailable to the contractor. The Court held that the Government's duty to disclose superior knowledge to its contractors exists independently of the theory of misrepresentation. The court outlined that the Government has a duty to disclose information to its contractors when:

1. the Government has knowledge of information vital to the contract;
2. the Government knows or should know of the detrimental effect which non-disclosure would have upon performance;
3. the contractor neither knows nor has reason to know of such information; and
4. the Government knows or should know of the contractor's ignorance.

MISREPRESENTATIONS

In the absence of a Differing Site Condition clause, a principal issue is whether the contractor justifiably relied on the Government representations. A misrepresentation occurs when the Government erroneously represents the existence or non existence of a fact material to contract performance, upon which a contractor reasonably relies to his detriment. If the Government is deliberately misleading about site conditions, and the contractor unknowingly relies on these inaccurate representations, the contractor may be eligible for additional compensation. Most of the cases decided under the theory of misrepresentation concern situations involving changed physical conditions.

Types of Misrepresentation

Fraudulent misrepresentation is when the representation made with intent to deceive and with the knowledge that it is false. This is generally a difficult type of misrepresentation to prove but allows for a remedy of both damages and recession. An action for fraudulent misrepresentation can also be brought as a tort.

Innocent misrepresentation is when the representation is made with an honest belief that it is true. This type of representation only allows for a remedy of recession.

Negligent misrepresentation is when the representation is made carelessly. This class of misrepresentation is relatively new and was introduced in order to allow for a remedy of damages in situations where neither a collateral contract nor fraud could be found.

The misrepresentation must have induced the contract : The false statement must have induced the representee to enter into the contract. The requirements here are that : (a) the misrepresentation must be material, and (b) it must have been relied on.

The misrepresentation must be material, in the sense that it would have induced a reasonable person to enter into the contract. Law of Restitution that, any misrepresentation which induces a person to enter into a contract should be a ground for rescission of that contract. If the misrepresentation would have induced a reasonable person to enter into the contract, then the court will presume that the representee was so induced, and the onus will be on the representor to show that the representee did not rely on the misrepresentation either wholly or in part. If, however, the misrepresentation would not have induced a reasonable person to contract, the onus will be on the misrepresentee to show that the misrepresentation induced him to act as he did. The representee must have relied on the misrepresentation. There will be no reliance if the misrepresentee was unaware of the misrepresentation. There will be no reliance if the representee does not rely on the misrepresentation but on his own judgment or investigations. There will be reliance even if the mis-representee is given an opportunity to discover the truth but does not take the offer up. The misrepresentation will still be considered as an inducement. There will be reliance even if the misrepresentation was not the only inducement for the representee to enter into the contract. Once an actionable misrepresentation has been established, it is then necessary to consider the remedies available to the misrepresentee. Setting aside the contract is possible in all cases of misrepresentation.

Restitution

The five basic remedies for breach of contract include the following: money damages, restitution, rescission, reformation, and specific performance. A money damage award includes a sum of money that is given as compensation for financial losses caused by a breach of contract. Parties injured by a breach are entitled to the benefit of the bargain they entered, or the net gain that would have accrued but for the breach. The type of breach governs the extent of damages that may be recovered. Parties that are induced to enter into contracts by mistake, fraud, undue influence, or duress may seek to have the contract set aside or have the terms of the contract rewritten to do justice in the case. Rescission is the name for the remedy that terminates the contractual duties of both parties, while reformation is the name for the remedy that allows courts to change the substance of a contract to correct inequities that were suffered.

Restitution is the act of restoring to the rightful owner something that has been taken away, lost, or surrendered. It is the act of making good or compensating for loss, damage, or injury. Also as a return to or restoration of a previous state or position. Also defined as a remedy associated with unjust enrichment in which the amount of recovery is typically based on the defendant's gain rather than the plaintiff's loss. Returning property or its monetary value to the rightful owner. The losing party in a negligence or contracts case may be ordered to make restitution. The general term *restitution* describes the act of restoration. The term is used in different areas of the law but carries the same meaning throughout.

The basic purpose of restitution is to achieve fairness and prevent the Unjust Enrichment of a party. Restitution is used in contractual situations where one party has conferred a benefit on another party but cannot collect payment because the contract is defective or no contract exists. For instance, assume that a person builds a barn on the property of another person. And that the owner of the property on which the barn sits refuses to pay the builder for the barn. Despite the absence of a contract, a court can order the owner to pay the builder the cost of the labour and materials under the doctrine of restitution.

The Principle of Estoppel

The principle is a rule of evidence incorporated in Section 115 of The Indian Evidence Act, 1872. The section reads as follows: *"When one person has, by his declaration, act or omission, intentionally caused or permitted another person to believe such a thing to be true and to act upon such belief, neither he nor his representative shall be allowed, in any suit or proceeding between himself and such person or his representative, to deny the truth of that thing."*

The doctrine of promissory estoppel is an equitable doctrine. Like all equitable remedies, it is discretionary . It is a principle evolved by equity to avoid injustice and though commonly named 'promissory estoppel', it is neither in the realm of contract nor in the realm of estoppel.

The true principle of promissory estoppel is where one party has by his words or conduct made to the other a clear and unequivocal promise which is intended to create legal relations or effect a legal relationship to arise in the future, knowing or intending that it would be acted upon by the other party to whom the promise is made and it is in fact so acted upon by the other party, the promise would be binding on the party making it and he would not be entitled to go back upon it. It is not necessary, in order to attract the applicability of the doctrine of promissory estoppel that the promisee acting in reliance of the promise, should suffer any detriment. The only thing necessary is that the promisee should have altered his position in reliance of the promise.

However, the government cannot be restrained from taking a policy decision and the principle of estoppel has no application nor does it operate at the level of the government policy. As a result of change in policy many people may become victim of the same but estoppel cannot be allowed to hinder the formation and implementation of the policy. The public authority cannot be disturbed from doing its duty.

Adhesion contract: These are designed by one party and offered on a take it or leave it basis. These are prone to one sidedness. There is no bargain or haggling in acceptance of such contracts. On the other side, everyone understands the importance of form contract as they serve important purpose in society. An adhesion contract *per se* does not precipitate an unconscionability ruling but it usually works in that direction.

Without Prejudice

Without abandonment of a claim, privilege, or right, and without implying an admission of liability. When used in a document or letter, *without prejudice* means that what follows (a) cannot be used as evidence in a court case. When a court case is dismissed, *without prejudice*, it means that a new case may be brought.

Quantum Meruit

In the law of contracts, quantum merit is a doctrine by which the law infers a promise to pay a reasonable amount for labour and materials furnished, even in the absence of a specific legally enforceable agreement between the parties.

A party who performs a valuable service for another party usually enters into a written contract or agreement before performing the service, particularly when the party is in the business of performing that service. For instance, most professional roofers hired to repair a roof insist on having a formal agreement with the owner of the house before beginning the repairs. In the absence of an agreement or formal contract, the roofer may be unable to recover losses in court if the transaction goes awry. Quantum meruit is a judicial doctrine that allows a party to recover losses in the absence of an agreement or binding contract.

By allowing the recovery of the value of labour and materials, quantum meruit prevents the Unjust Enrichment of the other party. A person would be unjustly enriched if he received a benefit and did not pay for it when fairness required that payment be made. Quantum meruit can be used to address situations where no contract exists or where a contract exists but for some reason is unenforceable. In such cases courts imply a contract to avoid an unjust result. Such contracts are called quasi contracts.

Unjust Enrichment

Unjust enrichment suffers from a confusion of nomenclature. Although it is referred to as "quasi-contract" and said to be based upon a "contract implied in law," it is not a contract at all. Rather, it is legal fiction described as "an obligation imposed by law to do justice even though it is clear that no promise was ever made or intended." By contrast with quantum meruit, recovery for unjust enrichment is not premised upon there having been "assent" between the parties. While quantum meruit arises out of the expectation of the parties, unjust enrichment is based upon society's interest in preventing the injustice of a person's retaining a benefit for which no payment has been made to the provider.

Revival of an Expired Contract

There is no rule of law that prevents the parties from agreeing to revive and/or amend an expired contract through an addendum or a new contract incorporating the old. To hold otherwise would defeat the parties' undisputed intent and create an arbitrary and unprecedented exception to the ordinary rules of contract. This is a case about mutual assent.When the contract has terminated or been extinguished, it is no longer subject to extension, for extension implies an existing agreement. *To bring the terms of an extinguished contract into renewed existence requires a new contract embodying such terms.*

No principle of law prohibited the parties from reviving and amending their contract by express agreement.

Force Majeure

If at any time, during the continuance of this contract, the performance in whole or in part by either party of any obligation under this contract shall be prevented or delayed by reason of any war, hostility, acts of public enemy, civil commotion, sabotage, serious loss or damage by fire, explosions, epidemics, strikes, lockouts or acts of God provided, notice of the happening of any such event is given by either party to the other within 30 days from the date of occurrence thereof, neither party shall by reason of such event, be entitled to terminate this contract nor shall either party have any claim for damages against the other in respect of such non-performance of delay in performance, and works under the contract shall be resumed as soon as practicable after such event has come to an end or ceased to exist.

15 Arbitral Immunity, Excepted Matters : Repudiation and Discretion

ARBITRAL IMMUNITY

In line with the immunity provided to judiciary , the courts have extended judicial immunity to arbitrators due to the functional similarities between the two positions. Arbitrators are neutral parties that are appointed to adjudicate on disputes submitted before them and render binding and final decisions. In this process, arbitrators determine the rights of the parties to the arbitration agreement. Similar to the public policy argument given to justify judicial immunity, the ground of independence and impartiality holds true for arbitral immunity. Thus, the courts have justified granting of judicial immunity to arbitrators. Arbitration proceedings are not like public courts, but are private and confidential. Arbitral proceedings lack rigid procedural formality and arbitral awards are subject to very limited judicial review.

With the rise of the use and demand for arbitration. There has arisen a corresponding demand of professional arbitrators and an industry of private business who provide arbitration support. Alongwith the growth in profession, there is perceived misconduct of arbitrators because of which the arbitration process is coming under attack. This has resulted in the questioning of justification of arbitral immunity.

The reason for providing immunity are the same as those that apply to Judges in courts. Arbitration and litigations share this in common that both provide a means of dispute resolution which depends upon a binding decision by an impartial third party. It is generally considered that an immunity is necessary to enable the third party to perform an impartial decision making function. Unless some degree of immunity is afforded, the finality of the arbitral process could be undermined.

In *Rajesh Batre* v. *Ranbir Singh Ahlawat* an arbitrator assumed jurisdiction on the unilateral nomination made by one party, without even bothering that there was no consent from the other party. The proceedings were conducted in the presence of proxy. The arbitrator stated in the court that the first party had sent legal notice to the other one informing regarding reference of dispute to the arbitrator. Since the other party did not raise any objection the consent was taken as implied. The arbitrator brazenly proceeded to conduct the proceedings and passed the award. High court observed that such parties can play havoc with the system by nominating an arbitrator unilaterally in breach of the agreement and obtain an award from arbitrator. The court imposed a cost of Rs. 20000 upon the first party and arbitrator.

Challenge to the appointment of the arbitrator can be made only on the ground of justifiable doubt with respect to his impartiality and independence or when the arbitrator does not possess the qualifications that the parties had agreed upon. Partiality occurs when the arbitrator favours one party over the other or when he is prejudiced about the subject matter of dispute, and dependence refers to a close relationship between one of the parties and the arbitrator or with someone close to the parties. The relationship can be a personal, direct or indirect professional business relationship and past relationships are important only if they are of a high magnitude that could eventually affect arbitrator's judgment. The arbitrator is under an obligation to disclose all facts and circumstances which might lead to such justifiable doubts.

Internationally also, a similar duty on the arbitrator is cast to remain independent and impartial at all times. The arbitrator should not act in the capacity of an advocate to any party and should not advice any party on the merits or outcome of the case, either before or after appointment. The arbitrator is liable to be removed in the event he acts in deliberate violation of the arbitration agreement or acts unfairly or impartially. A party can also challenge the appointment of arbitrator in an episode of impartiality or independence. The arbitrator remains liable, when he acts or omits to act with the intention of conscious or deliberately wrongdoing. The arbitrator can be challenged and removed on the grounds of lack of impartiality and independence. The allegation has to be made in writing.

Though there is a provision for arbitral immunity, it has been limited to the laws applicable and to intentional wrongdoing. A certain degree of immunity or exoneration from liability in favour of arbitrators is advisable to reinforce the independence and impartiality of the arbitrators with a free spirit rather than being concerned about later liability lawsuits.

Arbitration in our country is governed by the Arbitration and Conciliation Act, 1996. No provision under the Act, 1996 explicitly defines either 'serious misconduct' or 'biases' although misconduct was the basis for challenge to arbitrators under the Act of 1940. However, its implication can be inferred from a reading of sections 12, 13, 14, 15 and 34 of the Act. Though there is no direct provision or case law on arbitral immunity, in a combined reading of these provisions and relevant case law, gives us a clear picture of the extent of this protection in India. Under these sections suspicion by itself could not be made a ground for conclusion that the arbitrator would not act impartially or fairly. Hence, termination of the mandate is not allowed only on the apprehension of bias. To apply for a termination of a mandate, there must be actual bias. The court held that "the apprehension must be judged from a healthy, reasonable and average point of view and not on mere apprehension of any whimsical person". However, the remedies against this misconduct are the removal of the arbitrator, setting aside the arbitral award or the non-payment or partial payment of the arbitrator's fees. Reasonable apprehension or likelihood of bias of the arbitrator is sufficient ground for the removal of the arbitrator while actual bias must be proved for the setting aside of the award.

Under Indian scenario the remedies against misconduct are the removal of the arbitrator, setting aside award or non-payment or partial payment of the arbitrator's fee.

In no manner can the position of arbitrators be equated to that of judges. Hence though arbitral immunity has its roots from judicial immunity, it can in no manner supersede judges' immunity. In the process of arbitration, private arbitrators, not necessarily skilled in law, render final and binding determinations as to not only the parties' contractual rights, but also statutory rights and liabilities. Where the lapse is serious like that of bias, it seems right that the party who has suffered loss should be entitled to recover that loss from the offending arbitrator. On the flipside, it is equally important to protect the arbitrators from harassing parties and also to ensure their independence and impartiality in the interests of the public. Such a fine distinction has been drawn in the Indian law where the arbitral immunity though wide, is not absolute and there exists recourse against the arbitrator when he is biased under arbitration law in all circumstances. Hence, ultimately a balance must be struck between imposing sanctions on arbitrators to deter them from wilfully and recklessly abusing their duties and powers simultaneously making it possible for them to fulfil their quasi-judicial role without fear of undesirable attacks.

Excepted Matters

The term emanates from contractual disputes. During performance of contract disputes and differences are bound to arise between employer and contractor, resolution of which is essential. A mechanism of arbitration has been evolved where parties choose their own judge and refer disputes to him for adjudication. Now, there are certain disputes, specifically identified in the contract agreement the decision to which is specifically provided in the agreement. These matters are excluded from the purview of arbitration process. Rather these matters are not covered by valid arbitration agreement between the parties. Such disputes are not referred to arbitrator or if referred, the other party should bring them to the notice of arbitrator at the earliest opportunity stating that a particular dispute being 'excepted matter' is outside the jurisdiction of arbitration. The arbitrator if passes award on excepted matters, he is travelling beyond his jurisdiction creating situation for challenging the award under S. 34 of Act, 1996.

Following is the list of excepted matters appearing in the general conditions of contracts of IR:

(i) Assistance by the Railway for the Stores to be obtained by the Contractor
(ii) Illegal Gratification
(iii) Monetary dealings with any employee of the Railway
(iv) Meaning and intent of specification and drawings
(v) Rates for extra items of works
(vi) Payment to the Contractor
(vii) Signing of "No Claim" Certificate
(viii) Objections to recorded measurements within 7days

(ix) Provisions of payments of Wages Act
(x) Recovery from Contractor; wages paid to Contractor's labour
(xi) Provision of Workmen's Compensation Act
(xii) Provision of Mines Act
(xiii) Right of Railway to determine the contract
(xiv) Payment on determination of contract
(xv) Determination of contract owing to default of Contractor

REPUDIATION

Repudiation occurs where one of the parties renounces his liabilities under a contract, or if he evinces an intention no longer to be bound by the contract. If a breach of contract amounted to the manifestation of an intention on the part of the wrongdoer no longer to be bound by the terms of that contract, the breach will be treated as repudiatory and may be accepted as such by the innocent party. Refusal to perform all of the obligations under the contract wili amount to repudiation. Before a contract of employment was due to commence, the defendant told the plaintiff that his services were no longer required, repudiating his obligation. Repudiation may also occur where the promisor refuses to perform some of his obligations under a contract, provided the refusal is a sufficiently serious matter. Repudiation may be implied from the promisor's words or conduct, if a reasonable person in the shoes of the innocent party would clearly infer that the other party would not be bound by the contract. For repudiation, the breach must "go to the root of the contract". The general rule was that the contract is not terminated until the innocent party accepts the repudiation, although an act of acceptance requires no particular form .

A contract will be repudiated if there is an express declaration by words or conduct of an inability to perform. Repudiation for an inability to perform may be inferred by words or conduct of the promisor that the promisor is unable to perform e.g. A promises to sell his car to B but before completion sells it to C:

> An anticipatory breach will amount to a repudiation where a party, prior to the time for performance under the contract, evinces an intention to no longer be bound to the contract according to its terms. A promise may terminate for an anticipatory breach immediately without waiting for the date of actual performance if the breach is of a sufficiently serious

nature, i.e. an essential term or the repudiation goes to the root of the contract. Once the due date for performance has arrived, all rights for the anticipatory breach are lost and any termination must be based on the actual breach:

While the concept of repudiation is straightforward, its application is often difficult and one should be careful in cancelling a contract on the ground of repudiation. The injured party has a choice. He may affirm the contract or accept the repudiatory breach and treat the contract as at an end. Repudiation is nothing but a kind of breach which is not on account of performance. Where the injured party accepts a repudiatory breach, the contract comes to an end and both parties are released from their future obligations. Extant obligations remain binding and damages are payable by either party in respect of breach before termination.

Generally the injured party terminates the contract. If the party affirms the contract, it remains in force. If victim fails to rescind the contract, it also remains in force.

A breach in performance, even a serious breach, will not amount to repudiation unless it shows an intention not to be bound. Where the party in breach expressly states its willingness to be bound by the contract, it is very unlikely that party will be held to have repudiated the contract.

ERROR APPARENT ON THE FACE OF AWARD

It is the requirement of law that the award made should not be against law. An award is liable to be set aside where there is an objection to its validity apparent on the face of it. This happens where arbitrator has made a mistake and the mistake is apparent on the face of the judgment. Error apparent on the face of the award means some error of law and not error of fact. Error has to be one which can be discovered from the award itself or from documents incorporated into it. A defect apparent on the face means that on a mere reading of the award, and without more, it seems to be erroneous. An error in law on the face of the award means that one can find in the award some legal proposition which is the basis of the award and which itself is erroneous. An arbitrator is not entitled to ignore law or misapply it. An award which is not in accordance with the substantive law or Act or the agreement, would be liable to be set aside. When an award is based upon a proposition of law which is so unreasonable and irrational that no right thinking person could have come to such a conclusion on the basis of material on record, then such an award will be set aside.

If the arbitrator commits an error in construction of the contract or an error in construction of a statutory provision and makes an award, that error is an error within jurisdiction, and cannot be interfered with. As observed in *ONGC* v. *Saw Pipes Ltd.* reported in (2003) 5 SCC 705, if the illegality is of a trivial nature, the award cannot be said to be against public policy. An award may be set aside, if the construction of a contractual provision is so unreasonable and unfair that it shocks the conscience of the Court. The arbitrator has the authority to interpret the provisions of the contract based on his understanding of the law and the Court would not interfere with the interpretation unless the same is patently perverse, unreasonable, absurd, whimsical and shocks the conscience of the Court.

A case of the Arbitrator travelling beyond the jurisdiction from the case of an ordinary award when such award was challenged on the ground of error apparent on the face of record: "A dispute as to the jurisdiction of the arbitrator is not a dispute within the award, but one which has to be decided outside the award. An umpire or arbitrator cannot widen his jurisdiction by deciding a question not referred to him by the parties or by deciding a question otherwise than in accordance with the contract. He cannot say that he does not care what the contract says. He is bound by it. It must bear his decision. He cannot travel outside its bounds. If he exceeded his jurisdiction by so doing, his award would be liable to be set aside. It would be impossible to allow an umpire to arrogate to himself jurisdiction over a question which on the true construction of the submission was not referred to him. An umpire cannot widen the area of his jurisdiction by holding, contrary to the fact, that the matter which he affects to decide is within the submission of the parties" Evidence of matters not appearing on the face of the award would be admissible to decide whether the arbitrator travelled outside the bounds of the contract and thus exceeded his jurisdiction: In order to see what the jurisdiction of the arbitrator is, it is open to the Court to see what dispute was submitted to him.

If the arbitrator commits an error in the construction of the contract, that is an error within his jurisdiction. But if he wanders outside the contract and deals with matters not allotted to him, he commits a jurisdiction error. Such error going to his jurisdiction can be established by looking into material outside the award.

The arbitrator cannot act arbitrarily, irrationally capriciously or independently of the contract. His sole function is to arbitrate in terms of the contract. He has no power apart from what the parties have given him under the contract. If he has travelled outside the bounds of the contract, he has acted without jurisdiction. But if he has remained inside the parameters of the contract and has construed the provisions of the contract, his award cannot be interfered with unless he has given reasons for the award disclosing an error apparent on the face of it.

While passing the award, if, arbitrator makes a mistake of law or fact, that is no ground for challenging the validity of the award. It is only when a proposition of law is stated in the award and it is the basis of that award that is erroneous, can the award be set aside or remitted on the grounds of error of law apparent on the face of the record. An error of law on the face of the award means that you can find in the award or a document actually incorporated thereto stating the reasons for his judgment, some legal proposition which is the basis of the award and which you can say is erroneous.

An error in law on the face of award means, that one can find in the award or a document actually incorporated thereto, as for instance a note appended by arbitrator stating reasons for his judgment. Some legal proposition which is the basis of the award which one can then say is erroneous.

The word apparent in the expression 'error apparent on the face of award' does not mean obvious, but means 'made manifest to the understanding, by being stated in the order. An error of law appears on the face of the order if a proposition of law is stated in the order which then becomes speaking order. *(Union of India* v. *Ajanta Enterprises).*

DISCRETION

Unlike contracts for sale and purchase of goods, the construction contracts are very complex. Activites to be performed are many, and so is their quality and quantity to be monitored. Variables in such contracts are innumerable, especially sub-grade conditions and their effect on the over all project. External factors too contribute their might to influence the performance of contracts in undesirable manner. Under such odds the engineers are called upon to take decisions, in quite succession, many of which are discretionary in nature. At times the discretion exercised is not acceptable to contractor due to which dispute arise. Many contractual disputes have their origin in exercise of discretion. Therefore, a little enquiry into this matter will be of immense help.

Discretion is the power or right to make official decisions using reason and judgment to choose from among acceptable alternatives.

Legislatures, judiciary, and administrative agencies are among the public officers and offices charged with making discretionary decisions in the discharge of public duties. All discretionary decisions made are subject to some kind of review and are also subject to reversal or modification if there has been an abuse of discretion. An abuse of discretion occurs when a decision is not an acceptable alternative. The decision may be unacceptable because it is logically unsound, because it is arbitrary and clearly not supported by the facts at hand, or because it is explicitly prohibited by a statute or Rule of Law.

The keystone of the rule of law is the idea of the government of laws rather than the government of men. The keystone of the government of laws is legal control over human discretion. The existence of widespread discretion is therefore directly inimical to the existence of a liberal order. Discretions need to be exercised on the basis of justice or some real justification or even of mere reason. An unfettered discretion is an opportunity for temptation and for arbitrary, insolent, discriminatory, and corrupt government. Where there are fixed laws there is more or less certainty, there is certainly impartiality and consistency. A person may stand upon his legal rights without fear or favour. Discretion, on the other hand, undermines justice.

Executive discretion is the most dangerous of all forms of discretion. This is because its impact upon the citizens is immediate and uncertain. Legislative discretion is uncertain but not immediate. Judicial discretion is immediate but not uncertain. Executive discretions, is open to the greatest possible abuse. The administrator has unfettered power over the individual who stands at his mercy. The opportunities for arbitrary, insolent, discriminatory, intrusive and corrupt activities are maximised at this point. Administrative decisions often include the exercise of discretion. Discretion exists when the decision-maker has the power to make a choice about whether to act or not act, to approve or not approve, or to approve with conditions. The role of the decision-maker is to make a judgment taking into account all relevant information.

Departments should develop policies and guidelines to assist and provide guidance to decision-makers to exercise discretion. Unlike legislation, policies and guidelines do not have the force and effect of law and they should not be inconsistent with the legislation. If they are, the legislation takes precedence. Not every situation needs a policy or guideline and they may not cover all circumstances. However, they are an important means of providing guidance to decision-makers who are required to exercise discretion when delivering a government service and in making decisions and to those with an interest in the decisions. Policies and guidelines assist to ensure decisions are made consistently and fairly. Before preparing a policy or guideline, it is important to weigh up the costs and benefits of what outcomes might be achieved as a result. If better decision-making is likely to be achieved, there is likely to be an overall net benefit outcome.

Decision-makers must use discretionary powers in good faith and for a proper, intended and authorised purpose. Decision-makers must not act outside of their powers. No decision-maker has an unfettered discretionary decision-making power. It is not sufficient to exercise discretion and approve an application simply because it seems the right thing to do. When exercising discretion, decision-makers need to act reasonably and impartially. They must not handle matters in which they have an actual or reasonably perceived conflict of interest. It is important to apply the values that the legislation promotes, professional values and the values of the agency, not personal values. In exercising discretionary powers, decision-makers should have regard to any specific requirements as well as satisfy general administrative law requirements.

The act of exercising discretion can add a level of complexity into the decision-making process as the decision to be made may not be clear-cut. It may be necessary for the decision-maker to consider and weigh a number of factors and evidence. The legislation may state that certain matters must be taken into account in the decision-making process. When stated, these matters must be considered. The use of the word 'includes' or expression such as 'any other matters that in the opinion of the decision-maker are relevant' indicates that guidance from other sources will be necessary to determine what other factors might be relevant.

It is important to keep people informed in the decision-making process. Decision-makers also have a responsibility to inform the relevant parties of the outcome. There may also be a requirement to provide reasons for the decision reached.

Before exercising discretion, it is necessary to gather information and establish the facts. Some facts might be submitted with an application made to the decision-maker. Others might be obtained through inquiries or investigation.

Consider the Standard

The person taking action or making a decision must act reasonably. The decision-maker needs to act impartially. They must not handle matters in which they have an actual or reasonably perceived conflict of interest.

Observe the Rules

Before taking certain action or making some decisions, the decision-maker may be required to provide procedural fairness to anyone who is likely to be adversely affected by the outcome.

Although policies, previous decisions, and court and tribunal decisions may exist to guide the decision-maker, it is still important to consider the matter or application on its merits and to make a judgment about the matter under consideration.

Keep Parties Informed

The decision-maker should keep relevant parties informed during the decision-making process; they should inform the relevant parties of the outcome; and provide reasons for the decision reached.

Create and Maintain

It is vital that records are created and maintained about the issues that were taken into account in the process and why, the weight given to the evidence and the reasons for the decisions made.

Discretion refers to acting in a judicious or discreet manner. Whenever a person exercises prudence in actions and behavior, he is said to be observing discretion. A discreet person is known for his decisive powers and making them within certain boundaries. A discreet person is cautious and often employs tact and maturity while making decisions.

There is a popular proverb "discretion is a better part of valor," which means that one should not be blinded by risk-taking to such an extent that he does not weigh the repercussions of the act. The proverb is as good as "look before you leap," which implies taking calculated risks. Thus, learning to exercise discretion is solution of many problems. Rather it nips the problems before they come to surface.

16 Offer, Consent and Prevention Principle

'WILL" THEORY

Contracts are explained by "will theory" of contracts or "contracts as promises". It is also known as "will principle" or the "promise principle". According to the will or promise principle, commitments are enforceable because the promisor has "willed" or freely chosen to be bound by his commitment. The law of contract gives expression to and protects the will of the parties, since the will is something inherently worthy of respect. In this approach, the use of force against a reneging promisor is morally justified because the promisor himself has undertaken the obligation in question. A promisor cannot complain about force being used against him, since he created the obligation being enforced. An individual is morally bound to keep his promises because he has *intentionally* raised moral grounds for another to expect the promised performance.

In contract, the source of the obligation or duty being enforced is the promisor himself. The spirit of the will principle is that contracts require a "meeting of the minds." That mutual "assent" is thought necessary to create a contractual obligation in harmony with the will principle.

The principle depends upon the notion that contractual duties are binding because they are freely assumed by those who are required to discharge them. This position leads quite naturally to an inquiry as to the promisor's actual state of mind at the time of agreement—the so-called "subjective" viewpoint. Without a genuine commitment by the person who is to be subjected to a legal sanction, enforcement would seem to be unjustified by the "will" of the promise. Therefore it is necessary to inquire as to what was the actual state of mind of individual at the time of agreement which is called subjective view point. It must be established if obligation was chosen or not by the individual or it was imposed.

The other approach is to know 'objectively manifested intentions'. But where subjective intent can somehow be proved and it is contrary to objectively manifested behaviour, the subjective intent should prevail if the moral integrity of the will principle is to be preserved. However, inquiry into subjective intent would undermine the security of transactions by greatly reducing the reliability of contractual commitments. After all if the secret direction of the intentions could invalidate a contract, where is our security?

Despite the traditional sentiment that contracts require a "meeting of the minds," the objective approach has largely prevailed because a persons' objective manifestations generally do reflect his subjective intentions too. Yet, it has long been recognised that a system of contractual enforcement would be unworkable if it required a subjective enquiry into the promisor's mind. It is very difficult to discern the actual subjective intent or will of the parties.

CASE STUDY

From here we move on to a case study and attempt to find what went wrong and where. A contract was let out for construction of a bridge with pile foundations. As usual for such works the geotechnical investigations should be conducted in advance and construction drawings should be ready when construction work is awarded. Rightly so, the owner had engaged one agency for conducting geotechnical investigations and preparation of structural drawings.

The term of the construction tender was that the bidders would visit the site to familiarise themselves about the geology, geography of the area; availability of labour, material, etc. The contractor who bagged the work did visit the site and found one geotechnical agency working at bridge site. In the tender schedule, too, nominal quantity was kept for geotechnical investigations with a clear rider that this was optional and may or may not be operated.

Unfortunately the investigating agency failed. In the meanwhile construction contract was fixed and the contractor was asked to conduct geotechnical investigations which he did and submitted the analysed report. It took about two months and thereafter owner could not handover construction drawings for long time.

When contractor gave notice for repudiating the contract, the owner blamed him for taking long time in conducting investigations and submitting report. What happened later on is not of much relevance here. The question is can the owner heap the blame on to construction contractor for geotechnical investigations which were to be done by some other agency.

A look at the tender document indicates following:

1. **Schedule 'I'** of the agreement (Geotechnical investigations) is **OPTIONAL** i.e. this schedule may or may not be operated.
2. **Schedule 'II'** of the agreement is that RCC bore pile shall be 'constructed as per drawing'.
3. The work shall be done as per the following programme: "The work should be started from both ends. The excavation, PCC, foundation, concrete in solid/box abutment, hollow piers and abutment/pier caps for at least one abutment and two piers shall be taken up simultaneously. The hollow pier shall be executed by slip-form shuttering, etc.
4. **The bar chart in the document shows following activities:**
   i) Excavation for open foundation.
   ii) Piling.
   iii) Pile cap/foundation footing.
   iv) Substructure
   v) Bed block.
   vi) Earth work, and
   vii) Miscellaneous and finishing work

Therefore in the tender document no intention is reflected that investigations shall be done by construction contractor.

In order to resolve the knot the understanding of contract from legal point of view is necessary. A contract is defined as:

A contract is a *legally binding* or *valid* agreement between two parties. The law will consider a contract to be valid if the agreement contains all of the following elements:

1. offer and acceptance;

2. an intention between the parties to create binding relations;
3. consideration to be paid for the promise made;
4. legal *capacity* of the parties to act;
5. genuine *consent* of the parties; and
6. legality of the agreement.

An agreement that lacks one or more of the elements listed above is not a valid contract.

WHAT IS OFFER ?

An offer is a communication that gives the recipient the power to conclude a contract. The question of whether a party in fact made an offer is a common question in a contract case. The general rule is that it must be reasonable under the circumstances for the recipient to believe that the communication is an offer. The more definite the communication, the more likely it is to constitute an offer.

Offer is also defined as "an expression of willingness to contract on certain terms, made with the intention that it shall become binding as soon as it is accepted by the person to whom it is addressed", the "offeree". An offer is a statement of the terms on which the offeror is willing to be bound. It is the present contractual intent to be bound by a contract with **definite and certain terms** communicated to the offeree.

In a contract there must be an offer or a proposal which the person accepting has had an opportunity of considering and which when he accepts he knows, will form a binding contract. In other words, the proposer and acceptor must agree upon the same thing and in the same sense. Unless that is done, it is not a contract. The next thing which need explanation is offer or proposal. As to a proposal the **offeror must manifest or make known his intention of doing or not doing something,** and he must do so with the purpose of getting the offeree to assent to it. Here, intention is vital to determine whether his statement amounts to proposal.

Now we will examine the dispute between the parties from the angle of consent and offer. The distinction between "consent" and "promise" is that to promise is to commit to do or refrain from doing something. To consent to contract is to commit to be *legally* responsible for non performance of a promise. So consent is a commitment in addition to whatever moral commitment inheres in a promise.

From the tender document it can be easily inferred, as mentioned above and as witnessed at site by contractor that investigations by construction contractor was not the pre-intention. Neither the completion period of construction was designed for investigations as could be seen from bar chart in the contract. For geotechnical investigations separate time slot should have been provided, if it was the intention. Instead of indicating investigations as OPTIONAL, it should have been made as ' essential'. On the other hand bar chart shows that construction activity would commence within a week or two after issue of LOA. Nowhere directly or indirectly the contract condition conveys the intention of owner that drawings would be issued only after construction contractor had conducted the investigations. Therefore, not only impliedly but objectively, the construction activities were not contingent upon site investigations by the contractor. From the above discussion it is immensely clear and convincing that the contractor and owner had meetings of mind objectively and the contract created was valid one.This could be one interpretation. However, if the owner's intentions, as now revealed, was to issue design and drawings to contractor after conducting geotechnical investigations under construction contract, should other agency fail, then the contract was uncertain. And an uncertain contract (either this or that) is void on discovery u/s 29 of ICA which is reproduced below:

> **Section 29 of the ICA reads: "Agreements, the meaning of which is not certain or capable of being made certain are void"**: This section vindicates the view point since the contract is ambiguous with the different intentions of the owner. While making the promise and even now it is not clear if the owner would supply the drawings independent of geotechnical investigations done by contractor, or it is contingent upon investigations by contractor. It appears very plain and so does the contractor believe that supply of drawings was an independent activity as could be made out from the reading of various clauses and the bar chart in the contract. No one must have thought that agency would fail. Because of this in-built uncertainty the contractor remained at work site for considerable period, literally without work. Thus contractor was prevented from discharging his obligation. Thus the contract being uncertain is another view point.

Consent is said to be so caused when it would not have been given but for the existence of such coercion, undue influence, fraud, misrepresentation, or mistake.

Sometimes there may be apparent consent to the terms between the parties, real consent may not be found and hence the agreement negatived in the following circumstances:

i) Ambiguity, and
ii) Fundamental error as to the subject matter of the agreement.

In certain cases there may be all the usual external evidences of consent, but the apparent consent may have been given under a mistake which prevents formation of any real agreement. In the instant case contractor's consent was for the proposal which was nothing but tender document. But respondent was concealing a very vital fact which was not the subject matter of the proposal. Only after award of work he has let out his intentions which he had actively concealed. Thus the contractor's consent was not free but was caused by fraud which is defined u/s 18 of ICA. As such the contract was not valid *ab initio*. This is also another view point.

FRAUD DEFINED

"Fraud" means and includes any of the following acts committed by a party to a contract, or with his connivance, or by his agents, with intent to deceive another party thereto his agent, or to induce him to enter into the contract:

(1) the suggestion as a fact, of that which is not true, by one who does not believe it to be true;
(2) the active concealment of a fact by one having knowledge or belief of the fact;
(3) a promise made without any intention of performing it;
(4) any other act fitted to deceive; and
(5) any such act or omission as the law specially declares to be fraudulent.

Further, for a contract to be valid, there should be consent between the parties to contract. In this case contractor was under impression, as nothing contrary was mentioned, that immediately after issue of LOA drawings would be supplied whereas owner had in his mind that contractor would complete the investigations and based on that data design and drawings would be prepared as conveyed by owner to contractor. This thinking it appears is a later development after the agency had failed. Talking about the contract per se there was no meeting of minds; there was no common meaning of the contract and as such the contract was not valid.

According to Section 10 of the ICA, "all agreements are contracts if they are made by the free consent of parties competent to contract". Further section 13 of ICA reads: "two or more persons are said to consent when they agree upon the same thing in the same sense".

"FREE CONSENT" DEFINED

Consent is said to be free when it is not caused by :

(1) coercion, as defined in section 15,
(2) undue influence, as defined in section 16,
(3) fraud, as defined in section 17,
(4) misrepresentation, as defined in section 18, or
(5) mistake, subject to the provisions of section 20,21, and 22.

Mutual consent, which should also be a free consent, as defined in Section 13 and 14 of the ICA, is the sine qua non of a valid agreement. One of the essential elements which goes to constitute a free consent is that "*a thing is understood in the same sense by a party as is understood by the other party. It may often be that the parties may realise, after having entered into the agreement or after having signed the contract, that one of the matters which was essential to the agreement, was not understood by them in the same sense and that both of them were carrying totally different impressions of that matter at the time of entering into the agreement or executing the document. Such realisation would have the effect of invalidating the agreement under Section 20 of the Act. On such realisation, it can be legitimately said that the agreement was "discovered to be void". The words "discovered to be void", therefore, comprehend a situation in which the parties were suffering from a mistake of fact from the very beginning but had not realised, at the time of entering into the agreement or signing of the document, that they were suffering from any such mistake and had, therefore, acted bona fide on such agreement*". The agreement in such a case would be void from its inception, though discovered to be so at a much later stage.

An agreement, therefore, discovered to be void is one discovered to be not enforceable by law, and, on the language of the section would include an agreement that was void in that sense from its inception as distinct from a contract that becomes void." These observations were made by Supreme court of India in *Sri Tarsem Singh* v. *Sri Sukhminder Singh on 2 February, 1998.*

As explained earlier, the contract entered into shows ambiguity. The intention of owner and intention of contractor are different. There is no unanimity. Intentions of the promisor and promisee were not the same. They never intended the same thing in the same sense. Thus there was no meeting of minds and as such binding contract was not created between owner and contractor. This became apparent when contractor started looking for construction design and drawings. The contract must mean the same thing for the owner and the contractor which was not the situation here. Contractor never understood the contract terms in the manner in which owner intended them. Rightly so, because the intention of owner was concealed and some terms were subjective and not objective for contractor. There was indeed fundamental error in the transaction. And therefore the consent cannot be said to be genuine consent in legal terms. Hence the contract is void ab initio and repudiation of it by contractor is logical and legal. This is also one interpretation.

Now, at no stage the offer included the work of another agency which was engaged in geotechnical investigations at the bridge site. Such an intention was never expressed. The proposal was the schedule of work incorporated in the tender document. The assertion of the respondent that contractor gave the report of geotechnical after four and a half month and only after that respondent could issue the drawing is to confuse the issue deliberately. It was never part of the contract to do the investigations which were entrusted to other agency. Rather owner was to supply drawings when contractor approached him. It is altogether a different matter that contractor obliged and completed the investigations as directed by respondent since the main agency had failed. The failure of main agency in completing its task in no way shifts the responsibility towards contractor. However, if this was the intention of the owner, which he did not manifest while giving the proposal, then surely he has played a fraud upon contractor as defined u/s 17 which is reproduced below:

Thus, if we consider that intention of both parties was same, which indeed appears to be so, the issue of drawings was not contingent upon conducting geotechnical investigations by contractor and contractor had every right to repudiate the contract. The fault for no performance lies with owner. If we believe that second theory is correct, then there was no meeting of minds and therefore legal contract was not created. Analysis also indicates that it is a case of fraud u/s 17 of ICA since owner concealed the information.

THE PREVENTION PRINCIPLE

Most construction and engineering contracts require the contractor to complete the works by a specified date failing which the employer will be entitled to recover liquidated damages for delay at the rate stated in the contract. The contractor will only be relieved of its obligation to complete by the contractual deadline if an event occurs for which the contractor is entitled to an extension of time, but difficulties can arise if the employer causes delay to the completion of the works and the contract does not include a term providing for the award of an extension of time. Such a delay caused by the employer is often referred to as an 'act of prevention'.

The 'prevention principle' is a long established principle under law whereby a party may not enforce a contractual obligation against the other party where it has prevented the other party from performing that obligation. The prevention principle is closely aligned to the principle that no party may benefit from its own breach of contract.

In construction contracts, an employer's act of prevention could be either a breach of contract such as a failure to give access to site or a delay in issuing drawings or approvals, or a valid action ;for example instructing the contractor to perform additional works, or to suspend the works. In either case, if the contract does not provide for how the delay is to be dealt with, the employer will not be entitled to require the contractor to complete the works by the original contractual deadline and there will be no means in the contract for fixing a revised date. In such circumstances the original contractual deadline falls away and time becomes 'at large'.

If time is at large, the contractor is only required to complete the works within a reasonable period of time. However, this does not mean that the contractor has as much time as he wants to complete the works. The question of what will be a reasonable time for completion will be a matter of fact to be decided at the time the question arises and in light of all the circumstances. Invariably there will be a dispute between the employer and the contractor as to what is a reasonable time for completion.

Where time is at large, there will no longer be a fixed date from which liquidated damages can run and therefore the employer will lose its right to claim liquidated damages. This does not mean that the contractor is then relieved of all liability for delay; the employer will still be entitled to claim general damages if the contractor fails to complete the works within a reasonable time.

Given the complexity of construction projects, it is easy to see that without an extension of time clause an employer would almost invariably commit an act of prevention at some point during the contract.

Most standard forms of contract provide that the contractor will be entitled to an extension of time in the event of instructed variations or changes, suspensions, force majeure and changes in law. Depending on the type of project, and the parties' respective bargaining power, the contractor may also succeed in adding certain other neutral events to the list of events giving rise to an extension of time.

If time becomes at large under a construction contract as a result of an employer's act of prevention, this is likely to cause problems for the contractor as well as the employer. A well-drafted extension of time clause will benefit both parties by:

- Maintaining a contractual time for completion;
- Preserving the employer's right to liquidated damages;
- Giving the contractor relief from its strict duty to complete the works on time in the event that delays are caused by specified neutral events; and
- Construction contracts typically entitle contractors to an extension of time (an "EOT") to the contractually fixed completion date to the full extent of any delay for which the owner is contractually responsible. If a delay is caused for which the owner is responsible, the contractor will normally be entitled to an equivalent additional period of time to complete.

The "prevention principle" operates to invalidate a liquidated damages clause where the owner causes completion of the works to be delayed, leaving the owner to prove its damages at large, and the contractor obliged only to complete the works within a reasonable time. The exception to the operation of the prevention principle is where the contract contains a clear and specific mechanism for extending time for owner-caused delays, and the owner has validly extended time. The prevention principle is founded upon the broader notion that a party cannot impose a contractual obligation if that party has prevented the other party from complying with the obligation. The prevention principle is "grounded upon considerations of fairness and reasonableness". Many standard forms of construction contracts require a contractor to give notice of an event which may entitle him to an extension of time, with the rationale being that early notice enables the owner to verify the claim and to monitor the event and its impact upon progress of the work.

Most contractual arrangements contain a scope of works, a completion date and financial consequences for failing to complete by that completion date i.e. liquidated damages. However, if the scope of work is changed by the Employer such that the Contractor's progress of the works is delayed, or the Employer causes any other delay with the result that the Contractor misses the completion date, the Employer would be unable to apply the financial consequences as it was the Employer's actions that prevented the Contractor fulfilling his side of the bargain and completing by the contract date.

Prevention doctrine is a common-law principle of contract law which says that a contracting party has an implied duty not to do anything that prevents the other party from performing its obligation. A party who prevents performance of a contract may not complain of such non performance.

The prevention doctrine entails that, where one party to a contract takes an action that prevents the other party from being able to fulfill a condition precedent to that contract, the first party may not use its own action as a mechanism for avoiding performance of its contractual obligations. Prevention doctrine is also known as prevention of performance doctrine. The prevention principle can be used as an effective tool in arbitration to ward off levy of liquidated damages and reasonable extension of time without resorting to termination of contract by employer.

APPENDIX

INDIAN BARE ACTS

THE ARBITRATION AND CONCILIATION ACT, 1996

No. 26 of 1996

[16th August, 1996]

WHEREAS the United Nations Commission on International Trade Law (UNCITRAL) has adopted the UNCITRAL Model Law on International Commercial Arbitration in 1985:

AND WHEREAS the General Assembly of the United Nations has recommended that all countries give due consideration to the said Model Law, in view of the desirability of uniformity of the law of arbitral procedures and the specific needs of international commercial arbitration practice;

AND WHEREAS the UNCITRAL has adopted the UNCITRAL Conciliation Rules in 1980;

AND WHEREAS the General Assembly of the United Nations has recommended the use of the said Rules in cases where a dispute arises in the context of international commercial relations and the parties seek an amicable settlement of that dispute by recourse to conciliation;

AND WHEREAS the said Model Law and Rules make significant contribution to the establishment of a unified legal framework for the fair and efficient settlement of disputes arising in international commercial relations;

AND WHEREAS it is expedient to make law respecting arbitration and conciliation, taking into account the aforesaid Model Law and Rules; BE it enacted by Parliament in the Forty-seventh Year of the Republic of India as follows:

PRELIMINARY

1. Short title, extent and commencement.—(1) This Act may be called the Arbitration and Conciliation Act, 1996.

(2) It extends to the whole of India: Provided that Parts, I, III and IV shall extend to the State of Jammu and Kashmir only in so far as they relate to international commercial arbitration or, as the case may be, international commercial conciliation.

Explanation.—In this sub-section, the expression "international commercial conciliation" shall have the same meaning as the expression "international commercial arbitration" in clause (f) of sub-section (1) of section 2, subject to the modification that for the word "arbitration" occurring therein, the word "conciliation" shall be substituted.

(3) It shall come into force on such date as the Central Government may, by notification in the Official Gazette, appoint.

PART I – ARBITRATION

CHAPTER I
GENERAL PROVISIONS

2. Definitions.—(1) In this Part, unless the context otherwise requires :

(a) "arbitration" means any arbitration whether or not administered by permanent arbitral institution;

(b) "arbitration agreement" means an agreement referred to in section 7;

(c) "arbitral award" includes an interim award;

(d) "arbitral tribunal" means a sole arbitrator or a panel of arbitrators;

(e) "Court" means the principal Civil Court of original jurisdiction in a district, and includes the High Court in exercise of its ordinary original civil jurisdiction, having jurisdiction to decide the questions forming the subject-matter of the arbitration if the same had been the subject-matter of a suit, but does not include any civil court of a grade inferior to such principal Civil Court, or any Court of Small Causes; (f) "international commercial arbitration" means an arbitration relating to disputes arising out of legal relationships, whether contractual or not, considered as commercial under the law in force in India and where at least one of the parties is :

(i) an individual who is a national of, or habitually resident in, any country other than India; or

(ii) a body corporate which is incorporated in any country other than India; or

(iii) a company or an association or a body of individuals whose central management and control is exercised in any country other than India; or

(iv) the Government of a foreign country;

(g) "legal represntative" means a person who in law represents the estate of a deceased person, and includes any person who intermeddles with the estate of the deceased, and, where a party acts in a representative character, the person on whom the estate devolves on the death of the party so acting;

(h) "party" means a party to an arbitration agreement.

(2) This Part shall apply where the place of arbitration is in India.

(3) This Part shall not affect any other law for the time being in force by virtue of which certain disputes may not be submitted to arbitration.

(4) This Part except sub-section (1) of section 40, sections 41 and 43 shall apply to every arbitration under any other enactment for the time being in force, as if the arbitration were pursuant to an arbitration agreement and as if that other enactment were an arbitration agreement, except in so far as the provision of this Part are inconsistent with that other enactment or with any rules made thereunder;

(5) Subject to the provisions of sub-section (4), and save in so far as is otherwise provided by any law for the time being in force or in any agreement in force between India and any other country or countries, this Part shall apply to all arbitrations and to all proceedings relating thereto.

(6) Where this Part, except section 28, leaves the parties free to determine a certain issue, that freedom shall include the right of the parties to authorise any person including an institution, to determine that issue.

(7) An arbitral award made under this Part shall be considered domestic award.

(8) Where this Part—

(a) refers to the fact that the parties have agreed or that they may agree, or
(b) in any other way refers to an agreement of the parties, that agreement shall include any arbitration rules referred to in that agreement.

(9) Where this Part, other than clause (a) of section 25 or clause (a) of sub-section (2) of section 32, refers to a claim, it shall also apply to a counterclaim, and where it refers to a defence, it shall also apply to a defence to that counterclaim.

3. Receipt of written communications.—(1) Unless otherwise agreed by the parties—

(a) any written communication is deemed to have been received if it is delivered to the addressee personally or at his place of business, habitual residence or mailing address, and
(b) if none of the places referred to in clause (a) can be found after making a reasonable inquiry, a written communication is deemed to have been received if it is sent to the addressee's last known place of business, habitual residence or mailing address by registered letter or by any other means which provides a record of the attempt to deliver it.

(2) The communication is deemed to have been received on the day it is so delivered.

(3) This section does not apply to written communications in respect of proceedings of any judicial authority.

4. Waiver of right to object.—A party who knows that—

(a) any provision of this Part from which the parties may derogate, or
(b) any requirement under the arbitration agreement, has not been complied with and yet proceeds with the arbitration without stating his objection to such non-compliance without undue delay or, if a time limit is provided for stating that objection, within that period of time, shall be deemed to have waived his right to so object.

5. Extent of judicial intervention.—Notwithstanding anything contained in any other law for the time being in force, in matters governed by this Part, no judicial authority shall intervene except where so provided in this Part.

6. Administrative assistance.—In order to facilitate the conduct of the arbitral proceedings, the parties, or the arbitral tribunal with the consent of the parties, may arrange for administrative assistance by a suitable institution or person.

CHAPTER II
ARBITRATION AGREEMENT

7. Arbitration agreement.—(1) In this Part, "arbitration agreement" means an agreement by the parties to submit to arbitration all or certain disputes which have arisen or which may arise between them in respect of a defined legal relationship, whether contractual or not.

(2) An arbitration agreement may be in the form of an arbitration clause in a contract or in the form of a separate agreement.

(3) An arbitration agreement shall be in writing.

(4) An arbitration agreement is in writing if it is contained in—

(a) a document signed by the parties;

(b) an exchange of letters, telex, telegrams or other means of telecommunication which provide a record of the agreement; or

(c) an exchange of statements of claim and defence in which the existence of the agreement is alleged by one party and not denied by the other.

(5) The reference in a contract to a document containing an arbitration clause constitutes an arbitration agreement if the contract is in writing and the reference is such as to make that arbitration clause part of the contract.

8. Power to refer parties to arbitration where there is an arbitration agreement.—(1) A judicial authority before which an action is brought in a matter which is the subject of an arbitration agreement shall, if a party so applies not later than when submitting his first statement on the substance of the dispute, refer the parties to arbitration.

(2) The application referred to in sub-section (1) shall not be entertained unless it is accompanied by the original arbitration agreement or a duly certified copy thereof.

(3) Notwithstanding that an application has been made under sub-section (1) and that the issue is pending before the judicial authority, an arbitration may be commenced or continued and an arbitral award made.

9. Interim measures etc.by Court.—A party may, before, or during arbitral proceedings or at any time after the making of the arbitral award but before it is enforced in accordance with section 36, apply to a court—

(i) for the appointment of a guardian for a minor or person of unsound mind for the purposes of arbitral proceedings; or

(ii) for an interim measure or protection in respect of any of the following matters, namely:

(a) the preservation, interim custody or sale of any goods which are the subject-matter of the arbitration agreement;

(b) securing the amount in dispute in the arbitration;

(c) the detention, preservation or inspection of any property or thing which is the subject-matter of the dispute in arbitration, or as to which any question may arise therein and authorising for any of the aforesaid purposes any person to enter upon any land or building in the possession of any party or authorising any samples to be taken or any observation to be made, or experiment to be tried, which may be necessary or expedient for the purpose of obtaining full information or evidence;

(d) interim injunction or the appointment of a receiver;

(e) such other interim measure of protection as may appear to the Court to be just and convenient, and the Court shall have the same power for making orders as it has for the purpose of, and in relation to, any proceedings before it.

CHAPTER III
COMPOSITION OF ARBITRAL TRIBUNAL

10. Number of arbitrators.—(1) The parties are free to determine the number of arbitrators, provided that such number shall not be an even number.

(2) Failing the determination referred to in sub-section (1), the arbitral tribunal shall consist of a sole arbitrator.

11. Appointment of arbitrators.—(1) A person of any nationality may be an arbitrator, unless otherwise agreed by the parties.

(2) Subject to sub-section (6), the parties are free to agree on a procedure for appointing the arbitrator or arbitrators.

(3) Failing any agreement referred to in sub-section (2), in an arbitration with three arbitrators, each party shall appoint one arbitrator, and the two appointed arbitrators shall appoint the third arbitrator who shall act as the presiding arbitrator.

(4) If the appointment procedure in sub-section (3) applies and—

(a) a party fails to appoint an arbitrator within thirty days from the receipt of a request to do so from the other party; or

(b) the two appointed arbitrators fail to agree on the third arbitrator within thirty days from the date of their appointment, the appointment shall be made, upon request of a party, by the Chief Justice or any person or institution designated by him.

(5) Failing any agreement referred to in sub-section (2), in an arbitration with a sole arbitrator, if the parties fail to agree on the arbitrator within thirty days from receipt of a request by one party from the other party to so agree the appointment shall be made, upon request of a party, by the Chief Justice or any person or institution designated by him.

(6) Where, under an appointment procedure agreed upon by the parties—

(a) a party fails to act as required under that procedure; or

(b) the parties, or the two appointed arbitrators, fail to reach an agreement expected of them under that procedure; or

(c) a person, including an institution, fails to perform any function entrusted to him or it under that procedure, a party may request the Chief Justice or any person or institution designated by him to take the necessary measure, unless the agreement on the appointment procedure provides other means for securing the appointment.

(7) A decision on a matter entrusted by sub-section (4) or sub-section (5) or sub-section (6) to the Chief Justice or the person or institution designated by him is final.

(8) The Chief Justice or the person or institution designated by him, in appointing an arbitrator, shall have due regard to—

(a) any qualifications required of the arbitrator by the agreement of the parties and

(b) other considerations as are likely to secure the appointment of an independent and impartial arbitrator.

(9) In the case of appointment of sole or third arbitrator in an international commercial arbitration, the Chief Justice of India or the person or institution designated by him may appoint an arbitrator of a nationality other than the nationalities of the parties where the parties belong to different nationalities.

(10) The Chief Justice may make such scheme as he may deem appropriate for dealing with matters entrusted by sub-section (4) or sub-section (5) or sub-section (6) to him.

(11) Where more than one request has been made under sub-section (4) or sub-section (5) or sub-section (6) to the Chief Justices of different High Courts or their designates, the Chief Justice or his designate to whom the request has been first made under the relevant sub-section shall alone be competent to decide on the request.

(12) (a) Where the matters referred to in sub-sections (4), (5), (6), (7), (8) and (10) arise in an international commercial arbitration the reference to "Chief Justice" in those sub-sections shall be construed as a reference to the "Chief Justice of India". (b) Where the matters referred to in sub-sections (4), (5), (6), (7), (8) and (10) arise in any other arbitration, the reference to "Chief Justice" in those sub-section shall be construed as a reference to, the Chief Justice of the High Court within whose local limits the principal Civil Court referred to in clause (e) of sub-section (1) of section 2 is situate and, where the High Court itself is the "Court referred to in that clause, to the Chief Justice of that High Court.

12. Grounds for challenge.—(1) When a person is approached in connection with his possible appointment as an arbitrator, he shall disclose in writing any circumstances likely to give rise to justifiable doubts as to his independence or impartiality.

(2) An arbitrator, from the time of his appointment and throughout the arbitral proceedings, shall, without delay, disclose to the parties in writing any circumstances referred to in sub-section (1) unless they have already been informed of them by him.

(3) An arbitrator may be challenged only if—

(a) circumstances exist that give rise to justifiable doubts as to his independence or impartiality, or

(b) he does not possess the qualifications agreed to by the parties.

(4) A party may challenge an arbitrator appointed by him, or in whose appointment he has participated, only for reasons of which he becomes aware after the appointment has been made.

13. Challenge procedure.—(1) Subject to sub-section (4), the parties are free to agree on a procedure for challenging an arbitrator.

(2) Failing any agreement referred to in sub-section (1), a party who intends to challenge an arbitrator shall, within fifteen days becoming aware of the constitution of the arbitral tribunal or after becoming aware of any circumstances referred to in sub-section (3) of section 12, send a written statement of the reasons for the challenge to the arbitral tribunal.

(3) Unless the arbitrator challenged under sub-section (2) withdraws from his office or the other party agrees to the challenge, the arbitral tribunal shall decide on the challenge.

(4) If a challenge under any procedure agreed upon by the parties or under the procedure under sub-section (2) is not successful, the arbitral tribunal shall continue the arbitral proceedings and make an arbitral award.

(5) Where an arbitral award is made under sub-section (4), the party challenging the arbitrator may make an application for setting aside such an arbitral award in accordance with section 34.

(6) Where an arbitral award is set aside on an application made under sub-section (5), the Court may decide as to whether the arbitrator who is challenged is entitled to any fees.

14. Failure or impossibility to act.—(1) The mandate of an arbitrator shall terminate if—

(a) he becomes de jure or de facto unable to perform his functions or for other reasons fails to act without undue delay; and

(b) he withdraws from his office or the parties agree to the termination of his mandate.

(2) If a controversy remains concerning any of the grounds referred to in clause (a) of sub-section (1), a party may, unless otherwise agreed by the parties, apply to the Court to decide on the termination of the mandate.

(3) If, under this section or sub-section (3) of section 13, an arbitrator withdraws from his office or a party agrees to the termination of the mandate of an arbitrator, it shall not imply acceptance of the validity of any ground referred to in this section or sub-section (3) of section 12.

15. Termination of mandate and substitution of arbitrator.—(1) In addition to the circumstances referred to in section 13 or section 14, the mandate of an arbitrator shall terminate—

(a) where he withdraws from office for any reason; or
(b) by or pursuant to agreement of the parties.

(2) Where the mandate of an artibrator terminates, a substitute arbitrator shall be appointed according to the rules that were applicable to the appointment of the arbitrator being replaced.

(3) Unless otherwise agreed by the parties, where an arbitrator is replaced under sub-section (2), any hearings previously held may be repeated at the discretion of the arbitral tribunal. (4) Unless otherwise agreed by the parties, an order or ruling of the arbitral tribunal made prior to the replacement of an arbitrator under this section shall not b invalid solely because there has been a change in the composition of the arbitral tribunal.

CHAPTER IV
JURISDICTION OF ARBITRAL TRIBUNALS

16. Competence of arbitral tribunal to rule on its jurisdiction.—(1) The arbitral tribunal may rule on its own jurisdiction, including ruling on any objections with respect to the existence or validity of the arbitration agreement, and for that purpose—

(a) an arbitration clause which forms part of a contract shall be treated as an agreement independent of the other terms of the contract; and
(b) a decision by the arbitral tribunal that the contract is null and void shall not entail ipso jure the invalidity of the arbitration clause.

(2) A plea that the arbitral tribunal does not have jurisdiction shall be raised not later than the submission of the statement of defence; however, a party shall not be precluded from raising such a plea merely because that he has appointed, or participated in the appointment of, an arbitrator.

(3) A plea that the arbitral tribunal is exceeding the scope of its authority shall he raised as soon as the matter alleged to be beyond the scope of its authority is raised during the arbitral proceedings.

(4) The arbitral tribunal may, in either of the cases referred to in sub-section (2) or sub-section (3), admit a later plea if it considers the delay justified.

(5) The arbitral tribunal shall decide on a plea referred to in sub-section (2) or sub-section (3) and, where the arbitral tribunal takes a decision rejecting the plea, continue with the arbitral proceedings and make an arbitral award.

(6) A party aggrieved by such an arbitral award may make an application for setting aside such an arbitral award in accordance with section 34.

17. Interim measures ordered by arbitral tribunal.—(1) Unless otherwise agreed by the parties, the arbitral tribunal may, at the request of a party, order a party to take any interim measure of protection as the arbitral tribunal may consider necessary in respect of the subject matter of the dispute.

(2) The arbitral tribunal may require a party to provide appropriate security in connection with a measure ordered under sub-section (1).

CHAPTER V
CONDUCT OF ARBITRAL PROCEEDINGS

18. Equal treatment of parties.—The parties shall be treated with equality and each party shall be given a full opportunity to present his case.

19. Determination of rules of procedure.—(1) The arbitral tribunal shall not be bound by the Code of Civil Procedure, 1908 or the Indian Evidence Act, 1872.

(2) Subject to this Part, the parties are free to agree on the procedure to be followed by the arbitral tribunal in conducting its proceedings.

(3) Failing any agreement referred to in sub-section (2), the arbitral tribunal may, subject to this Part, conduct the proceedings in the manner it considers appropriate.

(4) The power of the arbitral tribunal under sub-section (3) includes the power to determine the admissibility, relevance, materiality and weight of any evidence.

20. Place of arbitration.—(1) The parties are free to agree on the place of arbitration.

(2) Failing any agreement referred to in sub-section (1), the place of arbitration shall be determined by the arbitral tribunal having regard to the circumstances of the case, including the convenience of the parties. (3) Notwithstanding sub-section (1) or sub-section (2), the arbitral tribunal may, unless otherwise agreed by the parties, meet at any place it considers appropriate for consultation among its members, for hearing winners, experts or the parties, or for inspection of documents, goods or other property.

21. Commencement of arbitral proceedings.—Unless otherwise agreed by the parties, the arbitral proceedings, in respect of a particular dispute commence on the date on which a request for that dispute to be referred to arbitration is received by the respondent.

22. Language.—(1) The parties are free to agree upon the language or languages to is used in the arbitral proceedings.

(2) Failing any agreement referred to in sub-section (1), the arbitral tribunal shall determine the language or languages to be used in the arbitral proceedings.

(3) The agreement or determination, unless otherwise specified, shall apply to any written statement by a party, any hearing and any arbitral award, decision or other communication by the arbitral tribunal.

(4) The arbitral tribunal may order that any documentary evidence shall be accompanied by a translation into the languages agreed upon by the parties or determined by the arbitral tribunal.

23. Statements of claim and defence.—(1) Within the period of time agreed upon by the parties or determined by the arbitral tribunal, the claimant shall state the facts supporting his claim, the points at issue and the relief or remedy sought, and the respondent shall state his defence in respect of these particulars, unless the parties have otherwise agreed as to the required elements of those statements.

(2) The parties may submit with their statements all documents they consider to be relevant or may add a reference to the documents or other evidence they will submit.

(3) Unless otherwise agreed by the parties, either party may amend or supplement his claim or defence during the course of the arbitral proceedings, unless the arbitral tribunal considers it inappropriate to allow the amendment or supplement having regard to the delay in making it.

24. Hearings and written proceedings.—(1) Unless otherwise agreed by the parties, the arbitral tribunal shall decide whether to hold oral hearings for the presentation of evidence or for oral argument, or whether the proceedings shall be conducted on the basis of documents an other materials:

Provided that the arbitral tribunal shall hold hearings, at an appropriate stage of the proceedings, on a request by a party, unless the parties have agreed that no oral hearing shall be held.

(2) The parties shall be given sufficient advance notice of any hearing and of any meeting of the arbitral tribunal for the purposes of inspection of documents, goods or other property.

(3) All statements, documents or other information supplied to, or applications made to, the arbitral tribunal by one party shall be communicated to the other party, and any expert report or evidentiary document on which the arbitral tribunal may rely in making its decision shall be communicated to the parties.

25. Default of a party.—Unless otherwise agreed by the parties, where, without showing sufficient cause—

(a) the claimant fails to communicate his statement of claim in accordance with sub-section (1) of section 23, the arbitral tribunal shall terminate the proceedings;

(b) the respondent fails to communicate his statement of defence in accordance with sub-section (1) of section 23, the arbitral tribunal shall continue the proceedings without treating that failure in itself as an admission of the allegations by the claimant.

(c) a party fails to appear at an oral hearing or to produce documentary evidence, the arbitral tribunal may continue the proceedings and make the arbitral award on the evidence before it.

26. Expert appointed by arbitral tribunal.—(1) Unless otherwise agreed by the parties, the arbitral tribunal may—

(a) appoint one or more experts to report to it on specific issues to be determined by the arbitral tribunal, and

(b) require a party to give the expert any relevant information or to produce, or to provide access to, any relevant documents, goods or other property for his inspection.

(2) Unless otherwise agreed by the parties, if a party so requests or if the arbitral tribunal considers it necessary, the expert shall, after delivery of his written or oral report, participate on an oral hearing

where the parties have the opportunity to put questions to him and to present expert witnesses in order to testify on the points at issue.

(3) Unless otherwise agreed by the parties, the expert shall, on the request of a party, make available to that party for examination all documents, goods or other property in the possession of the expert with which he was provided in order to prepare his report.

27. Court assistance in taking evidence.—(1) The arbitral tribunal, or a party with the approval of the arbitral tribunal, may apply to the Court for assistance in taking evidence.

(2) The application shall specify—

(a) the names and addresses of the parties and the arbitrators.

(b) the general nature of the claim and the relief sought;

(c) the evidence to the obtained, in particular—

(i) the name and address of any person to be heard as witness or expert witness and a statement of the subject-matter of the testimony required;

(ii) the description of an document to be produced or property to be inspected.

(3) The Court may, within its competence and according to its rules on taking evidence, execute the request or ordering that the evidence be provided directly to the arbitral tribunal.

(4) The Court may, while making or order under sub-section (3), issue the same processes to witnesses as it may issue in suits tried before it.

(5) Persons failing to attend in accordance with such process, or making any other fault, or refusing to give their evidence, or guilty of any contempt to the arbitral tribunal during the conduct of arbitral proceedings, shall be subject to the like disadvantages, penalties and punishments by order of the Court on the representation of the arbitral tribunal as they would incur for the likeoffences is suits tried before the Court.

(6) In this section the expression "Processes" includes summonses and commissions for the examination of witnesses and summonses to produce documents.

CHAPTER VI
MAKING OF ARBITRAL AWARD AND TERMINATION OF PROCEEDINGS

28. Rules applicable to substance of dispute.—(1) Where the place of arbitration is situate in India—

(a) in an arbitration other than an international commercial arbitration, the arbitral tribunal shall decide the dispute submitted to arbitration in accordance with the substantive law for the time being in force in India;

(b) in international commercial arbitration—

(i) the arbitral tribunal shall decided the dispute in accordance with the rules of law designated by the parties as applicable to the substance of the dispute;

(ii) any designation by the parties of the law or legal system of a given country shall be construed, unless otherwise expressed, as directly referring to the substantive law of that country and not to its conflict of laws rules;

(iii) failing any designation of the law under clause (a) by the parties, the arbitral tribunal shall apply the rules of law it considers to be appropriate given all the circumstances surrounding the dispute.

(2) The arbitral tribunal shall decide ex aequo et bono or as amiable compositeur only if the parties have expressly authorised it to do so.

(3) In all cases, the arbitral tribunal shall decide in accordance with the terms of the contract and shall take into account the usages of the trade applicable to the transaction.

29. Decision making by panel of arbitrators.—(1) Unless otherwise agreed by the parties, in arbitral proceedings with more than one arbitrator, any decision of the arbitral tribunal shall be made by a majority of all its members.

(2) Notwithstanding sub-section (1), if authorised by the parties or all the members of the arbitral tribunal, questions of procedure may be decided by the presiding arbitrator.

30. Settlement.—(1) It is not incompatible with an arbitration agreement for an arbitral tribunal to encourage settlement of the dispute and, with the agreement of the parties, the arbitral tribunal may use mediation, conciliation or other procedures at any time during the arbitral proceedings to encourage settlement.

(2) If, during arbitral proceedings, the parties settle the dispute, the arbitral tribunal shall terminate the proceedings and, if requested by the parties and not objected to by the arbitral tribunal, record the settlement in the form of an arbitral award on agreed terms.

(3) An arbitral award on agreed terms shall be made in accordance with section 31 and shall state that it is an arbitral award.

(4) An arbitral award on agreed terms shall have the same status and effect as any other arbitral award on the substance of the dispute.

31. Form and contents of arbitral award.—(1) An arbitral award shall be made in writing and shall be signed by the members of the arbitral tribunal.

(2) For the purposes of sub-section (1), in arbitral proceedings with more than one arbitrator, the signatures of the majority of all the members of the arbitral tribunal shall be sufficient so long as the reason for any omitted signature is stated.

(3) The arbitral award shall state the reasons upon which it is based, unless—

(a) the parties have agreed that no reasons are to be given, or
(b) the award is an arbitral award on agreed terms under section 30.

(4) The arbitral award shall state its date and the place of arbitration as determined in accordance with section 20 and the award shall be deemed to have been made at that place.

(5) After the arbitral award is made, a signed copy shall be delivered to each party.

(6) The arbitral tribunal may, at any time during the arbitral proceedings, make an interim arbitral award on any matter with respect to which it may make a final arbitral award.

(7) (a) Unless otherwise agreed by the parties, where and in so far as an arbitral award is for the payment of money, the arbitral tribunal may include in the sum for which the award is made interest, at such rate as it deems reasonable, on the whole or any part of the money, for the whole or any part of the period between the date on which the cause of action arose and the date on whichthe award is made.

(b) A sum directed to be paid by an arbitral award shall, unless the award otherwise directs, carry interest at the rate of eighteen per centum per annum from the date of the award to the date of payment.

(8) Unless otherwise agreed by the parties—

(a) the costs of an arbitration shall be fixed by the arbitral tribunal;
(b) the arbitral tribunal shall specify—
    (i) the party entitled to costs,

(ii) the party who shall pay the costs,

(iii) the amount of costs or method of determining that amount, and

(iv) the manner in which the costs shall be paid.

Explanation—For the purpose of clause (a), "costs" means reasonable costs relating to—

(i) the fees and expenses of the arbitrators and witnesses,

(ii) legal fees and expenses,

(iii) any administration fees of the institution supervising the arbitration, and

(iv) any other expenses incurred in connection with the arbitral proceedings and the arbitral award.

32. Termination of proceedings.—(1) The arbitral proceedings shall be terminated by the final arbitral award or by an order of the arbitral tribunal under sub-section (2).

(2) The arbitral tribunal shall issue an order for the termination of the arbitral proceedings where—

(a) the claimant withdraws his claim, unless the respondent objects to the order and the arbitral tribunal recognises a legitimate interest on his part in obtaining a final settlement of the dispute,

(b) the parties agree on the termination of the proceedings, or

(c) the arbitral tribunal finds that the continuation of the proceedings has for any other reason become unnecessary or impossible.

(3) Subject to section 33 and sub-section (4) of section 34, the mandate of the arbitral tribunal shall terminate with the termination of the arbitral proceedings.

33. Correction and interpretation of award; additional award.—(1) Within thirty days from the receipt of the arbitral award, unless another period of time has been agreed upon by the parties—

(a) a party, with notice to the other party, may request the arbitral tribunal to correct any computation errors, any electrical or typographical errors or any other errors of a similar nature occurring in the award;

(b) if so agreed by the parties, a party, with notice to the other party, may request the arbitral tribunal to give an interpretation of a specific point or part of the award.

(2) If the arbitral tribunal considers the request made under sub-section (1) to be justified, it shall make the correction or give the interpretation within thirty days from the receipt of the request and the interpretation shall form part of the arbitral award.

(3) The arbitral tribunal may correct and error of the type referred to in clause (a) of sub-section (1), on its own initiative, within thirty days from the date of the arbitral award.

(4) Unless otherwise agreed by the parties, a party with notice to the other party, may request, within thirty days from the receipt of the arbitral award, the arbitral tribunal to make an additional arbitral award as so claims presented in the arbitral proceedings but omitted from the arbitral award.

(5) If the arbitral tribunal considers the request made under sub-section (4) to be justified, it shall make the additional arbitral award within sixty days from the receipt of such request.

(6) The arbitral tribunal may extend, if necessary, the period of time within which it shall make a correction, give an interpretation or make an additional arbitral award under sub-section (2) or sub-section (5).

(7) Section 31 shall apply to a correction or interpretation of the arbitral award or to an additional arbitral award made under this section.

CHAPTER VII
RECOURSE AGAINST ARBITRAL AWARD

34. Application for setting aside arbitral award.—(1) Recourse to a Court against an arbitral award may be made only by an application for setting aside such award in accordance with sub-section (2) and sub-section (3).

(2) An arbitral award may be set aside by the Court only if—

(a) the party making the application furnishes proof that—

(i) a party was under some incapacity, or

(ii) the arbitration agreement is not valid under the law to which the parties have subjected it or, failing any indication thereon, under the law for the time being in force; or

(iii) the party making the application was not given proper notice of the appointment of an arbitrator or of the arbitral proceedings or was otherwise unable to present his case; or (iv) the arbitral award deals with a dispute not contemplated by or not falling within the terms of the submission to arbitration, or it contains decisions on matter beyond the scope of the submission to arbitration: Provided that, if the decisions on matters submitted to arbitration can be separated from those not so submitted, only that part of the arbitral award which contains decisions on matters not submitted to arbitration may be set aside; or

(v) the composition of the arbitral tribunal or the arbitral procedure was not in accordance with the agreement of the parties, unless such agreement was in conflict with a provision of this Part from which the parties cannot derogate, or, failing such agreement, was not in accordance with this Past; or

(b) the Court finds that—

(i) the subject-matter of the dispute is not capable of settlement by arbitration under the law for the time being in force, or

(ii) the arbitral award is in conflict with the public policy of India.

Explanation.—Without prejudice to the generality of sub-clause (ii), it is hereby declared, for the avoidance of any doubt, that an award is in conflict with the public policy of India if the making of the award was induced of affected by fraud or corruption or was in violation of section 75 or section 81.

(3) An application for setting aside may not be made after three months have elapsed from the date on which the party making that application had received the arbitral award, or, if a request had been made under section 33, from the date on which that request had been disposed of by the arbitral tribunal:

Provided that if the Court is satisfied that the applicant was prevented by sufficient cause from making the application within the said period of three months if may entertain the application within a further period of thirty days, but not thereafter.

(4) On receipt of an application under sub-section (1), the Court may, where it is appropriate and it is so requested by a party, adjourn

the proceedings for a period of time determined by it in order to give the arbitral tribunal an opportunity to resume the arbitral proceedings or to take such other action as in the opinion of arbitral tribunal will eliminate the grounds for setting aside the arbitral award.

CHAPTER VIII
FINALITY AND ENFORCEMENT OF ARBITRAL AWARDS

35. Finality of arbitral awards.—Subject to this Part an arbitral award shall be final and binding on the parties and persons claiming under them respectively.

36. Enforcement.—Where the time for making an application to set aside the arbitral award under award shall be endorsed under the Code of Civil Procedure, 1908 (5 of 1908) in the same manner as if it were a decree of the Court.

CHAPTER IX
APPEALS

37. Appealable orders.—(1) An appeal shall lie from the following orders (and from no others) to the Court authorised by law to hear appeals from original decrees of the Court passing the order, namely:

(a) granting or réfusing to grant any measure under section 9:
(b) setting aside or refusing to set aside an arbitral award under section 34.

(2) Appeal shall also lie to a court from an order of the arbitral tribunal—

(a) accepting the plea referred to in sub-section (2) or sub-section (3) of section 16; or
(b) granting or refusing to grant an interim measure under section 17.

(3) No second appeal shall lie from an order passed in appeal under this section, but nothing in this section shall affect or taken away any right to appeal to the Supreme Court.

CHAPTER X
MISCELLANEOUS

38. Deposits.—(1) The arbitral tribunal may fix the amount of the deposit or supplementary deposit, on the case may be, as an advance for the costs referred to in sub-section (8) of section 31, which it expects will be incurred in respect of the claim submitted to it:

Provided that where, apart from the claim, a counter-claim has been submitted to the arbitral tribunal, it may fix separate amount of deposit for the claim and counter-claim.

(2) The deposit referred to in sub-section (1) shall be payable in equal shares by the parties:

Provided that where one party fails to pay his share of the deposit, the other party may pay that share:

Provided further that where the other party also does not pay the aforesaid share in respect of the claim or the counter-claim, the arbitral tribunal may suspend or terminate the arbitral proceedings in respect of such claim or counter-claim, as the case may be.

(3) Upon termination of the arbitral proceedings, the arbitral tribunal shall render an accounting to the parties of the deposits received and shall return any unexpended balance to the party or parties, as the case may be.

39. Lien on arbitral award and deposits as to costs.— (1) Subject to the provisions of sub-section (2) and to any provision to the contrary in the arbitration, agreement, the arbitral tribunal shall have a lien on the arbitral award for any unpaid costs of the arbitration.

(2) If in any case an arbitral tribunal refuses to deliver its award except on payment of the costs demanded by it, the Court may, on an application in this behalf, order that the arbitral tribunal shall deliver the arbitral award to the applicant on payment into Court by the applicant of the costs demanded, and shall, after such inquiry, in any, as it thinks, fit, further order that out of the money so paid into Court there shall be paid to the arbitral tribunal by way of costs such sum as the Court may consider reasonable and that the balance of the money, if any, shall be refunded to the applicant.

(3) An application under sub-section (2) may be made by any party unless the fees demanded have been fixed by written agreement between him and the arbitral tribunal, and the arbitral tribunal shall be entitled to appear and be heard on any suchapplication.

(4) The Court may make such orders as it thinks fit respecting the costs of the arbitration where any question arises respecting such

costs and the arbitral award contains no sufficient provision concerning them.

40. Arbitration agreement not to be discharged by death of party thereto.—(1) An arbitration agreement shall not be discharged by the death of any party thereto either as respects the deceased or as respects any other party, but shall in such event by enforceable by or against the legal representative of the deceased.

(2) The mandate of an arbitrator shall not be terminated by the death of any party by whom he was appointed.

(3) Nothing in this section shall affect the operation of any law by virtue of which any right of action is extinguished by the death of a person.

41. Provisions in case of insolvency.—(1) Where it is provided by a term in a contract to which an insolvent is a party that any dispute arising thereout or in connection therewith shall be submitted to arbitration, the said term shall, if the receiver adopts the contract, be enforceable by or against him so far as it relates to any such dispute.

(2) Where a person who has been adjudged an insolvent had, before the commencement of the insolvency proceedings, become a party to a arbitration agreement, and any matter to which the agreement applies is required to be determined in connection with, or for the purposes of, the insolvency proceedings then, if the case is one to which sub-section (1) does not apply, any other party or the receiver may apply to the judicial authority having jurisdiction in the insolvency proceedings for an order directing that the matter in question shall be submitted to arbitration in accordance with the arbitration agreement , and the judicial authority may, if it is of opinion that, having regard to all the circumstances of the case, the matter ought to be determined by arbitration, make an order accordingly.

(3) In this section the expression "receiver" includes an Official Assignee.

42. Jurisdiction.—Notwithstanding anything contained elsewhere in this Part or in any other law for the time being in force, where with respect to an arbitration agreement any application under this Part has been made in a Court, that Court alone shall have jurisdiction over the arbitral proceedings and all subsequent applications arising out of that agreement and the arbitral proceedings shall be made in that Court and in no other Court.

43. Limitations.—(1) The Limitation Act, 1963 (36 of 1963), shall, apply to arbitrations as it applies to proceedings in court.

(2) For the purposes of this section and the Limitation Act, 1963 (36 of 1963), an arbitration shall be deemed to have commenced on the date referred in section 21.

(3) Where an arbitration agreement to submit further disputes to arbitration provides that any claim to which the agreement applies shall be barred unless some step to commence arbitral proceedings is taken within a time fixed by the agreement, and a dispute arises to which the agreement applies the Court, if it is of opinion that in the circumstances of the case undue hardship wouldotherwise be caused, and notwithstanding that the time so fixed has expired, may on such terms, if any, as the justice of the case may require, extend the time for such period as it thinks proper.

(4) Where the Court orders that an arbitral award be set aside, the period between the commencement of the arbitration and the date of the order of the Court shall be excluded in computing the time prescribed by the Limitation Act, 1963 (36 of 1963), for the commencement of the proceedings (including arbitration) with respect to the dispute so submitted.

PART II – ENFORCEMENT OF CERTAIN FOREIGN AWARDS

CHAPTER I
NEW YORK CONVENTION AWARDS

44. Definition.—In this Chapter, unless the context otherwise requires, "foreign award" means an arbitral award on differences between persons arising out of legal relationships, whether contractual or not, considered as commercial under the law in force in India, made on or after the 11th day of October, 1960—

(a) in pursuance of an agreement in writing for arbitration to which the Convention set forth in the First Schedule applies, and

(b) in one of such territories as the Central Government, being satisfied that reciprocal provisions have been made may, by notification in the Official Gazette, declare to be territories to which the said Convention applies.

45. Power of judicial authority to refer parties to arbitration.—Notwithstanding anything contained in Part I or in the Code of Civil Procedure, 1908 (5 of 1908), a judicial authority, when seized of an action in a matter in respect of which the parties have made an agreement referred to in section 44, shall, at the request of one of the parties or any person claiming through or under him, refer the parties to arbitration, unless it finds that the said agreement is null and void, inoperative or incapable of being performed.

46. When foreign award binding.—Any foreign award which would be enforceable under this Chapter shall be treated as binding for all purposes on the persons as between whom it was made, and may accordingly be relied on by any of those persons by way of defence, set off or otherwise in any legal proceedings in India and any references in this Chapter to enforcing a foreign award shall be construed as including references to relying on an award.

47. Evidence.—(1) The party applying for the enforcement of a foreign award shall, at the time of the application, produce before the court—

(a) the original award or a copy thereof, duly authenticated in the manner required by the law of the country in which it was made;
(b) the original agreement for arbitration or a duly certified copy thereof; and
(c) such evidence as may be necessary to prove that the aware is a foreign award.

(2) If the award or agreement to be produced under sub-section (1) is in a foreign language, the party seeking to enforce the award shall produce a translation into English certified as correct by a diplomatic or consular agent of the country to which that party belongs or certified as correct in such other manner as may be sufficient according to the law in force in India.

Explanation—In this section and all the following sections of this Chapter, "Court" means the principal Civil Court of original jurisdiction in a district, and includes the High Court in exercise of its ordinary original civil jurisdiction, having jurisdiction over the subject-matter of the award if the same had been the subject-matter of a suit, but does not include any civil court of a grade inferior to such principal Civil Court, or any Court of Small Causes.

48. Conditions for enforcement of foreign awards.—(1) Enforcement of a foreign award may be refused, at the request of the party against whom it is invoked, only if that party furnishes to the court proof that—

(a) the parties to the agreement referred to in section 44 were, under the law applicable to them, under some incapacity, or the said agreement is not valid under the law to which the parties have subjected it or, failing any indication thereon, under the law of the country where the award was made; or

(b) the party against whom the award is invoked was not given proper notice of the appointment of the arbitrator or of the arbitral proceedings or was otherwise unable to present his case; or

(c) the award deals with a difference not contemplated by or not falling within the terms of the submission to arbitration, or it contains decisions on matters beyond the scope of the submission to arbitration.

Provided that, if the decisions on matters submitted to arbitration can be separated from those not so submitted, that part of the award which contains decisions on matters submitted to arbitration may be enforced; or

(d) the composition of the arbitral authority or the arbitral procedure was not in accordance with the agreement of the parties, or, failing such agreement, was not in accordance with the law of the country where the arbitration took place; or

(e) the award has not yet become binding on the parties, or has been set aside or suspended by a competent authority of the country in which, or under the law of which, that award was made.

(2) Enforcement of an arbitral award may also be refused if the court finds that—

(a) the subject-matter of the difference is not capable of settlement by arbitration under the law of India; or

(b) the enforcement of the award would be contrary to the public policy of India.

Explanation.—Without prejudice to the generality of clause (b), it is hereby declared, for the avoidance of any doubt, that an award is in conflict with the public policy of India if the making of the award was induced or affected by fraud or corruption.

(3) If an application for the setting aside or suspension of the award has been made to a competent authority referred to in clause (e) of sub-section (1) the Court may, if it considers it proper, adjourn the

decision on the enforcement of the award and may also, on the application of the party claiming enforcement of the award, order the other party to give suitable security.

49. Enforcement of foreign awards.—Where the Court is satisfied that the foreign award is enforceable under this Chapter, the award shall be deemed to be a decree of that Court.

50. Appealable orders.—(1) An appeal shall lie from the order refusing to—

(a) refer the parties to arbitration under section 45;
(b) enforce a foreign award under section 48, to the court authorised by law to hear appeals from such order.

(2) No second appeal shall lie from an order passed in appeal under this section, but nothing in this section shall affect or take away any right to appeal to the Supreme Court.

51. Saving.—Nothing in this Chapter shall prejudice any rights which any person would have had of enforcing in India of any award or of availing himself in India of any award or of availing himself in India of any award if this Chapter had not been enacted.

52. Chapter II not to apply.—Chapter II of this Part shall not apply in relation to foreign awards to which this Chapter applies.

CHAPTER II
GENEVA CONVENTION AWARDS

53. Interpretation.—In this Chapter "foreign award" means an arbitral award on differences relating to matters considered as

commercial under the law in force in India made after the 28th day of July, 1924—

(a) in pursuance of an agreement for arbitration to which the Protocol set forth in the Second Schedule applies, and
(b) between persons of whom one is subject to the jurisdiction of some one of such Powers as the Central Government, being satisfied that reciprocal provisions have been made, may, by notification in the Official Gazette, declare to be parties to the Convention set forth in the Third Schedule, and of whom the other is subject to the jurisdiction of some other of the Powers aforesaid, and
(c) in one of such territories as the Central Government, being satisfied that reciprocal provisions have been made, may, by like notification, declare to be territories to which the

said Convention applies, and for the purposes of this Chapter an award shall not be deemed to be final if any proceedings for the purpose of contesting the validity of the award are pending in the country in which it was made.

54. Power of judicial authority to refer parties to arbitration.—Notwithstanding anything contained in Part I or in the Code of Civil Procedure, 1908 (5 of 1908), a judicial authority, on being seized of a dispute regarding a contract made between persons to whom section 53 applies and including an arbitration agreement, whether referring to present or further differences, which is valid under that section and capable of being carried into effect, shall refer the parties on the application of either of them or any person claiming through or under him to the decision of the arbitrators and such reference shall not prejudice the competence of the judicial authority in case the agreement or the arbitration cannot proceed or becomes inoperative.

55. Foreign awards when binding.—Any foreign award which would be enforceable under this Chapter shall be treated as binding for all purposes on the persons as between whom it was made, and may accordingly be relied on by any of those persons by way of defence, set off or otherwise in any legal proceedings in India and any references in this Chapter to enforcing a foreign award shall be construed as including references to relying on an award.

56. Evidence.—(1) The party applying for the enforcement of a foreign award shall, at the time of application procedure before the Court—

(a) the original award or a copy thereof duly authenticated in the manner required by the law of the country in which it was made;

(b) evidence proving that the award has become final; and

(c) such evidence as may be necessary to prove that the conditions mentioned in clauses (a) and (c) of sub-section (1) of section 57 are satisfied.

(2) Where any document requiring to be produced under sub-section (1) is in a foreign language, the party seeking to enforce the award shall produce a translation into English certified as correct by a diplomatic or consular agent of the country to which that party

belongs or certified as correct in such other manner as may be sufficient according to the law in force in India.

Explanation.—In this section and all the following sections of this Chapter, "Court" means the principal Civil Court of original jurisdiction in a district, and includes the High Court in exercise of its ordinary original civil jurisdiction, having jurisdiction over the subject-matter of the award if the same had been the subject matter of a suit, but does not include any civil court of a grade inferior to such principal Civil Court, or any Court of Small Causes.

57. Conditions for enforcement of foreign awards.—(1) In order that a foreign award may be enforceable under this Chapter, it shall be necessary that—

(a) the award has been made in pursuance of a submission to arbitration which is valid under the law applicable thereto;
(b) the subject-matter of the award is capable of settlement by arbitration under the law of India;
(c) the award has been made by the arbitral tribunal provided for in the submission to arbitration or constituted in the manner agreed upon by the parties and in conformity with the law governing the arbitration procedure;
(d) the award has become final in the country in which it has been made, in the sense that it will not be considered as such if it is open to opposition or appeal or if it is proved that any proceedings for the purpose of contesting the validity of the award the pending;
(e) the enforcement of the award is not contrary to the public policy or the law of India.

Explanation.—Without prejudice to the generality of clause (e), it is hereby declared, for the avoidance, of any doubt, that an award is in conflict with the public policy of India if the making of the award was induced or affected by fraud or corruption.

(2) Even if the conditions laid down in sub-section (1) are fulfilled, enforcement of the award shall be refused if the Court is satisfied that—

(a) the award has been annulled in the country in which it was made;
(b) the party against whom it is sought to use the award was not given notice of the arbitration proceedings in sufficient time to enable him to present his case; or that, being under

a legal incapacity, he was not properly represented;

(c) the award does not deal with the differences contemplated by or falling within the terms of the submission to arbitration or that it contains decisions on matters beyond the scope for the submission or arbitration; Provided that if the award has not covered all the differences submitted to the arbitral tribunal, the Court may, if it thinks fit, postpone such enforcement or grant it subject to such guarantee as the Court may decide.

(3) If the party against whom the award has been made proves that under the law governing the arbitration procedure there is a ground, other than the grounds referred to in clauses (a) and (c) of sub-section (1) and clauses (b) and (c) of sub-section (2) entitling him to contest the validity of the award, the Court may, if it thinks fit, either refuse enforcement of the award or adjourn the consideration thereof, giving such party a reasonable time within which to have the award annulled by the competent tribunal.

58. Enforcement of foreign awards.—Where the Court is satisfied that the foreign award is enforceable under this Chapter, the award shall be deemed to be a decree of the Court.

59. Appealable orders.—(1) An appeal shall lie from the order refusing—

(a) to refer the parties to arbitration under section 54: and
(b) to enforce a foreign award under section 57,

(2) No second appeal shall lie from an order passed in appeal under this section, but nothing in this section shall affect or take away any right to appeal to the Supreme Court.

60. Saving.—Nothing in this Chapter shall prejudice any rights which any person would have had of enforcing in India of any award or of availing himself in India of any award if this Chapter had not been enacted.

61. Application and scope.—(1) Save as otherwise provided by any law for the time being in force and unless the parties have otherwise agreed, this Part shall apply to conciliation of disputes arising out of legal relationship, whether contractual or not and to all proceedings relating thereto.

(2) This Part shall not apply where by virtue of any law for the time being in force certain disputes may not be submitted to conciliation.

62. Commencement of conciliation proceedings.—(1) The party initiating conciliation shall send to the other party a written invitation to conciliate under this Part, briefly identifying the subject of the dispute.

(2) Conciliation proceedings shall commence when the other party accepts in writing the invitation to conciliate.

(3) If the other party rejects the invitation, there will be no conciliation proceedings.

(4) If the party initiating conciliation does not receive a reply within thirty days from the date on which he sends the invitation, or within such other period of time as specified in the invitation, be may elect to treat this as a rejection of the invitation to conciliate and if he so elects, he shall inform in writing the other party accordingly.

63. Number of conciliators.—(1) There shall be one conciliator unless the parties agree that there shall be two or three conciliators.

(2) Where there is more than one conciliator, they ought, as a general rule, to act jointly.

64. Appointment of conciliators.—(1) Subject to sub-section (2)—

(a) in conciliation proceedings with one conciliator, the parties may agree on the name of a sole conciliator;

(b) in conciliation proceedings with two conciliators, each party may appoint one conciliator;

(c) in conciliation proceedings with three conciliators, each party may appoint one conciliator and the parties may agree on the name of the third conciliator who shall act as the presiding conciliator.

(2) Parties may enlist the assistance of a suitable institution or person in connection with the appointment of conciliators and in particular—

(a) a party may request such an institution or person to recommend the names of suitable individuals to act as conciliator; or

(b) the parties may agree that the appointment of one or more conciliators be made directly by such an institution or person;

Provided that in recommending or appointing individuals to act as conciliator, the institution or person shall have regard to such considerations as are likely to secure the appointment of an independent and impartial conciliator and, with respect to a sole or third conciliator, shall take into account the advisability of appointing a conciliator of a nationality other than the nationalities of the parties.

65. Submission of statements to conciliator.—(1) The conciliator, upon his appointment, may request each party to submit to him a brief written statement of his position and the facts and grounds in support thereof, supplement by any documents and other evidence that such party deems appropriate. The party shall send a copy of such statement, documents and other evidence to the other party.

(2) The Conciliator may request each party to submit to him a further written statement of his position and the facts and grounds in support thereof, supplemented by any documents and other evidence that such party deems appropriate. The party shall send a copy of such statement, documents and other evidence to the other party.

(3) At an stage of the conciliation proceedings, the conciliator may request a party to submit to him such additional information as he deems appropriate.

Explanation.—In this section and all the following sections of this Part, the term "conciliator" applies to a sole conciliator, to or three conciliators as the case may be.

66. Conciliator not bound by certain enactments.—The conciliator is not bound by the Code of Civil Procedure, 1908 (5 of 1908) or the Indian Evidence Act, 1872 (1 of 1872).

67. Role of conciliator.—(1) The conciliator shall assist the parties in an independent and impartial manner in their attempt to reach an amicable settlement of their dispute.

(2) The conciliator shall be guided by principles of objectivity, fairness and justice, giving consideration to, among other things, the rights and obligations of the parties, the usages of the trade concerned and the circumstances surrounding the dispute, including any previous business practices between the parties.

(3) The conciliator may conduct the conciliation proceedings in such a manner as he considers appropriate, taking into account the circumstances of the case, the wishes the parties may express, including any request by a party that the conciliator hear oral statements, and the need for a speedy settlement of the dispute.

(4) The conciliator-may, at any stage of the conciliation proceedings, make proposals for a settlement of the dispute.Such

proposals need not be writing and need not be accompanied by a statement of the reasons therefor.

68. Administrative assistance.—In order to facilitate the conduct of the conciliation proceedings, the parties, or the conciliator with the consent of the parties, may arrange for administrative assistance by a suitable institution or person.

69. Communication between conciliator and parties.—(1) The conciliator may invite the parties to meet him or may communicate with them orally or in writing.He may meet or communicate with the parties together or with each of them separately.

(2) Unless the parties have agreed upon the place where meetings with the conciliator are to be held, such place shall be determined by the conciliator, after consultation with the parties, having regard to the circumstances of the conciliation proceedings.

70. Disclosure of information.—When the conciliator receives factual information concerning the dispute from a party, he shall disclose the substance of that information to the other party in order that the other party may have the opportunity to present any explanation which he considers appropriate:

> Provided that when a party gives any information to the conciliator subject to a specific condition that it be kept confidential, con conciliator shall not disclose that information to the other party.

71. Co-operation of parties with conciliator.—The parties shall in good faith co-operate with the conciliator and, in particular, shall endeavour to comply with requests by the conciliator to submit written materials, provide evidence and attend meetings.

72. Suggestions by parties for settlement of dispute.—Each party may, on his own initiative or at the invitation of the conciliator, submit to the conciliator suggestions for the settlement of the dispute.

73. Settlement agreement.—(1) When it appears to the conciliator that there exist elements of a settlement which may be acceptable to the parties, he shall formulate the terms of a possible settlement and submit them to the parties for their observations.After receiving the observations of the parties, the conciliator may reformulate the terms of a possible settlement in the light of such observations. (2) If the parties reach agreement on a settlement of the dispute, they may draw up and sign a written settlement agreement. If requested by the parties, the conciliator may draw up, or assist the parties in drawing up, the settlement agreement.

(3) When the parties sign the settlement agreement, it shall be final and binding on the parties and persons claiming under them respectively.

(4) The conciliator shall authenticate the settlement agreement and furnish a copy thereof to each of the parties.

74. Status and effect of settlement agreement.—The settlement agreement shall have the and effect as if it is an arbitral award on agreed terms on the substance of the dispute rendered by an arbitral tribunal under section 30.

75. Confidentiality.—Notwithstanding anything contained in any other law for the time being in force, the conciliator and the parties shall keep confidential all matter relating to the conciliation proceedings.Confidentiality shall extend also to the settlement agreement, except where its disclosure is necessary for purposes of implementation and enforcement.

76. Termination of conciliation proceedings.—The conciliation proceedings shall be terminated—

(a) by the signing of the settlement agreement by the parties; on the date of the agreement; or

(b) by a written declaration of the conciliator, after consultation with the parties, in the effect that further efforts at conciliation are no longer justified, on the date of the declaration; or

(c) by a written declaration of the parties addressed to the conciliator to the effect that the conciliation proceedings are terminated, on the date of the declaration; or

(d) by a written declaration of a party to the other party and the conciliator, if appointed, to the effect that the conciliation proceedings are terminated, on the date of the declaration.

77. Resort to arbitral or judicial proceedings.—The parties shall not initiate, during the conciliation proceedings, any arbitral or judicial proceedings in respect of a dispute that is the subject-matter of the conciliation proceedings except that a party may initiate arbitral or judicial proceedings, where, in his opinion, such proceedings are necessary for preserving his rights.

78. Costs.—(1) Upon termination of the conciliation proceedings, the conciliator shall fix the costs of the conciliation and given written notice thereof to the parties.

(2) For the purpose of sub-section (1) , "costs" means reasonable costs relating to—

(a) the fee and expenses of the conciliator and witnesses requested by the conciliator, with the consent of the parties;

(b) any expert advice requested by the conciliator with the consent of the parties;

(c) any assistance provided pursuant to clause (b) of sub-section (2) of section 64 and section 68.

(d) any other expenses incurred in connection with the conciliation proceedings and the settlement agreement.

(3) The costs shall be borne equally by the parties unless the settlement agreement provides for a different appointment.All other expenses incurred by a party shall be borne by that party.

79. Deposits.—(1) The conciliator may direct each party to deposit an equal amount as an advance for the costs referred to in subsection (2) of section 78 which he expects will be incurred.

(2) During the course of the conciliation proceedings, the conciliator may direct supplementary deposits in an equal amount from each party.

(3) If the required deposits under sub-sections (1) and (2) are not paid in full by both parties within thirty days, the conciliator may suspend the proceedings or may make a written declaration of termination of the proceedings to the parties, effective on the date of that declaration.

(4) Upon termination of the conciliation proceedings the conciliator shall render an accounting to the parties of the deposits received and shall return and expended balance to the parties.

80. Role of conciliator in other proceedings.—Unless otherwise agreed by the parties:

(a) the conciliator shall not act as an arbitrator or as a representative or counsel of a party in any arbitral or judicial proceeding in respect of a dispute that is the subject of the conciliation proceedings;

(b) the conciliator shall not be presented by the parties as a witness in any arbitral or judicial proceedings.

81. Admissibility of evidence in other proceedings.—The parties shall not rely on or introduce as evidence in arbitral or judicial proceedings, whether or not such proceedings relate to the dispute that is the subject of the conciliation proceedings—

(a) views expressed or suggestions made by the other party in respect of a possible settlement of the dispute;
(b) admissions made by the other party in the course of the conciliation proceedings;
(c) proposals made by the conciliator;
(d) the fact that the other party had indicated to accept a proposal for settlement made by the conciliator.

PART IV – SUPPLEMENTARY PROVISIONS

82. Power of High Court to make rules.—The High court may make rules consistent with this Act as to all proceedings before the court under this Act.

83. Removal of difficulties.—(1) If any difficulty arises in giving effect to the provisions of this Act, the central Government may, by order published in the Official Gazette, make such provisions, not inconsistent with the provisions of this Act as appear to it to be necessary or expedient for removing the difficulty:

Provided that no such order shall be after the expiry of a period of two years from the date of commencement of this Act.

(2) Every order made under this section shall, as soon as may be after it is made, be laid before each Houses of Parliament.

84. Power to make rules.—(1) The Central Government may, by notification in the Official Gazette, make rules for carrying out the provisions of this Act.

(2) Every rule made by the Central Government under this Act shall be laid, as soon as may be, after it is made before each House of Parliament while it is in session, for a total period of thirty days which may be comprised in one session or in two or moresuccessive sessions, and if, before the expiry of the session immediately following the session or the successive sessions aforesaid, both Houses agree in making may modification in the rule or both Houses agree that the rule should not be made, the rule shall thereafter have effect only in such modified form or be of no effect, as the case may be; so, however, that any such modification or annulment shall be without prejudice to the validity of anything previously done under that rule.

85. Repeal and savings.—(1) The Arbitration (Protocol and Convention) Act, 1937 (6 of 1937), the Arbitration Act, 1940 (10 of 1940) and the Foreign Awards (Recognition and Enforcement) Act, 1961 (45 of 1961) are hereby repealed.

(2) Notwithstanding such repeal—

(a) the provisions of the said enactments shall apply in relation to arbitral proceedings which commenced before this Act came into force unless otherwise agreed by the parties but this Act shall apply in relation to arbitral proceedings which commenced on or after this Act comes into force;

(b) all rules made and notifications published, under the said enactments shall, to the extent to which they are not repugnant to this Act, be deemed respectively to have been made or issued under this Act.

86. Repeal of Ordinance 27 of 1996 and saving.—(1) The Arbitration and Conciliation (Third) Ordinance, 1996 (Ord. 27 of 1996) is hereby repealed.done or any action taken in pursuance of any provision of the said Ordinance shall be deemed to have been made, done or taken under the corresponding provisions of this Act.

THE FIRST SCHEDULE

(See section 44)

CONVENTION ON THE RECOGNITION AND EXPORCEMENT OF FOREIGN ARBITRAL AWARDS

Article I

1. This Convention shall apply to the recognition and enforcement of arbitral awards made in the territory of a State other than the State where the recognition and enforcement of such awards are sought and arising out of differences between persons, whether physical or legal. It shall also apply to arbitral awards not considered as domestic awards in the State where their recognition and enforcement are sought.
2. The term "arbitral awards" shall include not only awards made by arbitrators appointed for each case but also those

made by permanent arbitral bodies to which the parties have submitted.

3. When signing, ratifying or acceding to this Convention, or notifying extension under article X hereof, and State may on the basis of reciprocity declare that it will apply the Convention to the recognition and enforcement of awards made only in the territory of another Contracting State.It may also declare that it will apply the Convention only to differences arising out of legal relationships, whether contractual or not, which are considered as commercial undertaking national law of the State making such declaration.

Article II

1. Each Contracting State shall recognise an agreement in writing under which the parties undertaking to submit to arbitration all or any differences which have arisen or which may arise between them in respect of defined legal relationship, whether contractual or not, concerning a subject-matter capable of settlement by arbitration.
2. The term "agreement in writing" shall include an arbitral clause in a contract or an arbitration agreement, signed by the parties or contained in an exchange of letters or telegrams.
3. The court of a Contracting State, when seized of an action in a matter in respect of which the parties have made an agreement within the meaning of this article, shall, at the request of one of the parties, refer the parties to arbitration, unless in finds that the said agreement is null and void, inoperative of incapable of being performed.

Article III

Each Contracting State shall recognize arbitral awards as binding and enforcement them in accordance with the rules of procedure of the territory where the award is relied upon, under the conditions laid down in the following articles.There shall not be imposed substantially more onerous conditions or higher fees or charges on the recognition or enforcement of arbitral awards to which this Convention applies than are imposed on the recognition or enforcement of domestic arbitral awards.

Article IV

1. To obtain the recognition and enforcement mentioned in the proceeding article, the party applying for recognition and enforcement shall, at the time of the application, supply:
   (a) the duly authenticated original award or a duly certified copy thereof:
   (b) the original agreement referred to in article II or a duly certified copy thereof.
2. If the said award or agreement is not made in an official language of the country in which the award is relied upon, the party applying for recognition and enforcement of the award shall produce a translation of these documents into such language. The translation shall be certified by an official or sworn translator or by a diplomatic or consular agent.

Article V

1. Recognition and enforcement of the award may be refused, at the request of the party against whom it is invoked, only if that party furnishes to the competent authority where the recognition and enforcement is sought, proof that—
   (a) the parties to the agreement referred to in article II were, under the law applicable to them, under some incapacity, or the said agreement in not valid under the law to which the parties have subjected it or, failing any indication thereon, under the law of the country where the award was made; or
   (b) the party against whom the award is invoked was not given proper notice of the appointment of the arbitrator or of the arbitration proceedings or was otherwise unable to present his case; or
   (c) the award deals with a difference not contemplated by or not falling within the terms of the submission to arbitration, or it contains decisions on matters beyond the scope of the submission to arbitration, provided that, if the decisions on matters submitted to arbitration can be separated from those not so submitted, that part of the award which contains decisions on matters submitted to arbitration may be recognised and enforced; or

(d) the composition of the arbitral authority or the arbitral procedure was not in accordance with the agreement of the parties, or, failing such agreement, was not in accordance with the law of the country where the arbitration took place; or

(e) the award has not yet become binding on the parties, or has been set aside or suspended by a competent authority of the country in which, or under the law of which, that award was made.

2. Recognition and enforcement of an arbitral award may also be refused if the competent authority in the country where recognition and enforcement is sought finds that—

(a) the subject matter of the difference is not capable of settlement by arbitration under the law of that country; or

(b) the recognition or enforcement of the award would be contrary to the public policy of that country.

Article VI

If an application for the setting aside or suspension of the award has been made to a competent authority referred to in article V(1) (e), the authority before which the award is sought to be relied upon may, if it considers it proper, adjourn the decision on the enforcement of the award and may also, on the application of the party claiming enforcement of the award, order the other party to give suitable security.

Article VII

1. The provisions of the present Convention shall not affect the validity of multilateral or bilateral agreements concerning the recognition and enforcement of arbitral awards entered into by the Contracting States nor deprive any interested party of any right he may have to avail himself of an arbitral award in the manner and to the extent allowed by the law or the treaties of the country where such award is sought to be relied upon.
2. The Geneva Protocol on Arbitration Clauses of 1923 and the Geneva Convention on the Execution of Foreign Arbitral Awards of 1927 shall cease to have effect between Contracting States on their becoming bound and to the extent that they become bound by this Convention.

Article VIII

1. This Convention shall be upon until 31st December, 1958 for signature on behalf of any Member of the United Nations and also on behalf of any other State which is or hereafter becomes member of any specialised agency of the United Nations, or which is or hereafter becomes a party to the Statute of the International Court of Justice, or any other State to which an invitation has been addressed by the General Assembly of the United Nations.
2. This Convention shall be ratified and the instrument of ratification shall be deposited with the Secretary-General of the United Nations.

Article IX

1. This Convention shall be upon for accession to all States referred to in article VIII.
2. Accession shall be effected by the deposit of an instrument of accession with the Secretary-General of the United Nations.

Article X

1. Any State may, at the time of signature, ratification or accession, declare that this Convention shall extend to all or any of the territories for the international relations of which it is responsible.Such a declaration shall take effect when the Convention enters into force for the State concerned.
2. At any time thereafter any such extension shall be made by notification addressed to the Secretary-General of the United Nations and shall take effect as from the ninetieth day after the day of receipt by the Secretary-General of the United Nations of this notifications, or as from the date of entry into force of the Convention for the State concerned, whichever is the later.
3. With respect to those territories to which this Convention is not extended at the time of signature, ratification or accession, each State concerned shall consider the possibility of taking the necessary steps in order to extend the application of this Convention to such territories, subject, where necessary for constitutional reasons, to the consent of the Governments of such territories.

Article XI

In the case of a federal or non-unitary State, the following provisions shall apply:

(a) with respect of those articles of this Convention that come within the legislative jurisdiction of the federal authority, the obligations of the federal Government shall to this extent be the same as those of Contracting States which are not federal States;

(b) with respect to those articles of this Convention that come within the legislative jurisdiction of constituent States or provinces which are not, under the constitutional system of the federation, bound to take legislative action, the federal Government shall bring such articles with a favourable recommendation to the notice of the appropriate authorities of constituent States or provinces at the earliest possible moment;

(c) a federal State Party to this Convention shall, at the request of any other Contracting State transmitted through the Secretary General of the United Nations, supply a statement of the law and practice of the federation and its constituent units in regard to any particular provision of this Convention, showing the extent to which effect has been given to that provision by legislative or other action.

Article XII

1. This Convention shall come into force on the ninetieth day following the date of deposit of the third instrument of ratification or accession.
2. For each State ratifying or acceding to this Convention after the deposit of the third instrument of ratification or accession, this Convention shall enter into force on the ninetieth day after deposit by such State of its instrument of ratification or accession.

Article XIII

1. Any Contracting State may denounce this Convention by a written notification to the Secretary-General of the United Nations. Denunciation shall take effect one year

after the date of receipt of the notification by the Secretary-General.

2. Any State which has made a declaration or notification under article X may, at any time thereafter, by notification to the SecretaryGeneral of the United Nations, declare that this Convention shall cease to extend to the territory concerned one year after the date of the receipt of the notification by the Secretary-General.
3. This Convention shall continue to be applicable to arbitral awards in respect of which recognition or enforcement proceedingshave been instituted before the denunciation takes effect.

Article XIV

A Contracting State shall not be entitled to avail itself of the present Convention against other Contracting States except to the extent that it is itself bound to apply the Convention.

Article XV

The Secretary General of the United Nations shall notify the States contemplated in article VIII of the following:

(a) signatures and ratifications in accordance with article VIII;
(b) accessions in accordance with article IX;
(c) declarations and notifications under articles I, X and XI;
(d) the date upon which this Convention enters into force in accordance with article XII;
(e) denunciations and notifications in accordance with article XIII.

Article XVI

1. This Convention, of which the Chinese, English, French, Russian and Spanish texts shall be equally authentic, shall be deposited in the archives of the United Nations.
2. The Secretary General of the United Nations shall transmit a certified copy of this Convention to the State contemplated in article XIII.

THE SECOND SCHEDULE

(See section 53)

PROTOCOL ON ARBITRATION CLAUSES

The undersigned, being duly authorised, declare that they accept, on behalf of the countries which they represent, the following provisions:

1. Each of the Contracting States recognises the validity of an agreement whether relating to existing or future differences between parties subject respectively to the jurisdiction of different Contracting States by which the parties to a contract agree to submit to arbitration all or any differences that may arise in connection with such contract relating to commercial matters or to any other matter capable of settlement by arbitration, whether or not the arbitration is to take place in a country to whose jurisdiction none of the parties is subject.
   Each Contracting State reserves the right to limit the obligation mentioned above to contracts which are considered as commercial under its national law.Any Contracting State which avails itself of this right will notify the Secretary-General of the League of Nations in order that the other Contracting States may be so informed.
2. The arbitral procedure, including the constitution of the Arbitral Tribunal, shall be governed by the will of the parties and by the law of the country in whose territory the arbitration takes place.
   The Contracting States agree to facilitate all steps in the procedure which require to be taken in their own territories, in accordance with the provisions of their law governing arbitral procedure applicable to existing differences.
3. Each Contracting State undertakes to endure the execution by its authorities and in accordance with the provisions of its national law of arbitral awards made in its own territory under the preceding articles.
4. The Tribunals of the Contracting Parties, on being seized of a dispute regarding a contract made between persons to

whom Article I applies and including an Arbitration Agreement whether referring to present or further differences with is valid in virtue of the said article and capable of being carried into effect, shall refer the parties on the application of either of them to the decision of the Arbitrators.

Such reference shall not prejudice the competence of he judicial tribunals in case the agreement or the arbitration cannot proceed or becomes inoperative.

5. The present Protocol, which shall remain open for signature by all States, shall be ratified.The ratification shall be deposited as soon as possible with the Secretary, General of the League of Nations, who shall notify such deposit to all the Signatory States.
6. The present Protocol will come into force as soon as two ratifications have been deposited.Thereafter it will take effect, in the case of each Contracting State, one month after the notification by the Secretary-General of the deposit of its ratification.
7. The present Protocol may be denounced by any Contracting State on giving one year's notice. Denunciation shall be effected by a notification addressed to the Secretary-General of the League, who will immediately transmit copies of such notification to all the other Signatory States and inform them of the date on which it was received.The denunciation shall take effect one year after the date on which it was notified to the Secretary-General, and shall operate only in respect of the notifying State.
8. The Contracting States may declare that their acceptance of the present Protocol does not include any or all of the undermentioned territories; that is to say, their colonies, overseas possessions or territories, protectorates or the territories over which they exercise a mandate.

   The said States may subsequently adhere separately on behalf of any territory thus excluded.The 'Secretary-General of the League of Nations shall be informed as soon as possible of such adhesions.He shall notify such adhesions to all Signatory States.They will take effect on month after the notification by the Secretary-General to all Signatory states.

The Contracting States may also denounce the Protocol separately on behalf of any of the territories referred to above.Article 7 applies to such denunciation.

THE THIRD SCHEDULE

(See Sections 53)

CONVENTION ON THE EXECUTION OF FOREIGN ARBITRAL AWARDS

Article I

(1) In the territories of any High Contracting Party to which the present Convention applies, an arbitral award made in pursuance of an agreement, whether relating the existing or future differences (hereinafter called "a submission to arbitration") covered by the Protocol on arbitration Clauses opened at Geneva on September 24th. 1923, shall be recognised as binding and shall be enforced in accordance with the rules of the procedure of the territory where the award is relied upon, provided that the said award has been made in a territory of one of the High Contracting Parties to which the present Convention applies and between persons who are subject to the jurisdiction of one of the High Contracting Parties.

(2) To obtain such recognition or enforcement, it shall, further, be necessary:

(a) that the award has been made in pursuance of a submission to arbitration which is valid under the law applicable thereto;

(b) that the subject-matter of the award is capable of settlement by arbitration under the law of the country in which the award is sought to be relied upon;

(c) that the award has been made by the Arbitral Tribunal provided for in the submission to arbitration or constituted in the manner agreed upon by the parties and in conformity with the law governing the arbitration procedure;

(d) that the award has become final in the country in which it has been made, in the sense that it will not be considered as such if it is open to opposition, appeal or pourvoi en cassation (in the countries where such forms of procedure exist) or if it is proved that any proceedings for the purpose of contesting the validity of the award are pending;

(e) that the recognition or enforcement of the award is not contrary to the public policy or to the principles of the law of the country in which it is sought to be relied upon.

Article 2

Even if the conditions laid down in Article I hereof are fulfilled, recognition and enforcement of the award shall be refused if the Court is satisfied:

(a) that the award has been annulled in the country in which it was made;
(b) that the party against whom it is sought to use the award was not given notice of the arbitration proceedings in sufficient time to enable him to present his case; or that, being under a legal incapacity, he was not properly represented;
(c) that the award does not deal with the differences contemplated by or falling within the terms of the submission to arbitration or that it contains decisions on matters beyond the scope of the submission to arbitration.

If the award has not covered all the questions submitted to the arbitral tribunal, the competent authority of the country where recognition or enforcement of the award is sought can, if it thinks fit, postpone such recognition or enforcement or grant it subject to such guarantee as that authority may decide.

Article 3

If the party against whom the award has been made proves that, under the law governing the arbitration procedure, there is a ground, other than the grounds referred to in Article 1(a) and (c), and Article 2(b) and (c), entitling him to contest the validity of the award in a Court of Law, the Court may, if it thinks fit, either refuse recognition or enforcement of the award or adjourn the consideration thereof, giving such party a reasonable time within which to have the award annulled by the competent tribunal.

Article 4

The party relying upon an award or claiming its enforcement must supply, in particular:

(1) the original award or a copy thereof duly authenticated,

according to the requirements of the law of the country in which it was made;

(2) documentary or other evidence to prove that the award has become final, in the sense defined in Article 1 (d), in the country in which it was made;

(3) when necessary, documentary or other evidence to prove that the conditions laid down in Article 1, Paragraph (1) and paragraph (2) (a) and (c), have been fulfilled.

A translation of the award and of the award and of the other documents mentioned in this Article into the official language of the country where the award is sought to be relied upon may be demanded. Such translations must be certified correct by a diplomatic or consular agent of the country to which the party who seeks to rely upon the award belongs or by a sworn translator of the country where the award is sought to be relied upon.

Article 5

The provisions of the above articles small not deprive any interested party of the right of availing himself of an arbitral award in the manner and to the extent allowed by the law or the treaties of the country where such award is sought to be relied upon.

Article 6

The present Convention applies only to arbitral awards made after the coming into force of the Protocol on Arbitration Clauses opened at Geneva on September 24th, 1923.

Article 7

The present Convention, which will remain open to the signature of all the signatories of the Protocol of 1923 on Arbitration Clauses, shall be ratified.

It may be ratified only on behalf of those Members of the League of Nations and Non-member States on whose behalf the Protocol of 1923 on Arbitration Clauses, shall be ratified.

Ratification shall be deposited as soon as possible with the Secretary-General of the League of Nations, who will notify such deposit to all the signatories.

Article 8

The present Convention shall come into force three months after it shall have been ratified on behalf of two High Contracting

Parties. Thereafter, it shall take effect, in the case of each High Contracting Party, three months after the deposit of the ratification on its behalf with the Secretary-General of the League of Nations.

Article 9

The present Convention may be denounced on behalf of any Member of the League or Non-Member State.Denunciation shall be notified in writing to the Secretary-General of the League of Nations, who will immediately send a copy thereof, certified to the in conformity with the notifications, to all the other Contracting Parties, at the same time informing them of the date on which he received it

The denunciation shall come into force only in respect of the High Contracting Party which shall have notified it and one year after such notification shall have reached the Secretary-General of the League of Nations.

The denunciation of the Protocol on Arbitration Clauses shall entail, *ipso facto*, the denunciation of the present Convention.

Article 10

The present Convention does not apply to the colonies, protectorates or territories under suzerainty or mandate of any High Contracting Party unless they are specially mentioned.

The application of this Convention to one or more of such colonies, protectorates or territories to which the Protocol on Arbitration Clauses opened at Geneva on September 24th, 1923, applies, can be effected at any time by means of a declaration addressed to the Secretary-General of the League of Nations by one of the High Contracting Parties.

Such declaration shall take effect three months after the deposit thereof.

The High Contracting Parties can at any time denounce the Convention for all or any of the colonies, protectorates or territories referred to above.Article 9 hereof applied to such denunciation.

Article 11

A certified copy of the present Convention shall be transmitted by the Secretary-General of the league of Nations of every Member of the league of Nations and to every Non-Member State which sign the same.

K.L. MOHANPURIA
Secy. to the Govt. of India

Index